MAGIC CARPET RIDE

MAGIC CARPET RIDE

THE STORY OF MY LIFE

PHIL HARRIS

WITH IVAN FALLON

To Emily
Best wishes
Phil Harris

\Bb\
Biteback Publishing

First published in Great Britain in 2017 by
Biteback Publishing Ltd
Westminster Tower
3 Albert Embankment
London SE1 7SP
Copyright © Philip Harris and Ivan Fallon 2017

ISBN 978-1-78590-201-7

10 9 8 7 6 5 4 3 2 1

A CIP catalogue record for this book is available from the British Library.

Set in Adobe Caslon Pro

Printed and bound in Great Britain by
CPI Group (UK) Ltd, Croydon CR0 4YY

To Pauline and the family

Contents

CONTENTS

FOREWORD

The Rt Hon Sir John Major KG CH

I have known Phil and Pauline Harris for nearly forty years. It is a remarkable partnership and, although this book is a record of his own life, Phil would be the first to acknowledge the pivotal role that Pauline has played in it.

Phil Harris is an extraordinary man – yet modest. He does not forever remind people of his achievements, or his wealth, or his generosity to so many good causes. In his private life, he shares the everyday pleasures of most: his family, his friends, sport – pre-eminently football – and the ownership of fine showjumpers.

There is nothing especially noteworthy about any of this. But what *is* remarkable is the drive, the commitment, the sheer bloody-mindedness – where necessary – to achieve all he has done. That truly *is* extraordinary.

This book charts the rise from the modest circumstances of Phil's youth, to business super-stardom, to riches, to influence, to a knighthood, to a peerage. The highs and lows of this journey are set out in these pages, together with his strong sense of public service – most especially in improving the Health Service, and the quality of education.

The education of young people from backgrounds similar to Phil's is, perhaps, his most long-standing and deeply felt passion.

Phil has not forgotten from whence he came. Or what life at the bottom – with all its insecurities – is really like. He actively works to help young people who are not in a position to help themselves.

Many successful people care for the less advantaged, and will always dig deep when invited to do so. But Phil also takes it upon himself to *pro-actively* pursue plans to improve the education and life chances of young people. He has ploughed enormous time, energy and commitment – as well as money – into founding and funding the growing number of Harris Academies and, in doing so, has made a real and tangible difference. In fifty years' time, there will be many successful – even eminent – men and women, who will owe their success to the education that Phil Harris made possible for them.

This is the man at the heart of this book. It is a story that deserves to be told, not least so that it might inspire others to follow where Phil Harris has led.

PREFACE

The best thing you can be in life is lucky – and I've been very lucky. I was lucky with my parents and my family, blessed with my wife and my children and fortunate in business. Although I was born in the middle of a world war and grew up in a time of austerity and rationing, I wouldn't change anything about my life.

I was fortunate to inherit a small business started by my father in a stall in Peckham Market after the Second World War, just when the greatest consumer and house-building boom in Britain's history was getting under way. The biggest sadness of my life was inheriting it many years before I should have done, after both my parents died of cancer. But my good fortune, which he would have been the first to appreciate, was that my father got me off to a great start. The timing, and the kind of retail business I took over at the age of sixteen, could not have been better for a young man setting out on his career.

I had no great ambitions when I started: I just wanted to prove I could carry on with the business, which had just three shops, and make a living out of it. Then, when I had proved I could, I thought I might expand to ten shops, but when I got there, I just kept on going until eventually I controlled the biggest carpet retailing business in the land with 30 per cent of the market.

I have been fortunate in many other ways too. I didn't do well at school academically basically because I am dyslexic, but I was gifted with a good memory and a keen mathematical brain which can still compute with the speed of a calculator. I've never read a book, I can't write a letter and I can barely read a speech. But I can read a balance sheet, dictate letters, and if I've got to give a speech I can do it. Dyslexics have a way of finding creative ways around their difficulty.

At school, I was good at sport, which I have always loved, and I had an early taste of leadership when I was made school captain of both the cricket and football teams. I played tennis at Junior Wimbledon and I even nurtured ambitions to become a professional footballer for Arsenal, where I have been a life-long supporter through good and bad times (I became a director in 2005). I might have made the team if injury had not cut short a promising career. And thank goodness for that – another bit of good fortune to add to all the others.

When I took over the linoleum shops, people used to say: 'You'll never be like your father', which meant 'You'll never be *as good* as your father'. That made me even more determined to succeed, but in my own way. I admired my father greatly and I wanted to please him, but that didn't mean I had to be like him – I am happy to be myself. My father was a decent, modest, hard-working man who I only discovered, long after he passed away, had a distinguished war record and had been awarded the Military Cross by Field Marshal Montgomery in 1945. He taught me a great deal in the few precious years we had together, particularly the responsibilities of leadership, as I shall describe later. For years after he died, I would say to myself: 'What would Dad have thought? Would he be pleased?' I still do that sometimes.

Other people tell me I was born with an intuitive feel for retailing, a sense of knowing what a shop should look like and what will sell and what won't. I think I probably do, but I can't explain it or teach it to anyone. But building a business, any business, is as much about hard work as instinct and for many years I worked six days a week.

I have learned some hard lessons in life too. I enjoyed thirty-one good years with my first company, Harris Carpets, which became Harris Queensway. When I listed it on the London Stock Exchange the shares soared and everyone loved me. Then we had one bad year, and the company was taken over. I learned then how fickle a place the City can be. Although I came out of it well financially, within two years that great company, with 6,000 employees, was bust. I know that if I could have hung in there it would still be around today.

But time waits for no man and I started again and built another carpet company, this time even bigger and more successful. I called it Carpetright and it grew into a billion-pound company. I had twenty-four more good years as chairman but, approaching seventy, I decided I was too impatient for all the corporate governance and red tape that stifles entrepreneurs today. So, I stepped down and started a third one, Tapi Carpets, run by my son Martin, which at least for the moment we are keeping private.

Although retailing made me a relatively wealthy man, I have taken on many other challenges which have given me great satisfaction and, I hope, contributed in some modest way to a world which has been so good to me. The best job I ever had (unpaid) was chairman of Guy's and Lewisham Hospital Trust, which was to be the spearhead of Margaret Thatcher's ambitious plans to reform the National Health Service, as urgent a task then as it is now. She asked me to take it on in 1990, just months before she lost office, and in the first two years we cut costs by 20 per cent, saving £20 million a year – and treated 60,000 more patients.

Guy's was a bold experiment, opposed every inch of the way by unions, the Labour Party and even some of the medical staff. But, with the help of some superb managers, we made it work and I think we found a significant way forward for the whole NHS that could have made a real difference. But nerves failed, politics intruded and the momentum – and the opportunity – was lost before we had a chance to prove it. That's a great shame.

My real passion in the second half of my life has been the Harris Federation of academy schools. In 1989, Margaret Thatcher and Kenneth Baker asked me to sponsor a failing comprehensive in Crystal

Palace – Sylvan Grove School – which I transformed into one of the first City Technical Colleges (CTCs), the forerunner of the modern state academy school.

When we started, the pass rate (five GCSEs including maths and English) was 9 per cent, discipline and attendance were terrible, and many of the kids that emerged were basically unemployable. Five years later, the pass rate was 57 per cent and we won the award for most improved school in the country, which we've won again since (the only school ever to do so). Today, the pass rate is over 90 per cent and in 2016, 126 out of 144 of our sixth-formers went to university, and even more in 2017. Last year there were 2,000 applicants for 180 places, making it one of the most popular schools in the country.

The school in Crystal Palace may be my most important legacy, because it was the model for a chain of Harris schools and also led directly to the academy school, conceived by the Labour education minister Andrew Adonis and perfected by Michael Gove. These schools are all-ability state comprehensives that enjoy much more autonomy than they did under the local authorities, allowing head teachers to exercise their freedom to extraordinary effect. Academies have raised the whole level of education in Britain – and particularly in south London, which had the worst academic record and one of the highest crime rates in the country.

In June 2014, I was astounded when I was shown an article in *The Guardian* entitled: 'My hero: Lord Harris, the Conservative millionaire who is saving schools'. The author was Michael Gove, with whom I had worked closely when he was the Education Secretary.

'Harris changed everything about these schools – except the intake,' wrote Gove.

He introduced all the characteristics of the type of school middle-class parents pay thousands of pounds for. In came uniforms, house systems, academic subjects, strict discipline and zero tolerance of truancy. He also ensured his schools were led by traditionalist teachers who refused to accept excuses for failure. The result has been miraculous.

'What earns him hero status,' he added, 'is that this Conservative peer has done more to help working-class children than any Labour politician since Attlee and Bevan.'

Every school day, 30,000 students now attend Harris academies, primary and secondary, mostly in south London. There are forty-four of them, of which twenty-two were in need of serious improvement when we took them on – basically failing schools. Today, twenty-three are rated as 'outstanding', the highest ranking available, eleven are 'good' and the others are waiting to be inspected by Ofsted. Two of our schools are rated 'world class', which is off even the Ofsted scale. And nearly half our sixth form school leavers go on to universities – and hopefully successful careers after that.

Well before I became involved in schools, I was active in politics, not as a candidate or minister but as an adviser and supporter. My father voted Conservative all his life and so have I. In 1982, my friend Basil Feldman, a marvellous man and big fundraiser for the Tory Party, invited me to meet Mrs Thatcher in Downing Street, where she asked me to join one of her committees helping to advise the government on business. After that I saw her every couple of weeks, sometimes on my own, sometimes with her husband Denis, and my wife Pauline and I became regular guests at Chequers. The two jobs she gave me, Guy's and schools, were at the cutting edge of her radical policies to reform the Health Service and the education system in her final years in No. 10. For some reason, which I could never explain, she liked to call me 'Philly', which no one else ever had. I came to love her and stayed in touch for the rest of her life, often visiting her in old age.

I made many good friends in politics in those years, including Norman Tebbit, whom I also advised. I remember only too well visiting him at his sickbed after the IRA bomb in Brighton in 1984, which seriously injured him and left his wife Margaret paralysed. It was a really tough time for him, and when Jeffrey Sterling and Jonathan Aitken formed a little group to help Margaret, I happily supported it. I also got to know other senior party figures well too, including Chris Patten, Nigel Lawson, Kenneth Baker, Kenneth Clarke and Cecil Parkinson, but Norman has remained a special friend to this day.

After he won the 1992 election, John Major, whom I first met at one of Mrs Thatcher's lunches at Chequers, asked me to become treasurer of the Conservative Party. Its finances were in a terrible mess and it was on the brink of declaring itself bankrupt. It took a lot of doing, but, working with my co-treasurer Charles Hambro, we turned around the finances, raised £120 million and left the party in good shape.

Margaret Thatcher gave me a knighthood in 1985 and John Major made me a peer in 1996 and I have been an active member of the House of Lords since, often speaking (these days I talk about schools and education, about which I have strong views) and spending many hours in the lobbies on crucial votes.

One of the privileges of wealth is being able to give it away, and from the start Pauline and I decided we would donate 20 per cent of whatever we had to charitable causes, particularly relating to cancer. We raised the money for the first breast scanner in Britain, and, at Princess Diana's request, Pauline and I supported Birthright, her favourite charity, dedicated to improving the health of women and babies (it is now called Wellbeing of Women). Thirty years later, when my friend Sir Victor Blank held a special dinner to acknowledge our contribution, we were so moved that we donated another £1 million to build our sixth Harris Birthright Centre.

I have also been very lucky with the horses – not as a betting man, but as the owner or co-owner of some of the best showjumpers in the world. I desperately wanted David Broome to win an Olympic gold medal on one of them, but fate dictated otherwise, as I shall describe later. However, at the London Olympics in 2012, Scott Brash made up for it by winning team gold on Hello Sanctos, who we co-own with our friends Graham and Pauline Kirkham. What a moment that was.

I have been privileged to be involved with some of the country's most venerable and ancient institutions, including Westminster Abbey, where I donated three stained-glass windows to the abbey's King Henry VII Chapel, arguably the most perfect medieval building in the country. Pauline and I are immortalised as penitents at the bottom right-hand corner where we will stay on our knees praying to the heavens for ever. The chapel also bears my coat of arms, which includes two rolls of carpet.

The latest Harris Academy, Harris Westminster, a sixth form selective school a few minutes' walk from the 1,000-year-old abbey, arose out of a conversation I had with the dean, Dr John Hall, and operates in association with the Westminster public school where the fees are £12,000 a term and on average 50 per cent of its pupils go to Oxbridge colleges. Our school is free and in time we hope to match Westminster's academic record, providing a great opportunity for sixteen-year-olds, half of whom qualify for free school meals.

Harris Manchester College, which I have endowed, is the last Oxford college to gain full university status. It is named after my father and the quadrangle contains a life-size bronze statue of him in his full British Army uniform.

That would make him very proud.

CHAPTER 1

EARLY DAYS

Although I took the name Lord Harris of Peckham when I was awarded my peerage in 1996, I wasn't actually born in Peckham. It was 15 September 1942, Britain was at war and my mother was in St Albans, twenty miles north of London. She had presumably been sent there by my anxious father, Sergeant Charles William Harris, who was stationed with his regiment on Dartmoor, on standby to be shipped anywhere in the world – from Burma to the African desert where British soldiers were fighting with their backs to the wall.

Plaque at Diocesan House in St Albans. I was one of the 2,000.

My birth certificate lists the precise place as Diocesan House, Verulam Road, St Albans, and I often wondered about the connection with Peckham until I discovered a brass plaque in its hallway, which reveals that the maternity hospital in York Road, Lambeth, where I would have been born in peacetime, had been moved out of London in 1939 because of the threat of German bombs. Some 2,000 south-east London babies, including me, were born in Diocesan House in the war years.

It was a sensible precaution. Peckham, where the Harris family had lived for generations, was right under the flight path of the German bombers which pounded large parts of south-east London into huge heaps of rubble. My parents, uncles and grandparents had suffered three years of it, and even though the Americans had entered the war by then, the tide had not yet turned and the prospects must have looked bleak. In two years of marriage, my parents had seen each other for a total period of about two months.

Bombs or no bombs, my mother and I were back in Peckham six weeks later where we moved into our little home, a two-room rented flat at the top of a terraced house in Grenard Road, just off the high street. Like most of those Victorian houses in south London, there was no proper bathroom and the nearest toilet was in the backyard, two floors down. It was to be my home for the next seven years.

Mum and Dad had been born and grew up in the neighbourhood and my grandparents, all four of them, lived nearby, as did lots of uncles and aunts. Peckham was home, and that's where we stayed, my mother and I, for the rest of the war, taking shelter underground in Blake's Road when the air-raid warnings went off, which they often did, emerging only when we received the all-clear.

My earliest memory is of the wail of the sirens, and of the damp and darkness of the shelter, only a few minutes from home, and the smell, which was overpowering (bomb shelters were not known for their hygiene). I remember trying to rip my gas mask off and my grand-mother holding it on, and I can remember being frightened. I suppose everyone was, however much they got used to it. I often think now how brave that generation was to cope with their nights in the air-raid shelters, wondering if their homes would still be there in the morning, often emerging to find them flattened ruins. From the beginning of the Blitz on 7 September 1940, south-east London was bombed on fifty-seven consecutive days and nights, which destroyed large parts of Peckham. My wife Pauline lost a brother aged four to a direct hit on their home in Streatham, and a bomb landed on my nan's house, demolishing the washing and kitchen area.

Yet, somehow, life went on: shops opened, the trams ran, the milk was delivered, and people went about their business. Just about every family had fathers, husbands, brothers or sons in the forces, as my mother did, and they must have been desperately worried about them. Most had already lost close relatives in the First World War, just a generation before, and were fearful about losing another one – which many of them did. In later years, I would often hear about the defiant 'Dunkirk' spirit of Londoners during the Blitz and, as a boy, I heard enough tales from uncles and aunts to understand something of the humour and courage that helped get them through the darkest moments.

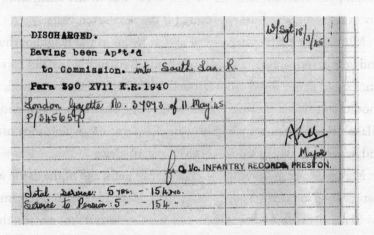

My father's discharge papers as a sergeant. He served for another year as an officer.

The air raids became less frequent by the time I was two years old, but the V-weapons that replaced them were even more frightening.

They came over any time of the day or night with almost no warning and they left open spaces where whole streets had been. A V-1, or 'doodlebug', fell on Peckham Rye, where my father had a shop after the war, killing twenty-three women who were just arriving for work at a corset factory.

I was three when the war ended but it was another year, 1946, before my father eventually came home from the army, almost a total stranger to his only child. My first real memory of him is his concerned face hovering over me when I was about four and got scarlet fever, which was followed by measles. One of these illnesses on its own was bad enough, but to have both was life-threatening. I was moved into the kitchen where I slept in a chair that my father adapted to recline into a bed. My nan, mum and dad took it in turns to watch over me day and night, and for a time it was touch and go as to whether I would pull through. They were told by the doctor to feed me chicken broth, the cure for everything in those days, but chickens after the war were almost unobtainable, so I was given rabbit broth instead, the taste of which I remember to this day. I was ill for a long time and right up to my teenage years I suffered from pleurisy and a weak chest, a direct result of that time. My father later told me I was lucky to have lived and in later years, talking to medical friends about it, I realised he was not exaggerating. Even now I suffer if I don't get away for a bit of sunshine in the damp English winters.

Both my parents came from large families, which made it even more surprising that I was an only child. My father, born in 1918, was one of six children and my mother, born Ruth Ellen Ward a year later, was one of ten, six of whom survived. Most of them lived in or around Peckham, the centre of the universe for the Harris and Ward families, and I saw a lot of them, particularly at Christmas, when everyone gathered at my nan's house in Blake's Road.

I was brought up to believe the Harrises had always lived in and around Peckham, which is what my father thought, but it wasn't so.

A few years ago, my son Martin and his wife Zoe presented me with a family history that showed they were originally from Hythe, on the Kent coast, where church records and gravestones show that they lived and died for at least seven generations. My earliest identifiable Harris ancestor, Jonathan, was baptised in Hythe in 1637 and was described in the records as a 'husbandsman', or farmhand, as was his son, but there is the occasional brewer and even a tailor recorded in the family history. Nicholas Harris, born in 1792, sailed with the East India Company, and is listed as a 'pensioner', presumably enjoying a well-earned retirement looking out over the English Channel.

It wasn't until the early nineteenth century that the Harrises, or at least my branch of them, arrived in Southwark where Edward Harris, my great-great grandfather, set himself up as a sail-maker and married into a prosperous tent-making family, presumably one peg up (so to speak) from sails. Tent-making was a big growth business in Victorian times as the Empire expanded and British troops spread out across the globe, and, judging from the increasingly prosperous addresses they lived at, the business thrived. Edward's son Charles, my great-grandfather (born in 1855), married a local girl Ann (or Ana) Beadle, and started a blind-making business, which I suppose was a logical progression.

My grandfather, Thomas George Harris, whom I remember well, inherited the business, which lasted into my father's time, closing I think during the Depression of the 1930s. As a small boy, I was terrified of him, although in fact he was probably a kindly old soul. He was born in Newington, not far from Peckham, in 1884, and was badly wounded in the trenches in the First World War, losing a leg. He recovered sufficiently to father two more children as well as the four he already had.

My father was born in Camberwell on 4 July 1918, four months before the end of the war, and his brother James – or Jimmy – came into the world two years later. The eldest, my uncle Tommy (who later had a linoleum shop, as did Jimmy), was thirteen years older, almost a different generation.

They lived a few streets away from us, in Hornby Road, and my parents would drag me over to see them, which I never looked forward to. I would dutifully stick my head around the door of my grandfather's room, shout 'Hello, Grandad', before dashing on to see my grandmother, a kindly lady who I remember as always being dressed in a long black dress. My grandfather died when I was seven or eight, by which stage he must still have been only in his sixties, without us having a conversation much beyond 'hello' and 'goodbye'. Now I wish I had talked to him more, because he would have had some stories to tell. This was a time when many families, like ours, had two generations who had served in world wars, my grandfather in the first and my father in the second. But they were unusual in both having survived.

I don't know a lot about my father's childhood, but I do know that he started his working life in the blind-making business before joining my uncle Tommy in his linoleum shop. He lived at home until he joined the army in 1939, and I think it was a happy enough household.

In his later years, my father seldom spoke about the war, but one of my aunts, his sister, had a framed photograph on her mantelpiece showing him in full officer's uniform getting a medal pinned to his chest by his hero Field Marshal Montgomery. That picture was never in our home and my mother seldom referred to his time in the army. It was only a few years ago, when my friend Robert Cranborne, now the 7th Marquess of Salisbury, presented me with my father's war records file, which he managed to dig out of the Ministry of Defence (where he was the minister), that I realised what he had been through.

This was a whole side of his history I had never known about. In researching this book, I have discovered a lot more about the father I knew all too briefly.

CHAPTER 2

MY FATHER, CHARLIE HARRIS

Regimental Chronicle, South Lancashire Regiment, January 1947.

When Britain declared war on Germany on 3 September 1939, my father was twenty-one, working in his elder brother Tom's lino shop in Deptford. He lived with his parents in 26 Hornby Road, Camberwell, and was courting my mother, Ruth Ward, whose home was in 109 Blake's Road, Peckham, less than a mile away. I know that from his army papers.

I can imagine the whole family sitting around the wireless listening to the Prime Minister, Neville Chamberlain, solemnly announcing that Hitler's troops had crossed the border into Poland and that 'consequently this country is at war with Germany'. To my grandparents, World War One must have seemed like only yesterday, and now, just a generation later, Britain was at war again. This time it would be my father's turn to serve.

And serve he did. Within days of war being declared, he signed up at the recruiting office in Kingston upon Thames and, when his papers came through a few days later, reported for a medical which, according to an account left by one of his fellow recruits, was pretty rudimentary: 'Shirt off, sound the chest, test the eyes, cough – you'll do. Move to the next room, hold up your right hand and repeat after me...' He was given a smallpox vaccination and that was about it.

His medical records list his height as 5ft 6½in, his weight at 124lbs, chest 32½in, with blue eyes and black hair. They also recorded his distinctive markings: 'one small mole on back, pigmentic patch 1x¾-inch on right forearm and 1 ear lobe deformed' (which I remember from childhood). He gave his religion as Church of England and his trade as 'lino salesman'. He was given a railway pass to report for training on 16 October 1939, told not to be late, and that was that: he was now No. 6144401, Private Harris C H. He was not yet assigned a regiment.

Like every other recruit, Private Harris, or Charlie as he was known all his life, must have expected his enlistment to last no more than a matter of months, a year at most. In fact, he would serve for six years and 154 days and end up as Major (Acting) William Charles Harris MC of the 1st Battalion, South Lancashire Regiment.

Charlie was one of an intake of half a million men conscripted into the British Army, which was desperately short of both weaponry and men, in the autumn of 1939. He was sent to an infantry training centre in Seaford, a quiet seaside resort in East Sussex, where for the next five months he drilled, learned how to use a rifle and bayonet, chuck a grenade, clamber over assault courses and dig trenches. He was an active, self-confident and fit man, gregarious and adventurous by nature, and

I can imagine him adjusting pretty well. He was a more than competent boxer, good enough to have fought at semi-professional level as a promising bantamweight in the local boxing arenas, and could have held his own against most of his fellow recruits.

The training was tough, the weather was awful, and the recruits collapsed into their bunks at night, cold and exhausted, only to be roused up three hours later to go on forced marches in the middle of winter. Charlie spent that first Christmas away from his family and then, on 2 February 1940, he was ordered to disembark for France, where the British Expeditionary Force, consisting of over 300,000 men – just about every trained soldier in the country – sat along the French and Belgian borders waiting for the Germans to attack. This was the period of World War Two known as the Phoney War, when scarcely a shot was fired.

Charlie embarked for France on 13 March 1940 and was posted to the 1st Battalion of the East Surrey Regiment, a seasoned regiment of regular army soldiers, most of whom came from south London. He joined them on the Belgian border, and dug in with the rest of them.

But he had only been there a month when he was suddenly taken ill and rushed to a field ambulance from where he was transferred to a general hospital. There is no record of what his illness (or injury) was – the best guess is a burst appendix – but it was serious enough for him to be evacuated back to England on 1 May 1940, where he was still recovering when the balloon went up. On 10 May 1940, the German Army smashed through the Allied lines, destroyed the French Army and forced the British to retreat to the channel port of Dunkirk. Charlie's colleagues in the East Surreys were in the thick of it, and I have some eyewitness accounts of it from his fellow soldiers: 'At midnight we were ordered back to the beach to await embarkation at Dunkirk at dawn on 1 June,' a soldier wrote in his diary.

What a sight we encountered! The beaches were crowded with men waiting their turn to be taken to the ships laying offshore, enemy

aircraft dive-bombed and machine-gunned us and the men in the boats
fired back defiantly. We, the Surreys, kept together and dug slit trenches
around a large sand dune which we named Surrey Hill.

Most of them got off, but a sister regiment, the 2/6th East Surreys, was
forced to surrender at St Valery and the majority of its soldiers spent
the next five years in prisoner-of-war camps. An estimated 384,000
British and French servicemen were brought back, many of them on
small boats that had been put out from the Kent and Sussex coasts, but
for every seven British soldiers who escaped from Dunkirk, one man
was left behind.

Charlie was still in hospital and missed the fighting, but I can imagine how he felt for the men of his old regiment who finally landed
back in Dover on 2 June. On 15 July 1940, he was recovered sufficiently
to be posted to the 10th Battalion of the East Surrey Regiment, a new
battalion raised for the purposes of civil and coastal defence duties,
and was promoted to lance-corporal. An invasion was expected im-
minently and there wasn't much to withstand it. Tanks, trucks and
heavy weapons had been abandoned in France and there were barely
enough rifles to go around. Charlie's regiment was sent to a camp at
Ilfracombe, on the north Devon coast, and given a thirty-mile stretch
of beaches and cliffs to guard. The summer was spent training, digging
trenches, laying down barbed wire and building concrete pillboxes and
underwater obstructions, ready to repulse the German forces massing
across the Channel.

Invasion or no invasion, Charlie had other important matters on his
mind, and on 3 October 1940 he was granted two weeks of 'privilege'
leave, took a train back to London and arrived in Peckham where, two
days later, on 5 October, he married Ruth Ward at St Luke's Church,
just down the road from my grandmother's house in Blake's Road. His
father, Thomas George Harris, listed his profession on the marriage
certificate as 'blind-maker' and my granddad Ward described himself

as a 'general dealer' (he was actually the local rag-and-bone man). It wasn't a big ceremony, but they all went back to my nan's house to celebrate before the happy couple departed on a brief honeymoon. I don't know where they went, but it certainly wasn't to the seaside, which was by then covered in barbed wire and mines – strictly out of bounds. In any case, my father couldn't afford much on a corporal's pay and the rest of the family just about had enough to go around.

Peckham had suffered a lot of damage in the short time Charlie had been away. The Battle of Britain was just ending, but the Blitz was at its height when my parents started their married life. The Luftwaffe came over night after night, forcing both my grandmothers to carry their bedding, Thermos flasks and food down into the airless shelters. Shortly after their wedding, poor St Luke's suffered a direct hit and was only partly rebuilt when I was growing up.

Charlie's 'privilege' leave was followed by another two weeks of 'compassionate' leave and in all he was away for a month, the longest period he was to spend with my mother for the next six years. By 9 November 1940, he was back with his regiment, which in January was transferred to an army camp at Plympton, on the edge of Dartmoor, a major training ground for the army with firing ranges and assault courses.

The war records show flashes of Charlie's military record over the next three years, which were fairly uneventful. In November 1940, a month after his marriage, he forfeited two days' pay for some offence or other, but it obviously did him no damage as in April 1941 he was promoted to lance-sergeant. In September that year he suffered an injury that was considered 'not severe', although it again put him in hospital. A month later he was admitted to Stoke Military Infirmary in North Staffordshire, the nearest general hospital to his base, where he was kept for a week. He was discharged on 1 October and must have been given some home leave at Christmas 1941, because that's when I was conceived. I was born almost nine months later on 15 September, my mother's birthday.

At first, the threat of invasion kept the regiment alert but that wore off after June 1941, when Hitler attacked Russia, effectively ending the invasion threat, although the troops continued to man the coastal defences. The Americans entered the war in December 1941 and Britain found itself fighting in the Far East, where the Japanese promptly invaded Malaya and Burma. Units of the British Army were now being sent to the Far East or the North African desert, but the 10th East Surreys remained at home where there were now over a million men under training.

In the middle of 1942, Charlie was sent on an advanced training course at the 77 Division Battle School in Tavistock, which involved forced marches, assault courses, night exercises and the new tactics the army had learned over three years of warfare. The men were graded on their performance, Q1 being exceptional (likely to be given to officers), Q2 good, Q3 satisfactory and Q4 poor. My father passed out with an honourable Q2 and a few months later was promoted to the rank of sergeant 'under conditions of war' – which meant that when peace came he would lose the rank. He listed himself as a 'sergeant' on my birth certificate.

But still there was no action, and for the next two years the regiment spent most of its time training, practising landing on beaches in Devon and Somerset, street fighting in Hull, and even jumping out of airplanes. For most of this time it was based in the west of England, including Helston in Cornwall, and the regimental joke was: 'Join the army and you see England'. Early in 1944, with an invasion of Northern Europe widely expected that year, Charlie applied for a transfer and was sent for yet more specialised training, this time rehearsing large-scale landings on beaches at night-time in all sorts of weather. By June, fitter and more hardened than at any time in his life, he was ready for the opening of the Second Front, which everyone knew was imminent. It came on 6 June 1944, when the Allies finally landed in France.

To his great chagrin, Charlie missed D-Day, just as he had missed

Dunkirk – two of the biggest events of the war in Europe. In 1940 he had been evacuated, through no fault of his own, just days before the Germans broke through the Maginot Line. Now, four years later, he was left out of the Normandy landings, held in reserve while a beach-head was established by the first troops ashore. On 7 July, he was moved to Sussex ready for embarkation as part of the first wave of reserves, and on 13 July, he left for France. He was posted to the 1st Battalion of the South Lancashire Regiment, which he finally caught up with on 17 July outside the besieged town of Caen where, within a day, he was thrown into one of the fiercest battles of the war in north-west Europe.

His first taste of battle came just after dawn on a beautiful summer's day on 18 July 1944, when, from his slit trench to the south of the town, he watched wave after wave of Allied bombers, 2,000 of them, fly over to bomb the German positions around Caen. Out to sea, the Royal Navy battleships joined in the bombardment until, as Antony Beevor wrote in his book *D-Day*, 'for those watching, it was unthinkable that anyone could survive such an onslaught'.

Then the British armoured divisions, followed closely by the infantry, went in, initially encountering dazed Germans rising out of the corn with their hands up. The South Lancashires were first off the mark, and the regimental war diaries, which diligently recorded each day's events, show them initially making good progress, although at one point my father's company lost direction in the heavy woodland and stumbled about before rejoining the main body of the regiment. There were German bodies everywhere, some of them killed by the shock waves, and prisoners streamed past the advancing troops, Charlie's first close contact with the enemy. At 0830 hours, a machine gun opened up and mortar fire began coming in from behind a line of sandpits, but the troops pressed on and by early afternoon they had cleared out a clump of enemy-occupied farm buildings, their objective for the day.

All that night – my father's first under fire – the Germans continually shelled the South Lancashires' positions, shooting at random in the dark, forcing the troops to keep their heads down in their hastily dug trenches. Early the next morning, Charlie's regiment moved up again and dug in around the town of Sannerville, which was nothing more than a heap of rubble. They 'stood to' in expectation of a German counter-attack which didn't materialise and, according to the battalion records, 'the rest of the day was passed in comparative quiet although there was fairly heavy mortaring and the enemy artillery increased in intensity through the day'.

Meanwhile, the British armoured brigades, spearheading the attack, suffered heavy losses from camouflaged Tiger tanks, and the accompanying infantry were cut down with ferocious machine-gun fire which stopped the advance in its tracks. By the end of the second day, few of the objectives had been taken. Most of the regiments, including the South Lancashires, were down to half-strength. It was quite an introduction for my father to modern warfare.

The first two days were fought in exhausting, intense heat, dust and mosquitoes, in a landscape littered with wreckage and so badly cratered it looked, according to one report, 'like a landscape of the moon'. But that night the rain started, flooding the trenches and turning everything to mud. They had to stay where they were, under continual shelling and mortar fire, for the next two days before moving forward again on 22 July. They were, according to the war diaries, 'in close contact with the enemy throughout', and a German sniper shot and killed the regiment's commanding officer, Lieutenant-Colonel Bolster, the third commanding officer the South Lancashires had lost since D-Day.

The rain was followed by oppressive heat so intense it reminded the hardened veterans of the desert, with hordes of mosquitoes and dust which got in everywhere until the soldiers could barely see or breathe. Then the rain came again, an almighty downpour turning the sludge and slit trenches into a sea of mud into which tracks sank eighteen inches. One tank commander wrote home: 'Thank God I am not an infanteer who has to choose between keeping dry above ground or dodging the mortars by jumping into a trench with three foot of water in it.'

The attack had now clearly failed but Charlie and his mates had to put up with the conditions for another five days, all the time under fire from weapons ranging from 5 cm mortars to the dreaded Nebelwerfer, a five-barrelled rocket launcher that made a sound like a banshee. 'Such was this summer,' remarked an officer in a letter home, 'there was no summer at all.' On the afternoon of 27 July, they were finally relieved and moved back to Escoville for a well-earned forty-eight hours of rest. By 31 July, however, they were back in the line, ready for the next decisive phase of the Normandy battle.

* * *

In the last week of July 1944, the American Army, led by General Patton, finally broke out of the Normandy bridgehead and smashed through the enemy lines beyond Avranches, forcing the Germans to abandon Caen, disengage their Panzer divisions and fall back on Falaise, ten miles to the south. On 11 August, the 8th Infantry Brigade, which included the South Lancashires, set off down the main road towards Falaise as part of a grand plan to encircle the German Army before it could withdraw its tanks and heavy equipment. The South Lancashires led the way, transported on self-propelled artillery from which the guns had been removed, or sitting on the tanks. It was very hot, and their biggest problem was the clouds of choking dust, thrown up by the column of moving vehicles, which infiltrated through eye-shields and clothes and masked the perspiring faces. But, after fighting for every yard of ground around Caen, it was exhilarating – 'as near to great fun as men can expect to get in battle,' according to the official history of the 3rd Division.

It couldn't last, however, and in the afternoon the South Lancashires came under heavy fire from anti-tank weapons and machine guns and stood fast for the night, moving off again the next morning to find signs of a hasty enemy withdrawal. Progress now became rapid again and the only enemy encountered were stragglers and deserters, eager to give themselves up.

Although the Germans, particularly the fanatical *Hitlerjugend* and SS divisions, continued to fight, the end was now very near in Normandy. By the middle of August, the South Lancashires had advanced seventy-five miles inland from the D-Day beaches; and by the 16th they had taken the town of La Rivière, which they found clear of enemy troops. With their part of the mission accomplished, they were taken out of the line and my father spent three pleasant days on a farm before moving to a training area near La Chapelle-au-Moine. It was there that he heard the momentous news on 24 August that the Free French, under General Leclerc, had entered Paris. A few weeks later, on 3 September 1944, the British 2nd Army liberated Brussels. The next target was Germany itself.

*   *   *

It would take another nine months of often bitter fighting against fanatical resistance in the coldest winter for years before they got there. The South Lancashires took part in one of the toughest battles of the campaign around Overloon, in Holland, between 12 and 18 October 1944 and survivors later described D-Day as 'a picnic by comparison'. The regimental crest of the 1st battalion is still displayed in the military museum in Overloon, presented after the war by Major Donald Urry, my father's commanding officer. Many officers and men of the regiment, whom my father would have known well, are buried in the town's military cemetery.

In December 1944, a brutal cold spell brought progress on the north-western front to a stop and the South Lancashires reluctantly left the comparative comfort of Overloon, and moved further upriver to Oostrum to prepare for the crossing into Germany. They spent Christmas 1944 on the front line and the war diaries record that patrols heard sounds of revelry from the enemy lines across the Maas River. As was the custom, Christmas dinner – treacle pudding and a couple of cans of Belgian beer – was served by the officers. The war diaries present it as a jolly occasion, but it wasn't. 'Christmas Day on the Maas was a sad time,' recorded one of the officers. 'Every man got a can of beer. Some did not drink. Each received a plum duff.' He recorded the general low spirits of the troops who, after years of war, just wanted to be home with their folks. My father had now been in the army for five years and he had only been home for Christmas once.

In January 1945, extensive flooding put back the operation to cross the Rhine, but the South Lancashires' war diaries record a grimly fought battle near Goch, an ancient town on the German–Dutch border, in February, where casualties were heavy. My father's role in the fighting was recognised in a commendation he received, one of the few papers he left behind. It reads:

It has been brought to my notice that you have performed outstanding good service, and shown great devotion to duty, during the campaign in North West Europe. I award you this certificate as a token of my appreciation, and I have given instructions that this will be noted in your Record of Service.

It bears Montgomery's signature.

A few days later he was promoted to the rank of 2nd lieutenant and presented with his Officer's Record of Service army book, which my researchers found in his army records in the Ministry of Defence, and which lists his 'Nature of Commission' as 'Emergency'. He kept it with him for the rest of his time in the army.

I wonder now what he felt about his promotion. Pride obviously, but probably also regret at leaving the soldiers of his platoon with whom he had bonded during the winter months when the freezing weather on the Maas prevented offensive activity. People tell me I have a natural ability for creating loyalty among the little teams I have built around me from my earliest days in the shops, and I probably inherited that from my father. Unfortunately, I never got a chance to see that side of him, but researching this book has given me a better understanding of the forces that shaped him into the man he was. I just wish he had talked to me more about it, but he never wanted to and I have to respect that.

By the third week in March 1945, the Allied armies were positioned along the entire length of the Rhine and on the night of 23 March began streaming across into Germany. My father followed six days later at a place called Mühlenfeld at 0530 on 29 March 1945 and the 1st Battalion of the South Lancashires was ordered to head north, where it soon began picking up prisoners of war and German stragglers, including a U-boat instructor who turned out to be on leave but had got caught up in the retreat. But their rapid advance ran into stiffer opposition from fanatical German SS and parachute troops along the River Ems at Lingen, holding up the whole of General Horrocks's XXX Corps, which the 3rd Division was attached to.

The South Lancashires were given the task of clearing the northern exits of the town and had almost completed the task when the enemy counter-attacked vigorously, taking one of the bridges they were holding. A troop of tanks came to the rescue and the Germans pulled back, taking some prisoners with them. The South Lancashires were in the thick of that little battle, according to the war diaries.

They pressed on again and on 11 April 1945, my father's big day, they received orders to relieve the battered 5th Durham Light Infantry, who had taken the town of Wildeshausen, and hold it against the expected counter-attack until the armour got there. Advance parties reported back that it was empty of enemy soldiers, but during the night the Germans had crept back and opened fire as the British troops entered the town. 'A' Company, with my father in command, was first on the scene.

'A Company reported small pocket of enemy with MG [machine gun] and said they were dealing with it,' the war diaries recorded laconically. Charlie's commanding officer later wrote a detailed account of what followed, which became part of his citation for a medal. It describes how my father led a section forward through the narrow streets towards the last reported location of the enemy, but had only gone 200 yards when two machine guns opened up at close range, catching the lead section in the crossfire and causing several casualties. Everyone dived for cover and tried to fire back, but they were pinned down and there was no way forward. Charlie ordered the first section (about ten men) to cover him and draw the enemy fire, and then led a second section round the right flank with the intention of turning the enemy's position. But he again came under fire, this time from a third machine gun which had been sited there to anticipate just that tactic. There was nothing for it but to charge.

According to his commanding officer in the citation for a medal he wrote after the event, Charlie jumped to his feet and, shouting for the troops to follow, he leapt forward, shooting from the hip. The Germans were overrun and the survivors retreated through the backstreets, followed hotly by the British troops. After a thorough search of the area, Charlie reported back that it was clear of the enemy.

Charlie's day was not over yet, however, and he was back in action a few hours later. At 1800 hours, a column of returning British troop carriers was fired at by a group of enemy soldiers who had again slipped back into the town, and the leading vehicle was hit by a *Panzerfaust*, the German equivalent of a bazooka. This time the details of Charlie's actions went unrecorded apart from another laconic entry in the war diaries: 'A Company reported their small pocket cleared.'

Shortly before nightfall, the Wehrmacht cut the only supply road into Wildeshausen, and for the next forty-eight hours, the troops in the town had to beat off a series of German counter-attacks, including one led by a company of parachutists. Later, one of the British officers described how the German officer leading the attack was wounded and fell six yards in front of their guns. 'He was brought in, and stated that he had been ordered to capture the railway station and to hoist the Nazi flag on the roof as a success signal, for the rest of his battalion to come in and mop up Wildeshausen.' One of the Middlesex soldiers, who had arrived to strengthen the defences, collected the flag that night 'and the C.O. sent it to the Mayoress of Finchley as one of the Battalion's trophies of war'. As far as I know it's still there.

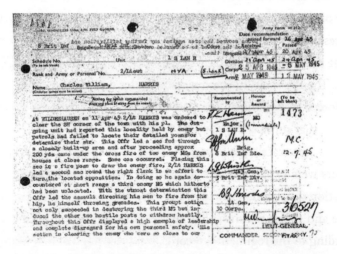

My father's commendation for his MC. It is signed by Field Marshal Bernard Montgomery as well as General Brian Horrocks and General 'Bolo' Whistler.

After that, they moved on again, deeper and deeper into Germany, and Charlie was in Bremen, taken by the Allies in the final days of the war in more bitter fighting, on 6 May 1945 when the news came through that Hitler was dead and the Russians were in the Reichstag. Two days later Germany formally surrendered, and the regiment held a thanksgiving service followed the next day by a requiem for the fallen, of whom there were many. In my father's papers, I found a list of all the officers who served in his regiment from Normandy to the end of the war, sent to him by a fellow officer who had painstakingly compiled it. It records twenty officers, including two colonels and three majors, killed and nearly forty seriously wounded in that eleven-month period alone. The list of casualties is longer than the survivors.

At the end of May, they moved out of the Bremen area, which was to be in the American sector, to the pretty Westphalian town of Lemgo where they took over a huge camp that had housed thousands of Russian prisoners of war in unimaginable conditions. They experienced some grim satisfaction in making the local civilians clean out the appalling mess, but then began the even grimmer task of processing some of the thousands of 'displaced people', or 'DPs', left behind by the ravages of war. The diaries record them processing 5,000 pathetic souls in just three days, but as fast as they could do so, the camps filled up again. The Russians, in particular, had suffered terribly, starved, beaten and forced to work until they died in their millions. These poor souls were all that survived.

It was not exactly the heroic end to the war my father and his fellow soldiers were expecting, but after it had been cleaned up, the accommodation was good, particularly for the officers, and they organised a dance and sports fixtures. Charlie was put in charge of boxing, which, according to the regimental records, was 'very popular'.

If they were expecting to be de-mobbed and sent home immediately, the troops of the 3rd Division were to be disappointed. Other divisions were breaking up, their conscript soldiers already packing to go back to Britain. But there was still a war on in the Far East and the regiment was moved to Detmold, in the Ruhr, where it began training for operations in the Pacific Theatre. Charlie and his fellow officers were ordered to be ready to ship out any day to the US, where they would be transported to the Far East on American ships.

Britain was now headed into an election and 4 July 1945 was polling day for the armed forces in Germany. I'm sure my father would have voted for the Conservatives and his hero, Winston Churchill, and would have been as shocked as anyone when Churchill lost and Britain elected a Labour government under Clement Attlee.

His mood, however, must have been lightened by the news he received early in the middle of a hot, sticky July: he had been awarded the Military Cross, the third highest military decoration that was awarded to officers for an act 'of exemplary gallantry during active operations against the enemy'. Charlie's actions at Wildeshausen had not gone unrecognised and his acting commanding officer, Major J. K. Warner, had recommended him for an immediate Military Cross. Major Warner sent his citation to brigade HQ, where it was signed by the brigade commander and passed on up to Major General 'Bolo' Whistler, the legendary commander of the 3rd Division. Aware of the importance of the action in Wildeshausen, Wheeler duly signed the recommendation on 24 April and sent it to General Horrocks, commander of XXX Corps, who signed it and sent it up again until, finally, on 6 May 1945, it reached the headquarters of the commander-in-chief himself, Field Marshal Bernard Montgomery, who added his signature of approval to all the others.

I have a copy of the citation, with all those signatures on it, and am very proud of it. I am even prouder of the regimental photo of Montgomery pinning the medal on his chest in July 1945. I have had a life-size bronze statue of him made from that picture and it now stands in the quad in Harris Manchester College in Oxford University.

In August, as they were packing to leave for the US, news came through that the Japanese had surrendered and the war in the East was over and a few days later, on 20 August 1945, General Whistler called the officers and NCOs together to brief them on their future. They would not be going to the Pacific Theatre, he told them, but nor would they be going home just yet. The 3rd Division had been chosen to become Britain's new 'Imperial Strategic Reserve', a fast reaction force that could be sent into trouble spots in the British Empire at short notice to deal with emergencies. They would be relieved from their occupational duties in Germany, and stand ready on five days' notice to fly to any part of the world. The most likely arena in the short term was the Middle East.

This posed a real dilemma for my father. Most of the soldiers recruited into the forces in the war years were now being discharged and were returning home. He had served in the army for nearly six years, he was twenty-seven, with a wife and a three-year-old son, and he could return to civilian life knowing he had done his duty to his country – which mattered a lot to him. At the same time, he felt a loyalty to his regiment and to the 3rd Division, which, out of the whole British Army, had been chosen for this new strategic role. Staying on would mean certain promotion to captain, but it would also mean signing on for a minimum of three years.

He came home to see me and my mother at the end of July 1945, and I assume discussed his future with her and the rest of his family. My mother, I know, was appalled at the thought of him signing on again, and did everything she could to dissuade him. But I think he had already made up his mind. My uncle Fred, who had just been de-mobbed from the navy, used to joke that my father offered to take him along as his batman if he was sent to the Middle East but he indignantly refused. 'I'm not going to work for you,' he told him in the pub one night when my father, half-seriously, suggested it.

At any rate, my father went back to his regiment in Moorsel, Belgium, signed on for three years and the deed was done. It was one of the biggest mistakes of his life, and came close to ending his marriage. I now know that my mother never fully forgave him, although neither of them ever raised it in my hearing and I only discovered all this much later, long after they had both passed on.

On 20 September, confirmation came through that the division was to be sent to the Middle East 'to deal with the Palestine question' and they set off by train on 6 October, 'amid tearful farewells of the Belgian belles', as one soldier put it. In Toulon, they boarded the SS *Mataroa*, where, according to the same soldier, the accommodation was not 'the acme of comfort', and docked in Port Suez ten days later where they were issued with tropical uniform – shorts – and new equipment. I remember seeing a picture of my father in shorts in the desert but never knew until now where he was or what he was doing there.

They spent the next six weeks at a large First World War camp near Ismailia, where Charlie gave boxing lessons to the young troops. Training involved playing endless war games, and exercises where Charlie, now a senior officer, often acted as umpire. On 12 November, they performed an exercise bizarrely codenamed 'Sinn Fein', where the 1st battalion competed against the Moonbeams, 'a well-organised and armed guerilla [*sic*] group'. Captain Harris is listed as an umpire. Over 100 new recruits arrived from Britain and the diaries record that 'R Company formed under Captain Harris MC to deal with battalion reinforcements'. His complement included a batman.

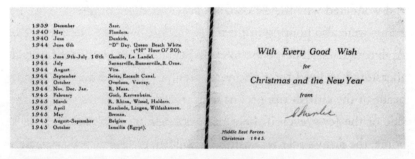

Regimental 1945 Christmas card home from Egypt. On the left it lists the battles the South Lancs had been through, including Dunkirk and D-Day. Charlie joined them in July 1944 outside Caen.

In early December, they finally left for Haifa, some by road, some by train, my father in charge of the rear echelons. They found Palestine cold and wet after the Egyptian desert, and they quickly changed back into long trousers and winter gear. They spent a bleak Christmas 1945 in Haifa and my father joined the other officers in serving dinner, after which there was a football match where the officers played the sergeants. 'Result: chaotic,' the war diaries record. On Boxing Day, there was a concert 'at which many impromptu performances were given', and then it was back to serious business.

On 27 December, there were terrorist attacks in Jerusalem and Jaffa and the regiment now patrolled the streets of Haifa in armoured cars. 'It was a very strenuous time,' wrote one of the officers for the regimental journal, 'patrolling the town night after night. We never got more than one night in three in bed.' On 4 January 1946, they were given instruction on the use of batons and shields and 'methods of mob dispersal'.

Their job basically was to keep order between the Jews and the Arabs and prevent the flow of 'illegal immigrants' into Palestine, still under British mandate, which largely meant preventing uprooted and homeless Jews, including Holocaust survivors, from entering the territory. The troops had seen pictures of the German concentration camps where six million Jews had perished (there was a big one at Bremen), and wondered why they should keep the survivors out. Jewish immigrants were also pouring in from Iraq, Iran, Libya and North African Arab countries, all desperate to claim back the Holy Land where their ancestors had lived for 3,000 years. The politics were well above the heads of the British troops, but their natural sympathies were on the side of the Jews, even if the sentiments were not reciprocated. Back home, the army's role was wildly unpopular, as it was internationally, and the US Congress had even delayed granting Britain vital loans for reconstruction because of its troops in Palestine. Before the election, the Labour Party had promised to allow mass Jewish migration into Palestine but once it was in government it reneged because of Arab pressure on the Foreign Office. Anti-British Jewish militancy increased and the Zionist movement, whose objective was to drive the

British out of Palestine and establish a Jewish state, stepped up its military campaign, blowing up the British headquarters in the King David Hotel in Jerusalem with the loss of nearly a hundred lives.

On 8 January 1946, Charlie was promoted again, this time to second-in-command of D Company with the rank of Acting Major. Many years later, in one of the very rare moments he spoke about it, he told me he had been promoted because his major had been killed, but I think, reading the records, it was more likely his major left for another regiment. The diaries record that notification was received 'that Major Holmes MC had been granted a regular commission in the Essex Regiment' and my father would have stepped into his place. The promotion was never ratified.

A few days later, he witnessed for himself the arrival of the pathetic souls the British were trying to keep out. On 18 January 1946, Royal Navy destroyers picked up a ship sixty miles off the coast and escorted her into the port of Haifa. She was a tiny craft, just 500 tonnes, packed with Jewish refugees who had somehow, against terrible odds, got this far. Charlie was at the dock the next morning as 537 males and 357 women filed off her, clutching what few possessions they had taken from Europe, where most of their families had died in the Nazi extermination camps. Charlie helped escort them to a temporary immigrant area where the conditions were pretty basic (the film *Exodus*, made in 1960, was based on this incident or one like it).

By that stage my father was deeply disillusioned with the role of the army in the post-war world. There had been honour and glory fighting Hitler, however tough it was, but here there was no honour and even less glory, and he had no taste for street fighting against Jewish civilians given the name 'terrorists'. Within a month of arriving in Palestine, urged on by the increasingly strident demands of my mother, who had not seen him in six months, he had made up his mind. He would leave the army.

That was not so easy though. He had contracted for three years and the army had every intention of holding him to it. Experienced officers were in short supply in an army that now consisted predominantly of raw recruits who had never seen action. His request was refused, but on 29 January 1946, my father was abruptly taken out of the Palestinian theatre and sent back to the UK. The only reference in the records to his departure is a note that 'Lt Hopkins was appointed Unit Boxing Officer in the absence of Capt Harris MC'. After that, he is listed on the monthly roll-call as 'on course UK', implying he was sent back to England for further training. But I don't think he was – he was done with the army. He remained on the strength of the regiment for another two months, regularly marked as 'absent – on course UK'.

It was, I believe, my mother who engineered his release with an extraordinary degree of determination and persistence that I never thought she possessed until I read the records.

She wrote to the War Office demanding my father be released immediately, saying he had done his bit for the country, was a decorated hero, and should be allowed to come home to his wife and his young son who had barely seen him. When that got her nowhere, she worked her way through the signatures on my father's commendation for his MC, getting higher and higher up the ranks. Although the letters were written in her own hand, they were clearly drafted by someone else, as I cannot imagine my mother, who had a limited formal education, using the official language she did. But the sentiments were all hers, and she wrote with a certainty and authority that leaves me in awe – as indeed it did the brass in the War Office.

She wrote to General 'Bolo' Whistler again, making a powerfully emotional case for the release of her husband, but he replied to the effect that he couldn't set a precedent. Then she wrote to Lieutenant General Sir Brian Horrocks, stressing my father's service under his command and his MC, threatening to leave my father if he was not released from the army. Next up would have been Montgomery himself, and she was clearly prepared to remind him of the medal he had pinned on my father's chest.

In total, she must have written more than twenty letters, each one carefully handwritten, until General Horrocks finally relented. In the middle of April 1946, Charlie was finally discharged from the British Army.

My mother had her husband home at last. And I had my father back.

CHAPTER 3

'ANY OLD IRON?'

Back in London in the summer of 1946, my father initially found life hard. Unable to find a job to look after his wife and growing son, he took up boxing for a living and fought as a professional for a couple of years, hoping to save enough to start his own business. In those days, before television, boxing had a huge public following and London was full of arenas that attracted large crowds. My father fought as a lightweight at some of the popular east London venues: Manor Place Baths in Bow (a favourite of his), Hoxton Baths, Leyton Baths, Streatham Ice Rink and others – all well-known London landmarks when I was a boy.

Professional boxers were expected to fight up to ten bouts a year and could make a decent living out of it, although obviously their careers were short. My father was already twenty-eight when he turned professional and I think he fought about a dozen or so fights before he saved enough money to open a lino stall in the covered market in Rye Lane. I was only six when he retired from the ring and I never saw him fight, but until recently, when it was rebuilt, there were still pictures of him on the wall of Bradfield Club in Commercial Road (now the Bradfield Youth and Community Centre), his home club where he trained and later coached the local hopefuls.

Until he got his lino business off the ground a few years later, he didn't earn very much and we were far from rich. But we didn't go hungry either and I don't remember lacking for anything – people's expectations were more modest in those days. Once he was back, we settled down as a family. We were an interesting lot. My mother's father, Grandad Ward, was the local rag-and-bone man, who would cheerily drive his horse and cart through the streets with the traditional cry of his trade, 'Any old iron?', accompanied by the clanging of his brass bell. He collected scrap iron, old furniture and clothes, anything people wanted to throw out, which he would later sort and sell for what he could – an early form of recycling. He was a great trader, swapping an old pram for a kitchen table, or pennies for old iron, often handing out sweets and once even a goldfish for something he thought he could make a few bob out of. Every town had at least one rag-and-bone man, who was a respected and essential member of the local community, and long after the war they still used horse-drawn carts. My grandfather preferred the term 'totter', and he always talked of 'goin' tottin'', but it was the same thing. I often sat beside him on the cart and rang the bell as he did his rounds, driving his horse down streets which are still familiar to me. Later, back in the yard, I would go through the treasure trove he had collected, finding old books and interesting bric-a-brac that people had thrown out.

He sometimes went on benders, getting so drunk he forgot where he'd left his horse. He was arrested several times for being drunk and disorderly and my father, his son-in-law, would have to bail him out. On one occasion, he actually lost his horse, or it was stolen, and he was so devastated by it that Dad, whose lino business must have been doing well by then, bought him a new one. The first one never did turn up.

Horse-drawn vehicles were still common on the streets of Peckham in the late 1940s, delivering coal or furniture or pulling hearses, and the milkman did his daily round on a horse-drawn float. Our horse was kept in the stables around the back of the house and one day I went in to see her and shouted excitedly: 'Dad, Grandad – come quick! We've got two horses now.' They didn't believe me of course, but I was right – the mare had given birth overnight and there was a new foal.

The better-off houses in Peckham had small gardens, and boys like me could earn some extra pocket money by gathering up the horse dung from the streets and selling it as manure. In the summer, it was the weekly task of husbands to mow the lawns, energetically pushing hand-mowers across their tiny patches, and we used the cuttings for the horses – but we could never give them too much or they got colic.

Another early memory I have is of one Christmas time, when I was about seven, when my father and grandad took me to Herne Hill to sell mistletoe at a penny a bunch. After a while they decided I was doing a better job than they were and went off to the pub. It was freezing but I didn't mind, proudly displaying my takings when they eventually staggered back. I probably paid for their beer – and they gave me a lemonade afterwards.

My father, with his war medals and prowess as a boxer, was a well-respected individual in a community where everyone knew everyone else, but I always remember him as a modest man and never heard him boast. He enjoyed going to the pub with his friends, of which he had many, but in comparison to my uncle Fred and my grandfather, who liked their tipple, he was a relatively abstemious man.

I adored my nan, my mother's mother, and the highlight of my week was when we visited her on Sundays at her house in Blake's Road, where she gave me winkles and cockles and thick slices of bread with lots of butter – my favourite meal. Sometimes she would take me down to the East Street market, off Walworth Road, where she would treat me to a sarsaparilla – a hot, carbonated raspberry drink that I don't think exists any more. These were real treats at a time when basic commodities such as butter, meat, tea and coal were still rationed. So was confectionery until well into the 1950s, and I can clearly remember getting my coupons clipped in the sweet shop on Sundays when I bought bon-bons with my pocket money.

At home in our two-room flat we had no bathroom, just a sink, and the toilet was at the bottom of the garden, which was not unusual in the immediate post-war years in our part of London. Nan made up for our lack of a bath by giving me a weekly scrub in an old tin tub, boiling the water in the kitchen and putting it in the tub in front of the open fire. One of my favourite times was when the whole family would gather at her house for a Christmas Day dinner, which started at lunchtime and went on well past my bedtime. My uncle Fred, who took over from my grandfather as the rag-and-bone man in Peckham, was always the life and soul of the party and I loved listening to him until I would eventually fall asleep and some kind soul, probably my father, would carry me upstairs to Uncle Fred's bed on the first floor.

Of all her grandchildren, I was my nan's favourite and she always made a fuss of me, and I couldn't wait to get to her house for my favourite tea after Sunday school.

My memory of my childhood in Peckham, maybe coloured by time, is that people were generally happier and more content with their lot, more secure and with less stress in their personal and professional lives. I think austerity and the bombings brought people together and made them much more self-reliant. My mother worked in the local laundry in the mornings, making sure she was home by the time I arrived back from school. There was little surplus money to spend, and there wasn't much to spend it on anyway. Few people went further than Brighton or the south coast for holidays, and no one I knew ever went abroad, unless they were in the armed forces. Very few families had cars.

For my parents' generation, the post-war years were a time of enormous political, social and economic change with the introduction of the National Health Service and the welfare state. Life for most people, many of whom had lived through two world wars and the depression of the '30s, began to improve as the country recovered, and my father expanded from his market stall to take over the one opposite. But he still refused to vote Labour and was delighted when Churchill became Prime Minister again in 1951.

I remember the year of 1951 for a different reason: it was the year of the Festival of Britain, a huge exhibition on London's South Bank, near Waterloo station, which I must have visited half a dozen times, sometimes with my parents or with my nan. The central attractions were the huge dome, the largest in the world, and the Skylon, which was the London Eye of its day, a cigar-shaped tower supported by cables that made it look as if it was floating in the air. I remember my father chuckling at Churchill's joke that the Skylon reflected the British economy under the Labour government: 'no clear means of support'.

Even more exciting for an active young boy and his mates was the fun fair in Battersea Park, which had a terrifying rollercoaster called the Big Dipper (there was a big accident there twenty years later when lots of children were killed), which I rode with my dad, as well as huge roundabouts and slides on a scale we had never seen before.

But I think my most bonding times with my father were when he took me to boxing matches, or we listened to them together on the radio. Like every boy at the time, I was brought up on boxing legends such as Joe Louis, Rocky Marciano and our own home-grown champions Jack Dempsey, Bruce Woodcock and Freddie Mills, who lived down the road at Denmark Hill. Dad would get up in the middle of the night to tune in to fights broadcast from the US, and as I got older I was allowed to join him, sitting hunched over a crackling radio as overexcited commentators brought every punch from more than 3,000 miles away into our living room.

The most memorable fight he took me to was between the world light-heavyweight champion, Sugar Ray Robinson, and the British contender Randolph Turpin in June 1951. Sugar Ray was a legendary fighter whom my father regarded as the greatest boxer of all time 'pound for pound'. He famously arrived for the fight in a pink Cadillac while Turpin, an unassuming 23-year-old from Warwickshire with a black Guyanese father, travelled on the London Underground. His elder brothers were in his corner along with his manager, George Middleton, whose day job was a scrap metal dealer.

The fight was in Earls Court Arena and my father and I drove across London in the little old Ford van he had acquired soon after the war when he started his small lino business. To say it was temperamental would be an understatement: to start it, you had to hold the dashboard in place with one hand while pulling the starter out with the other, which as like as not didn't work, and often we had to push it down the road. My mother hated it, but it was all we could afford and we were lucky to have any transport at all. The only decent car in the family was an old Wolseley owned by my uncle Tom, who was thirteen years older than my father, and my mother used to love going for jaunts in that, down the Old Kent Road or, on special occasions, to the Dreamland funfair at Margate.

The van managed to get us safely across London to watch the fight of a lifetime. No one gave Turpin a chance, and some of my father's friends were saying that he wasn't ready for it and Sugar Ray would destroy him. But he didn't – the fight went the full fifteen rounds and at the end the referee held up Turpin's glove, pronouncing him the new light-heavyweight champion of the world. The cheer that greeted him could probably have been heard in Peckham and the rejoicing in the streets and pubs was afterwards compared to the VE Day celebrations. It didn't last long, however – two months later they had a rematch in New York and Sugar Ray knocked our British hero out in the tenth round. We listened to that one on our radio in Peckham.

We had our own local boxing star from neighbouring Balham, Don Cockell, who turned professional around the same time my father did and they must have known each other from the London boxing circuits. Cockell initially fought as a light-heavyweight and, after a string of stunning knockouts, challenged Turpin for the British and Commonwealth championship. They were Britain's two best boxers in a generation and my father took me to the White City Stadium on 10 June 1952 to see the fight. Cockell was knocked down three times and lost on a technical knockout in the eleventh round. Later he had a successful career as a heavyweight until he challenged Rocky Marciano for the World Heavyweight Championship. Marciano, one of the deadliest punchers of all time, half-killed him, remarking afterwards: 'He's got a lot of guts. I don't think I ever hit anyone else any more often or harder.' Cockell never won another fight and became a rather sad figure, ending up working as an emergency maintenance man in Tooting. He later died of cancer, aged fifty-three.

My father had high hopes for a young flyweight called Henry Carpenter (not to be confused with the boxing commentator of the same name who was serving in the Royal Navy at the time), a local lad from Peckham he sparred with at the Bradford Club. He was Britain's flyweight entry in the 1948 London Olympics (known as the 'Austerity Games' because of the post-war shortages and rationing), where he was thought to have a good chance, but lost in the second round, after which he turned professional. We went to see him several times at the Manor Place Baths in Walworth, where he often fought, and he had a string of victories until April 1951, when he came up against Terry Allen, the British lightweight champion. The fight went the distance but to Dad's great disappointment Henry lost on points. As so often happened, he was never the same after that and he lost three out of his next four bouts and then retired. Allen had been a barrow boy before he turned professional and when he retired he opened a fruit and vegetable shop in Islington.

I still treasure those precious times I had with my father, talking about boxing, going to fights, conducting post-mortems afterwards and just spending precious time on our own. At home, he was always busy in the shops or talking to Mum, but boxing was our private space that my mother was never allowed to enter. I think I probably talked to him more when we were going to boxing matches than at any other time of my life. I was a voluble youngster and he was a good talker and loved to share his deep knowledge of the sport with his only son.

I have retained my interest in boxing all my life, but it was never the same without my father.

* * *

There were no state nursery schools in Peckham when I was growing up, so like everyone else I started school when I was five, attending Gloucester Road Primary, an imposing red-brick Victorian building which is still there (and where, I am told, they list me as one of their distinguished alumni). My main memory of it is of disliking the school milk, provided by the state and which every child in the country was expected to drink, a third of a pint a day, and the malt, introduced in schools to supplement the child's diet. Both made me feel sick and put me off school from an early age.

But I enjoyed Sunday school at St Luke's Church, or what was left of it after the bombing (it was rebuilt in the early 1950s as a squat, brick structure). For some reason, St Luke's registered my birth as 1943, making me a year younger, and I still have that certificate today.

From my earliest school days, I had difficulties with basic reading and writing, something that has lasted all my life. Only many years later, when my sons were assessed, did I discover that I was dyslexic, which no one knew about then and that teachers and parents alike put down either to laziness or stupidity. Yet they could see I was neither, and the teachers never picked on me. I was an active, keen boy, good at sport and even better at maths. I was always able to compute numbers in my brain faster even than the teachers, a habit I have retained all my life (the only person I have ever met who could do mental arithmetic faster than me was (Lord) Leonard Wolfson, who later put me on the board of Great Universal Stores).

Dyslexic people learn to cope by finding different ways of getting around problems, approaching things from an unconventional angle. And that's what I did from a very early age, without realising what I was doing or why I was doing it. I managed to get by in English basically because I had a good memory and learned by rote, convincing my teachers I was a better reader than I actually was (writing was more difficult and I never really mastered that). My memory also helped me with history, where I could memorise dates and names, and with geography. Like my father, I was also good at sport, mostly ball sports, and that helped me gain respect as well as give me confidence (which I never lacked in any case).

By the early 1950s, my father's lino business was going well enough for us to buy our first house, which also meant moving school. Our new home, 155 Millfield Road in Thornton Heath, a few miles from Croydon, was a semi-detached house with two bedrooms and a little garden but, much more important, it had a proper bathroom and the type of kitchen my mother had dreamed of, with a washing machine and a fridge. My father paid £1,950 for it, probably with the help of the building society, and it was a major step up from our old flat which we were not sorry to leave. He also bought our first real car, a Standard Vanguard, with the number DRD 333, which I've always tried to get for one of my cars but never managed it.

Unfortunately, in the year or so we lived in the new house, I was ill a lot with ear trouble and pleurisy, a hangover from my childhood illness. I still remember the crotchety old doctor in Thornton Heath who attended me and who I was afraid of, but he knew what he was doing and eventually I got better. I was not helped by the London smogs, or 'peasoupers' as we called them, fogs so thick with smoke that you could barely see your hand in front of your face, and which affected my weak chest. There was at least one every winter, which regularly brought the City to a near-standstill and caused thousands of early deaths from asphyxia and bronchial asthma. I remember well the 'Great Smog' of December 1952 that killed an estimated 12,000 Londoners and stopped all trains, cars and public events for four days. The local newspapers reported that in some of the theatres it was so thick 'that the actors could not be seen upon the stage'.

I spent only one year at my new school, Kensington Avenue, but it was a defining one for me as they made me captain of the football team.

I had played football on and off all my life, kicking a ball around the local park with friends or my father, but this was the first time I had played with a proper team against other schools, and I excelled at it.

I was also approaching the time when I would be expected to take the Eleven Plus test, which I was dreading. The saving grace was that a large part of it was oral, including mental arithmetic, which I could cope with fairly easily, and I was also pretty good at general knowledge. But the English essay was torture and I struggled with it. Somehow I scraped through and was accepted by Streatham Grammar, where I would spend the rest of my school days.

At home in the garden in Millfield Road.

In 1954, when I was twelve, we moved to a new house again, this time to the more upmarket Gibson's Hill from where I travelled every day to school by bus. Although I still struggled with English, once again I learned to compensate for my dyslexia and managed somehow to keep up with the class in most subjects. Every day we had to learn to spell twelve new words and get at least half of them right – or we got the cane. I knew I could never remember twelve so I learned seven, which gave me a spare if I got another one wrong. I don't think the teachers ever tumbled to this little trick. I memorised some of the most difficult words so well that I remember them to this day, and a little test I still use is to ask people to spell the word PHLEGM. You'd be surprised at the number who can't – try it some time.

I continued to do well at maths, which was a huge advantage for me, and any of the other subjects which involved numbers or memory, preferably both. But I was hopeless at languages and got the cane regularly for French and Latin, which I could never grasp, and my German was even worse. I gave up on learning a foreign language a long time ago.

Nor could I get my head around drawing. One day we were set the task of drawing a pig and I drew a round face with two little ears and four sticks for legs. The teacher thought I was taking the Mickey and I got a caning for it. But I was simply not good at it and never mastered it. I have always been good at getting what I want, but getting there was not always easy, which is why I had to approach things from a different angle. That is how I have lived my life.

The teachers might have been tough disciplinarians, but they also did a fine job. Mr Gutteridge, who administered punishment with a ruler on the back of the knuckles, later became a friend whom I saw a lot of long after leaving school.

My real forte was sport and within two years I was captain of both the cricket and football teams. That gave me a status in the school that more than compensated for my reading problems, and kept me out of trouble with the masters. At the age of twelve, I was picked to play football for London Schoolboys and dreamed of even higher things. The highlight of my career was playing at Highbury, home of Arsenal. Unfortunately, in the first twenty minutes I damaged a cartilage in my knee and had to limp off. It required an operation, a big affair in those days, and I was too scared to have it, so a promising football career ended there.

Forced to give up football, I took up tennis, and my uncle Tom presented me with a wooden-framed Dunlop racquet that I kept religiously in its wooden press and which lasted me for years (I've still got it). It was the last present Uncle Tom ever gave me, as he died soon afterwards, aged forty-nine. With that racquet I won the Sutton championship and qualified to play at the Junior Wimbledon, where I lost to an American. I have played tennis most of my life and still love it.

In Millfield Road, with the Baker brothers.

My most abiding memory of cricket is captaining the school team in the opening match of a tournament in Dulwich Park. My parents, who seldom saw me play, came to watch and I wanted to make my father really proud. I batted at number six and was the highest scorer in the first innings, getting eight out a total of twenty-eight, which was enough to set us up for a win. I took a couple of quick wickets and was feeling so pleased to be playing so well in front of my father. Then I fielded a ball awkwardly and bruised my thumb-nail, which aggravated an existing whitlow (I've still got the scar). We won the game but I was in such pain as I came off the pitch that I went over to my dad and showed it to him, asking him to take me to a doctor. But if I expected sympathy, I didn't get it. 'No,' he told me sternly. 'When you're the captain, you go home with the team – not before.' And he got into his car and drove off, leaving me open-mouthed and ashamed. I went back to the pavilion to join the others and travelled home with the team on the bus. My father looked at me with approval and took me straight to casualty to have it treated.

I didn't think much of it at the time, but I realised later that I had learned something of lasting importance: you stay with your team and look after the people you are responsible for. It was something he had learned as a soldier in the war and I suspect was why he had become such a good officer. It is a principle I have followed all my life since.

CHAPTER 4

THE CARPET TRADE

My father was twenty-nine when he quit boxing and started in the lino trade. My uncle Tom was already in the business with three shops, two in Tooting and one in Battersea, and my cousin Denny, Tom's son, later started his own business with two shops, one in Edmonton and the other in Haringey. Uncle Jimmy also had a lino shop, so there was something of a family tradition about it, just as there had been a tradition of making blinds.

I don't know whether Uncle Tom helped him get started, but at any rate, in about 1949, when I was seven, my father opened a stall under the name C W Harris Linoleum in the covered Peckham Market where most local people did their weekly shopping. It was a large stall, more like a shop really, with the walls stacked with rolls of lino and the floor piled up with rugs and the narrow stair carpets that were popular then. He had a good sales manner and worked hard and was soon doing well enough to take over another stall across the aisle. He ran the two as a single unit, with two men working for him, and he did a roaring trade. That stall remained the heart of the business until well into my time, producing the cash flow that paid the bills and allowed us to expand. I used to go and help out from an early age, particularly on Saturday afternoons after I finished school at twelve noon. I remember clearly the rugs we sold and even the price: the rugs were £1 9s 6d each (twenty-seven inches by fifty-four inches) and the stair carpet was 3s 11d a yard (eighteen inches wide).

The market in Rye Lane was so busy on a Saturday that it could take ages just to get from the covered entrance to our stall. Rye Lane itself was probably the most important shopping street in south-east London and Jones & Higgins, where I was sometimes taken at Christmas time as a special treat, was regarded as one of the best department stores outside the West End (it was closed in 1983 but the building remains and I opened a carpet shop there in 2007).

My father was ambitious, hard-working and keen to expand, but I suspect he never expected the business to take off as it did. The early years, with Britain still in the throes of rationing and austerity, were tough, and his main interest was probably just to earn enough to put bread on the table. However, in the early 1950s, he was able to lift his head and look around for new opportunities – which is when he opened his first real shop, on Peckham High Street, followed a few years later by another one in Penge. I'm sure he would have gone on to open many more stores if he'd had the chance, but in 1956, when he had been operating the business for about seven years, fate intervened.

*   *   *

My life up to the age of fourteen was a contented, fulfilled and, overall, happy one. I struggled academically at some subjects but that didn't worry me because I had my sports and for several years I was more interested in becoming a professional footballer than I was a retailer. I was always the leader of our little gang, consistently captaining teams in different schools and different sports, and I think my father was proud of me, although he never said it – that was not his style. After my initial illness, I was a healthy, fit boy with seemingly boundless energy and enthusiasms, which I was able to share with both friends and family.

But then life changed. In 1956, Dad, still only thirty-eight, was diagnosed with cancer of the stomach and had an operation in the Charing Cross Hospital (which was then still in the Strand) where I went to see him. I didn't often go up to the West End, which was a very different world to our more innocent Peckham and south-east London, and my anxious mother carefully counted out the bus fare – I think it was about sixpence each way – and sent me on my way. I got off at Trafalgar Square and was walking across it when one of those professional photographers who used to hang around tourist sites took a photo of me with the pigeons. He then demanded money for the picture, which I hadn't asked him to take and didn't want, in such a menacing way that I would probably have given it to him if I'd had it. As it happened, I had nothing other than my bus fare home and fled the scene with him still shouting abuse at me.

It really upset me and I was still shaking when I arrived at the hospital, where I found my dad sitting up in bed after his operation, looking weak but cheerful. The news, he told me, was good. The doctors believed the cancer had been cut out and he was going to be all right. He came home a few weeks later but still had to go back for radiotherapy, then the only treatment available for cancer other than surgery, and he used to come back from hospital and get my mother to apply talcum powder on his front, right up to his neck, to ease the pain of his burnt skin. He didn't forget the staff in the hospital who had looked after him: many years later I found a letter in his effects from the head of the radiotherapy department in Charing Cross thanking him for his 'very kind gift', which they promised to use to buy 'some little things' they couldn't get on the NHS. That letter touched me deeply. He was a really kind, generous man.

A year passed and he seemed to be getting better, going to work most days and trying to carry on the business. I helped in the shops as much as possible, and so did my mother, but he was the boss, the person the staff looked up to, and they could see he was no longer the man he was. I was a busy teenager and just assumed, as everybody else seemed to, that he would get better. Besides, by then, I had a girlfriend.

* * *

I first met Pauline Chumley in 1956, when we were both fourteen. It happened like this. I had a friend from across the road, Peter Holmes, who I used to play football and cricket with, part of our gang that hung out around Norwood Grove, a park on the edge of Gibson's Hill in Norbury where we both lived. In the long summer evenings, we would all meet up for an impromptu game of cricket, one of us bringing the stumps, another the bat (that was usually me) and someone else the ball. They were informal games, with everyone taking their turn to bat and bowl, and they were great fun.

We didn't have umpires of course, and that sometimes led to disputed decisions. Peter Holmes, known as 'Omo' because of his red hair and freckles, likes to tell the story of how, on one occasion, I didn't take kindly to being given out leg before wicket and threatened to take my bat home if it was not reversed. 'So, we had a big negotiation as to whether you were out or not,' Peter recalled recently, 'and we finally agreed we would continue playing but you'd have to wait for the second innings. Typical Phil!' I think I was a good sportsman but I hated to be bested by anyone – even my best friend.

When I had to give up football, Peter and I found a couple of tennis courts on the other side of the park and we used to play there. Peter, although a couple of years younger than me, was a decent player with a wicked swerving serve, and in my build-up to the Sutton lawn tennis championship we practised as much as we could.

One day, when we had nothing much to do, Peter and I rode our bikes up to the riding school stables in Streatham thinking we might learn to ride. I can't remember now why we had this notion, and nor can Peter, but I suppose it was just something to do and we both fancied having a go. It turned out to be one of the luckiest days of my life.

At the stables was a tall, fair-haired, pretty girl of about fourteen, about six months older than me, looking very assured and at home in the saddle. She was giving lessons to some of the younger riders, riding a horse and leading another across the common. I wondered if I could ever ride like that, and decided I would at least give it a try – if she would help me. She was very friendly and soon we were chatting away.

She introduced herself as Pauline Chumley and she was from Streatham, where my school was and, like me, she was an only child. She told me her mother was a seamstress in one of the fancy tailors in Savile Row where she worked on trousers and suits for members of the royal family, and her father, who was often away on big jobs, was a foreman in a company specialising in roofs for commercial buildings. I wondered how she could be such a competent rider at such a young age and she told me she had been riding horses since she was seven, dropping out of school early to take a job in the local riding school where she now worked full time. She offered to help Peter and me master the art, which we did with more enthusiasm than skill, in my case with some extra lessons that my father, who encouraged my new interest, arranged for me in Bexley. I never learned to be as stylish as she was, but at least I could sit in the saddle and get over the occasional jump – as long as they were not too high.

Soon we were good friends and she began hanging out with our gang in the evenings and at the weekends. We both had bikes, our main means of transport, and one day, when we had known each other for about three months, she suddenly challenged me: 'I'll race you home.' She lived about two miles from me, but it was in the same direction, so I accepted, thinking I would easily beat her. She was already on her bike and heading down the road with a head start when I went to mount up and give chase. That's when I discovered she had let the air out of my tyres and hidden the pump. It took me ages to get home.

My father presented me with my first horse, an ex-point-to-pointer from Eridge called Vixen, which he bought for £75. I think he was pleased I could ride and Vixen was a present for getting into Norwood Technical College, where I intended to study after I left Streatham Grammar. She was a feisty animal and soon after I got her, she took off, completely out of control, galloping along the side of Streatham

Common with me clinging on for dear life. I was only saved from certain injury, or worse, by Pauline coolly riding up beside me and grabbing the bridle of my charging mare.

I eventually learned to control her and, as I became more experienced, Pauline used to take me eventing, travelling long distances across south London on horseback, competing in horse shows along with lots of other young hopefuls whose mothers spoke in distinctly upper-middle-class accents and drove Land Rovers trailing horseboxes. On one memorable day, we went as far as Wimbledon and another day to Sanderstead, near Croydon, nearly two hours there and back, riding our horses on busy roads.

Life was much more innocent in those days and I don't think we even held hands until much later, and even then, that's about as far as it got. But our relationship must have progressed because I invited her back to my house one Sunday to meet my parents. I gave her elaborate instructions about which bus to catch and what time to be there and then went to the bus stop to meet her – and waited and waited. Finally, I gave up and traipsed off home wondering how I could explain this early romantic setback to my parents, who had been looking forward to meeting the first girl I had ever invited home.

When I arrived, she was sitting in front of the television, cool as anything and eating a peach that my father had peeled for her. She had misunderstood my directions and got off the bus at the stop before, so made her own way. My father must have liked her because he later said to me: 'One day, that's the girl you should marry.'

A few months after that, my mother told me what she had probably suspected for some time: my father's cancer was back, this time inoperable and there was no point even in having more radiotherapy. A month later, on 1 October 1957, he passed away in the Catholic hospital in Lambeth, aged thirty-nine. I had just turned fifteen.

He was buried in the Thornton Heath cemetery, near my uncle Tom, his brother.

CHAPTER 5

STARTING OUT

I had just left Streatham Grammar in 1957 with one O-level (in maths) and was starting on a business studies course at Norwood Tech when my father passed on and I left school to work full time in the carpet shops. My father probably always intended – or at least hoped – I would go into the business, although he was also keen I should finish my course at Norwood. He had encouraged me to work in the shops on Saturdays and school holidays, which I loved, and I had picked up a lot of the basics from watching him. That experience was about to come in useful.

Initially my mother, who was not really a businesswoman, decided she would carry on with the help of the senior people who didn't much welcome any intervention from her fifteen-year-old son. All the staff were much older than me and resentful of any suggestions I made, and I'm afraid my mother sided with them, at least at the beginning. I couldn't really blame her. These were people who had worked for my dad for years and they would say to her, behind my back: 'Your husband would never have done it this way.' They included my uncle Jimmy, my father's youngest brother, who had his own carpet business and who my mother listened to.

In the final year of my father's illness, our little company, with its three shops, had probably gone backwards, losing out even to the local competition, which was making the transition from lino to carpets faster than we were. Our staff just tried to carry on running the shops in the way my father had, and no one had any new ideas of their own

– including my mother, who was too reliant on the old staff. I was convinced one of the managers was on the take but my mother didn't want to know.

I started work in the Penge shop where I didn't have enough to do to occupy me and on my half days (Wednesday in Penge, Thursday in Peckham) I travelled around London looking at other lino and carpet shops, trying to understand what worked and what didn't. Lino shops in those days were fairly drab premises, and ours were no exception, with unappealing displays and a cramped, gloomy space inside. The big department stores, then in their heyday, dominated the flooring business but usually relegated lino and carpets to the basement; they made no real attempt to provide anything much in the way of service.

In the lino shop in Rye Lane as a sixteen-year-old. The rolls of lino were stacked against the wall, with the cheapest on the right, 2s 6d a square yard, and the more expensive, 6s and more, on the left.

Lino was still the mainstay of the business, but carpets that came in two sizes, 9ft x 7ft 6in. and 12ft x 9ft, were just coming in, and the new trend was to put a carpet in the middle of the room and fill in the surround with lino. Fitted carpets were still a few years away but I could see the potential for them if ever someone could make them cheaply enough. The carpets we sold were mostly made from cotton – wool was too expensive – but viscose and other artificial fibres such as nylon, which would revolutionise the industry within a few years, were on the horizon. When Latex backing came in, it gave the business another stimulus.

My one-man research project took me to many parts of London and into many shops, and along the way I picked up some useful ideas. Fashion and shoe shops were already responding to the more sophisticated shoppers of the era, with clever window displays, sales promotions and in-store presentations. My father tended to have two big sales a year, one in the summer and one in the New Year, but the most successful shops I saw seemed to have something going all the year round. The best shops were always busy. I think I probably got some of my best ideas from Tooting market, which was more competitive than any of the shops.

The main lesson I took back from this little exercise, and which has guided me all my life, was that price, or value for money, was paramount. Get that wrong and it didn't matter what else you did – you would be out of business. Even a penny off a price of 2s 6d a yard could make all the difference. That was a principle I always taught to people who worked for me, and it's as relevant today as it was then. You can't be the cheapest today because of the internet – but you do have to offer the best value for money, which includes price, quality and, above all, service, which today is more important than it ever was.

* * *

As I was starting out in business, I couldn't help but be aware of the transformation that post-war Britain was going through. The era of austerity and rationing was finally left behind and the biggest consumer boom in the country's history was getting under way – which would have an enormous impact on me and my nascent business. In 1958, Harold Macmillan made his famous 'most of our people have never had it so good' speech, telling his supporters: 'Go around the country, go to the industrial towns, go to the farms and you will see a state of prosperity such as we have never had in my lifetime – nor indeed in the history of this country.'

And I could see it for myself. Cars, TV sets, electrical appliances and other consumer goods were suddenly becoming accessible to an emerging middle class that had money to buy them, often on credit and hire purchase, which grew in leaps and bounds in the late 1950s and 1960s. Before the war, very few households took on debt. But now credit was easily available and retailers and mail order companies were offering hire purchase on easy terms. Britain, for the first time, was becoming a nation of borrowers.

There was full employment, rapidly rising wages and living stand-ards, and people were scrambling to get on the housing ladder, with the result that house-building was going through the roof – and every new house built required new lino or carpets. Between 300,000 and 400,000 homes were built every year, twice the level of today, and bomb sites were being replaced with new high-rise blocks of flats, with bathrooms, running water and even lifts, unknown in the Peckham I grew up in.

It was a great time to be in the carpet business – if we could only get our act together. Back in Penge, I expounded on my thoughts to Bill Wertley, the manager of the shop, a wonderful man who had worked for my father for years. We travelled to work together every day in his little Wolseley, which was always running out of petrol, usually on the way home just as I had to be on court to play tennis or meet the lads. On one occasion, when I had to be somewhere urgently, the car chugged to a stop and I dashed over to a sweet shop and bought four tins of lighter fuel, all that was available. I poured that into the petrol tank and the car started and chugged rather jerkily down the road. I made my appointment but Bill complained the car was never the same again. Bill stayed with me until the early 1980s but he never wanted to move higher than store manager and never did. He was an important friend when I needed one.

With Bill's support, I gradually tightened my grip on the business as my mother loosened hers and the old guard drifted away. And I began to implement some of my own ideas. When I began, we used to store carpet, then delivered in squares rather than rolls, upstairs and lino in the basement, and you could cut your hands to shreds carrying the lino about. Shops carried large quantities of stock, piled up untidily on the floor or stacked against the walls, difficult to display in a limited space and uncomfortable for both the customer and for the staff. In our Peckham shop, we carried Belgian rugs which had to be folded up like blankets, piled up on the floor, and then laboriously opened for customers to see.

One day I said to the staff: 'This is no good – we have to find a better way.' We had some lino squares downstairs, and I hit upon the idea of rolling them into cylinders, wrapping the cotton rug around them and displaying them against the wall. They looked much more attractive and our sales immediately increased. Later we did the same with broadloom carpets, which meant we didn't have to keep huge rolls of carpet in the store – an enormous saving on cash flow that revolutionised our business. Other carpet chains copied us, but we were the first.

We worked on tight margins which I watched closely. A yard of lino cost us 1s 8d and there was purchase tax on that; we sold it at 2s 6d a yard, so the profit margin was a slender 8d on every yard we sold. We bought rugs for £7 and sold them for £11 19s 6d, a decent gross profit, but when you took the rental, staff, utilities, unsold stock and other costs off, there wasn't much room for error, which is why the casualty rate in the industry was so high.

In the clothing industry, fashions change overnight and a colour or style popular one season will barely sell the next. In carpets, customers' tastes change too but over a longer period, two to three years, and I could see from an early age the importance of anticipating that change and being ahead of it if possible. I watched carefully as shoppers made their choices and talked to them, as well as to the suppliers, trying to get a sense for how tastes were moving. Getting it wrong could mean the end of the business.

By the time I was sixteen, I was ready to open my first new shop and I found the perfect property at 182 Balham High Road at a rental of £850 a year. I was all ready to go when I hit an unexpected snag: I was too young to sign any documents (you had to be twenty-one) and my mother initially refused to sign for me. Fortunately, Ian Harris, who had been my father's lawyer for years, took my side and, after a bit of a row, she agreed.

The Balham shop, the first of many thousands I would open over the next fifty years, made a profit in its first year and grew in leaps and bounds after that. Over the next two years I opened another four shops, using the same formula, bringing the number of stores to eight by the time I was eighteen.

It was still a small business, but it was growing fast. I've got the accounts for 1959 that show that our total sales that year were £94,000, on which we made a profit after all costs and taxes of £500. I remember thinking at the time that it was a lot of money and maybe I could give myself a raise. The next year the figures were several times higher and went on growing in double digits.

I didn't need to see written accounts to know what my figures were – I kept them in my head, and always knew what we had in the bank. I may have struggled to fill out an invoice, but I could leave that to others. My invoices, bits of paper, were a hopeless scrawl which even I struggled to read. A few years ago, an old customer, who had kept an invoice, presented it to me – and even now I can't even work out the date.

*   *   *

When we were about sixteen, Pauline Chumley moved to Windsor to look after some polo ponies and we stopped seeing each other for a bit. For a year or so I had another girlfriend called Carol, who lived in Bagshot, and I used to catch the train down to see her on Saturdays after the shops closed (which they did at six). I often stayed overnight on a bed her parents made up for me in the living room, or Carol came up to Gibson's Hill to stay with me and my mother. Carol liked rock 'n' roll and we used to go bopping, or listen to our favourite records on her parents' gramophone, which included Neil Sedaka singing 'Oh Carol', a big hit at the time.

One year I was due to spend Christmas with her and, to help out, I offered to get a Christmas tree. There was an army barracks across the road and I had noticed young pine trees growing nearby. So, I enlisted the help of a friend who had a Land Rover and we dug one up, roots and all, and were proudly taking it back when the police stopped us. I hadn't realised I had committed an offence, but they took it seriously and I had quite a job to talk my way out of it. Carol's parents were not impressed.

Our relationship ended abruptly when, one Thursday, I took Peter Holmes down by train with the intention of practising our tennis. I was due to play in a lawn tennis tournament that weekend and a neighbour of Carol's family very generously let us play on his grass court. Carol's mother, however, accused me of selfishly neglecting her daughter and we ended up catching the train back to London. I never saw Carol again until twenty-five years later, when she came to the opening of one of our stores in Bristol with her mother. She was married with two children, and we had a friendly chat about our respective families before going our separate ways.

After my tiff in Bagshot, I tracked Pauline down and invited her out. Her reaction was typically blunt: 'What's the matter? Has your girlfriend given you up then?' But she agreed and, although we were still only seventeen, things began getting serious after that and we went out almost every night. My wages were £5 2s 6d a week, which even in the 1950s wasn't a fortune, but it was enough to have a good time and we went ten-pin bowling in Streatham high street with Peter and the gang, or to see the occasional film. The first time we went to the cinema together we saw a horror movie called *The Mummy*, and Pauline says I spent most of it under the seat. I do remember I had my hands over my eyes.

There were plenty of discos in the area but Pauline and I didn't dance much, although I briefly fancied myself as a jiver. I never wore the skin-tight jeans and winkle-picker shoes that were all the rage at the time, but I did use Brylcreem, basically because it was promoted by my favourite cricketer, Denis Compton. We tended to go to each other's homes and play games such as Monopoly, which I always tried very hard to win and hated losing. We never encountered drugs and never smoked pot – and no one even offered it to us. Nor did we drink more than the occasional shandy. It all sounds very tame now, and maybe it was, but we enjoyed ourselves at least as much as teenagers do today.

By 1960, the business was doing well enough to afford an increase in my wages to £10 2s 6d a week and my mother bought me a second-hand Zephyr Zodiac, a fine big car in its day, out of company profits. I was hoping to impress Pauline with it and took her to Chertsey by the river where I asked her to marry me. Her reply was: 'Why not?', which I took as an acceptance, so I took her to a jeweller's and bought her an engagement ring which she still wears from time to time. We were both only eighteen when we were married in December 1960 in Wandsworth Town Hall and we moved into a semi-detached house in Purley where the rent took up half my wages.

Shortly after the wedding, my mother, who had always been in good health, went into Croydon Hospital for what was supposed to be a minor operation. I was dashing around visiting the shops all day and called the hospital from a phone box to check on her and tell her I'd be in to see her later. I got through to the ward and the news they gave me, and the way they delivered it down the phone, still shocks me to this day. She had breast cancer, I was told, and did not have long to live.

I went home to Pauline in a daze to tell her the news, and then went to see my mum in hospital where she was blissfully unaware of her diagnosis. The doctors told me she was too far gone even for treatment and having seen how my father suffered during radiotherapy, I agreed with them that we should not even try it. I decided, rightly or wrongly, to keep it from her and never told another soul, not even my nan, her mother, who didn't forgive me for a long time. I was fearful that if anyone else knew they would give it away and I wanted my mother to spend the last few months of her life as happy as possible.

She was diagnosed in February 1961 and died four months later, on 27 June, so it was mercifully quick. She is buried beside my father at Thornton Heath and I visit their graves every Christmas and on their birthdays and anniversaries. Our big consolation was that our daughter Susan was born on 26 June, the day before my mother died. The sadness is that Mum never lived to see her – or any of her grandchildren.

Four years later, my beloved nan followed her. She had been a remarkably fit and determined woman all her life, travelling up to the City on the bus every day to clean offices, and she outlived not just my grandfather but two of her children, my mother and my Aunty Rose, who died in the same year. She had lived in Blake's Road all her life but in the mid-1960s she was told by the council that her house, where I had enjoyed so many happy times in my childhood, was to be knocked down to make way for more council flats. She was eighty-three and I helped her move to a new flat nearby, where I laid the carpet and the lino in the bathroom and toilet (not very well, as I recall).

Then, still worried about her, I left her to go back to Beckenham where Pauline and I were living at the time. I arrived to find Pauline ashen-faced and weeping: she had just had a call to say my nan had passed away. That was a sad, sad day in my life. I will always remember the way her face lit up when I went around for my special Sunday tea and those wonderful Christmases with all the family. I miss her still.

CHAPTER 6

FATHER FIGURES

My mother left me everything she and my father ever owned: the house in Gibson's Hill, Norbury, with all its furniture and belongings, and a business which by that stage had eight shops and was making a decent profit. For probate purposes, her estate was valued at £12,655, which was a substantial enough sum in those days for a nineteen-year-old to inherit. My father had bought the house in Gibson's Hill in 1954 for £3,450 (they now sell for around £700,000), and it was worth a lot more by then, as was the business.

My father was thirty-nine when he died, my mother forty-one – too young. With modern cancer treatments, they would almost certainly have lived a lot longer, but who can tell? Great advances have been made, and we always seem to be on the edge of a breakthrough, but we're still not there.

I was still too young to sign leases on new shops but fortunately people rallied around me and I was lucky enough to have sage and wise heads to advise me. There was Jimmy Downs, a next-door neighbour of my parents, who had a fashion clothing business in the West End, and was a great family friend. He later became one of my trustees.

I could never have opened my first shop without the backing of Ian Harris, my parents' solicitor, who must have seen something in me when he took my side against my mother. He was there for me for years, an experienced and sensible counsellor whenever I needed him – as I did a lot in those early years.

Even more important was my accountant, who all my life I called

'Mr Smith' – he did have a first name which was Cliff – but even as a grown man I never used it. He was always just plain 'Mr Smith'. He operated out of a little office above a shop in Denmark Hill that you had to get to by a dark, winding staircase, and twice a week I would take all the invoices and bills over to him and he would patiently deal with them. He could always find the papers I couldn't, fill in the forms that baffled me and took a huge burden off my young shoulders.

I never had a proper finance director until many years later – although I had difficulty writing things down, I could remember all the rents, the prices of every carpet we sold, the profit margin, the cash we had in the tills and how much we had made that week. But I had great difficulty putting it onto paper – Mr Smith did all that brilliantly. Later he came to work for me full time as finance director, right up to the point I floated the company in 1978.

I had total faith in both Ian Harris and Mr Smith and they never let me down. The converse was true too. I never let them down either, never reneged on a debt or broke a contract, all of which was very important for our relationship – and for my reputation in a world where carpet retailers were not renowned for their longevity.

My third mentor and father figure came into my shop one day, introduced himself as David Biderman, and offered to sell me carpets. He was a slight, balding man, nearly twenty years older than me (he was born in 1923), and clearly knew a great deal more about the carpet trade than I did – which he was prepared to share with me. We were too small to buy direct from the manufacturers, so had to deal with wholesalers, who bought from several sources. David was the best I ever came across.

He never talked about himself and I never knew about his extraordinary past until many years later, when he wrote his life history and sent me a copy. His family were Polish Jews who emigrated to Britain before he was born and he was brought up in Islington, north London – 'not the posh bit', he liked to emphasise. His father, an engineer, died when he was a teenager and David worked for an uncle in the fur trade in Belgium before the war. Then Hitler invaded and David, who lost many family members in the Nazi concentration camps, got back to England, where he joined the RAF and was trained as a bomb aimer.

In December 1943, he was on his thirteenth bombing mission over Germany when his plane was hit by anti-aircraft fire. He bailed out, landed in the middle of Nazi Germany, was captured and ended up in the prisoner-of-war camp Stalag Luft III. David faced a serious problem because he was a Jew, a fact he kept very secret. He was involved in two famous escapes, the first described in the film *Trojan Horse*, in which three men successfully escaped, and the second in March 1944, which was immortalised in the (highly inaccurate, according to David) film *The Great Escape* in which seventy-six men got out of the camp (David got left behind), fifty of whom were recaptured and executed by the Nazis; only three got home. It was April 1945 before he was liberated by the Americans after some horrific times.

Eighteen years later, he turned up in my shop, we got chatting, and he and his elegant wife Pearl, who I still see, invited Pauline and me out for dinner. We had such fun that after that the four of us went out at least once a week. David became particularly fond of Pauline and always jokingly took her side – she was the 'good girl' who was always right, while I was the 'bad boy' who was always wrong, which probably had an element of truth in it. Or so Pauline thought.

He became a mentor to us both, and whenever I had a problem, I would talk it through with him. I consulted him before I made any big decisions, including buying a house or a new car, and I even turned to him for advice on my clothes – I'd ask him whether my suit or shirt was 'too flashy', when I should wear a tie, and so forth. He also taught me the importance of punctuality – if I was five minutes late he would storm at me: 'Where have you been?'

David was the agent for a carpet company called Beurstel Carpets, which made cheap copies of Persian rugs that sold well and gave my

shops a real boost. He also had very good relations with a manufacturer
in Yorkshire, whom he cajoled and bullied into making the carpets
he and I wanted and which I knew would sell. 'Eventually, I virtually
had to design them myself,' he told me grumpily. They did well for me,
as did a line of cheap Czech-made carpets made from hemp that we
promoted as 'wall-to-wall carpets for the average man at affordable
prices'. He also introduced me to a Czech-made rug, made from 100
per cent wool, very thin and very cheap but very good quality, which
was another great seller. Those products, and others like them, really
helped make my business prosper and in the mid-1960s we moved
heavily into broadloom carpets (4ft 6in. wide, and later 9ft) which
could be fitted wall-to-wall, and became the staple of the industry.
David was always ahead of his time, coming up with a new and better
product or hunting down a bargain even if he had to travel thousands
of miles behind the Iron Curtain.

I was the perfect client for him; young, enthusiastic and as eager to
learn as he was to teach. He took me to carpet fairs and exhibitions
around the country, travelling by train, when we would talk endlessly,
mostly about carpets but sometimes about my business strategy. In
truth, in my early twenties, I didn't have much of a strategy beyond
buying carpets as cheaply as possible and selling as many of them as I
could for the best price through as many new shops as I could open.
He was brilliant at dealing with the manufacturers, but he didn't know
the customers like I did, and after a while he learned to trust my judgement more than he did his own. I used to say to David: 'Look, we need
this, we don't need that. Get out of this – it's finishing. Get out of
cotton carpets – no one's buying those anymore.' I had an instinctive
feel for the market, he negotiated great prices for me, and together we
made a formidable team, always aiming to be at the cutting edge of
fashion, price and the fast-changing technology of the industry.

'Look, Phil will only give you this or that for that carpet and that's
all it's worth,' he would tell a big manufacturer in his authoritative

manner that no one argued with. That got the respect of the manufacturers, who always treated me well (and still do).

We had our fall-outs too, usually over price, but later made it up after one or the other of us gave way. On one occasion, we set off for a carpet fair in Harrogate and we were arguing so hotly by the time we stopped at Luton station that I got off the train, carrying my suitcase, telling him I was going back home. When he jumped off too, I said: 'Oh no, if you're not going, I'm going,' and I climbed back on the train. He followed and we both collapsed onto our seats, out of breath and panting. 'What are you doing to me?' he groaned, holding his chest. On another occasion, we had such an argument on the way to a carpet exhibition in Brighton – over a penny on the price of a £6-a-yard carpet – that when we arrived he crossed the platform and caught the next train back to London.

Rocking on Muffin the Mule.

But he could be wrong, too. In my early boyhood, there was a popular TV puppet show called *Muffin the Mule*, which became a bit of a craze. It sparked a wide range of spin-off merchandise, including books, records, games and toys, and a professional photographer hit on the idea of toting around a Muffin the Mule rocking horse, offering to take pictures of children posing in the saddle. My mother must have fallen for it because I have one of myself, which I think was taken on the beach in Margate, which stood on our mantelpiece for years. I've still got it at home.

David's daughter Ruth also had a photograph of herself sitting on an identical Muffin, possibly taken by the same photographer. David remembered that and, well after the Muffin craze had faded, bought a huge stock of old Muffin the Mule rugs and offered them to his retail customers. He was highly offended when I wouldn't take them, but I told him they were awful, well past their sell-by date and there would be no demand for them. Everyone else thought the same, but he managed to persuade a gullible merchandiser at Littlewoods to take 250 of them, and then got his friends and relatives to go around the stores and buy them all up. Littlewoods bought the rest of his stock and were stuck with them for years.

CHAPTER 7

TAKING OFF

The four years from the ages of fifteen to nineteen were the most formative and defining of my life. I lost my father, I quit school, I started work, I got married, my mother died and I became a father. And a year later I made my first takeover.

After the success of Balham, I set ten shops as a target. When I got there, I aimed for twenty – and so it went on, rising every year. In 1974, I had fifty-four shops, and by 1977 it was ninety-three. Eventually it would get to 1,750 shops. I could never stand still – I was too impatient for that, and I was only happy when I was expanding, which, as we shall see later, was not always the right thing to do. But good or bad, right or wrong, that's my nature and I can't change it.

Opening new shops in the early days was not simple. The big property and insurance companies, which owned many of the outlets on the high streets, were not keen on lino and carpet shops, which were much less glamorous than jewellery, fashion and electrical retailers. We were regarded as a bit too dowdy for the smarter set, and all too often we were offered secondary positions that I refused to take. Ideally, we preferred shops with a selling area of between 1,000 and 2,000 square feet, located in prime sites near the major multiple retailers, such as Marks & Spencer, Dixons, Currys or even Woolworths, where there was a decent footfall. But they were not easy to come by, and I spent long and frustrating hours trying to find the right site, negotiate a decent rent and opening it.

There was another problem: bankruptcies were frequent in the flooring business and the suppliers, who worked on thirty-day payment terms, were often reluctant to allow credit. When my uncle Tom died, he left his business to his son Den, who ran into trouble two years later and I had to take him into our business. Then my uncle Jim also ran into difficulties and I took him on too (he worked for me for five years and ran the Balham shop). That made the suppliers a bit wary of me, but fortunately my cash flow was strong enough for me not to need much credit. However, it held me back for a little while.

There had to be a better way of expanding and, in 1962, when I was still only twenty, I made my first takeover. It was a modest enough start, a local retailer called Carpetways, which had three shops, one in Lewisham, one in North End, Croydon and a third in Surrey Street, Croydon. I had known the owner, who also had a wholesaling business, for some time, and I sometimes bought carpets from him, as had my father. He followed my career closely, always with a friendly word of encouragement, and several times he told me: 'One day I'll sell you my shops.'

He was getting on a bit and the day came when he called to say he was ready to do a deal, and I leapt at the opportunity. Without a lot of haggling, I bought the business for £75,000, or £25,000 a store, which was pretty much the value of the stock. I didn't need to borrow the money: my business, largely as a result of getting the stock out of the shops, was spinning off cash and one of the stores, Penge, made a profit of £28,000 that year. I got my money back in less than a year, and after that both the bank and the manufacturers couldn't do enough for me. My creditworthiness was never questioned again.

Expansion, however, brought other complications. In the beginning, all my shops were grouped around home, so I never had to travel very far. I always drove myself – I still do – and as the business expanded north of the river I was spending half the day in the car. My biggest and most modern shop was in East Ham, and the daily journey across London and back, often in rush-hour traffic, was a wearying one. It took me over an hour to drive from Gibson's Hill, where I was living in my parents' old house with Pauline and baby Susan, and more if the Blackwall Tunnel was blocked. My solution was to hire my first area manager, a man called Stan who had worked for my father on Saturdays for some years. I put Stan in charge of East Ham and the shops north of the river, while I looked after the south, as well as doing all the buying and finding new sites. I was fond of Stan and he and his wife often came around for tea with us. He could easily have become my first managing director if things had gone differently.

I had no real office, just a secretary, Ruth Penny, and a part-time girl based above the shop in Balham. I had no formal finance director either – only Mr Smith, who did all the books for me. I visited him every Tuesday and Thursday, carrying all my invoices and receipts, and we went through the bills that had to be paid, every one of which I personally signed (years later, when I went through some of my father's old papers, I was amazed to see his signature was remarkably like mine).

That's how I kept track of the cash. There could be substantial sums in the stores at close of business and I insisted it was banked daily, deposited in the night safe facility in the local bank. The total of the weekly takings was phoned in on Saturdays at close of business by the store managers and I consolidated it, mostly in my head. Some years later a journalist asked me what my business philosophy was and I had to think about it before I replied: 'It is to look constantly at cash flow, which is more important than profit.' I always knew, within a few pounds, how much should be in the bank at the weekend. And that's how I caught Stan out. It's also how I met David Stockwell, who was to play a huge role in my business life.

It came about like this. I had noticed on my visits to East Ham that the quality of the ticketing and point-of-sale promotions in the windows was very good, much better than in my other shops. When I queried Stan about it, he told me that they were done by a talented local designer who came in off the street one day looking for business.

He had his own studio nearby and was doing in-house sales material for the W. J. Harris (no relation) pram company, which, under the ownership of Selim Zilkha and Jimmy Goldsmith, grew into Mothercare a few years later. He also did work for the local Debenhams and other nearby stores and cinemas. Stan had got to know him well and clearly liked him and had already taken on his younger brother Tony to work in the store where he was showing great promise. We agreed that the next time I was in the store we should get together with the elder brother.

Stan seemed to be doing a good job, but what I didn't realise was that he was a gambler, betting on the horses and losing money heavily. I think the staff in East Ham probably knew, but no one told me, and I only began to suspect when the takings didn't match my calculations. His undoing was a heavy bet he placed on the Epsom Oaks, won that year by a horse called Noblesse, while his horse was not even placed. That week our cash takings were almost £3,000 short of what I was expecting and when I confronted him, he admitted he had taken money to pay for his bets, hoping to put it back from his winnings before I noticed. I had no option but to report the matter to the police.

I arrived in the East Ham store soon after Stan was arrested (he did six months in prison) to find everyone very jittery. I was trying to calm them down when I noticed this man hanging about, clearly waiting to see me, but I had to deal with the staff situation first and take charge of the shop myself until things settled down. Finally, I turned to the designer that Stan had been so impressed with, who introduced himself as David Stockwell. We got chatting and he showed me some of the point-of-sale promotions he had prepared, which I thought were excellent. 'What else can you do for us?' I asked him, and he immediately said: 'For a start, there's a lot you can do with this shop.' What was wrong with it? I asked defensively – it was my best shop and I was very proud of it. He then took me around to show me how unattractive the layout was – carpets were piled up untidily and prices were still written in biro and stuck on. 'The service is really bad,' he added. 'I see customers coming in and walking out again because the staff don't know where anything is.'

So, I asked him if he would help redesign it for me, and over the next few months, I discovered he had a real flair for it. By doing seemingly simple things, such as repainting everything in brighter colours, improving the ticketing and rearranging the displays, the shop looked like a different place after he'd finished with it. I put his brother Tony, young as he was, in daily charge and that worked very well too. I could see they were both smart as whips, with that quick Cockney wit that East Enders were well known for. They regarded me as privileged for having been to a grammar school and living in a house in a posh area. I never saw myself as in the least posh – I came from Peckham, after all, where no one was posh.

David and I soon became friends and Pauline and David's wife Valerie got on well. David recalls, not long into our relationship, the time I suggested we come over and spend the weekend with them in their tiny flat in Wanstead, east London. Neither Pauline nor I realised it at the time, but they had to put us up in their only bed while they slept on the floor. When I suggested they come to us the next weekend and we would go riding, David looked aghast. 'The only horse I've ever seen is the one that delivers the milk,' he exclaimed. I never got him onto a horse.

He was a really clever and talented man and his little design business was growing as Mothercare expanded and his reputation spread. But I wanted him close, and offered to let him have the space above the East Ham shop at a good rental. In truth, I often used it as my own East End office and after the shop closed at six in the evening, I would climb the stairs to use his phone, which he still complains about. He wasn't actually working for me at the time, but it felt as though he was and I was able to talk through all my problems and opportunities with him. We were that close.

Meanwhile, I was building the rest of the team that would grow with me over the next twenty years. I took on a boy called Ted Wright, who had started life as a milkman, and Kingsley Elton, who played football with Ted and came in as a 'Saturday boy'; when I asked him what he did in the week, he told me he worked in a glue factory as a trainee chemist and had done shifts in the Palais dance hall at Ilford.

My working uniform: white polo neck and jacket. And my faithful accountant, Mr Smith.

My cousin Ron Poole also joined me, and was to become my most loyal of lieutenants, remaining with me for years. As a teenager, he had helped out in our shops and he was a really hard worker with a flair for the business. He took responsibility for fitting out and opening new shops and without him I could never have expanded the business at the rate I did.

I never worried about qualifications – I didn't have any myself – and tried to create an informal yet efficient and organised atmosphere where these young men could use their initiative but understand very clearly the principles on which I ran the business. They always called me 'Phil' but, although we were all very friendly, they also treated me as the boss. I paid good wages and commissions, and never found getting and keeping good people a problem. We all worked hard but I liked to have fun too, and took them on trips to the seaside at weekends or invited them and their wives to the company dinners that I began at that stage, often in the local Chinese or Indian restaurants. I never imposed a dress code – I always wore white polo-neck sweaters and slacks – but insisted all the staff were smart and polite.

And that's how I built up the business, taking over new stores, upgrading existing ones, constantly innovating, finding new ranges of cheaper carpets and designing clever promotions, moving at ev-er-greater speed with a close band of people who settled into the fast rhythm of it, all of us learning as we went along.

I knew all the staff by their Christian names and my quirky memory meant I could keep every detail of the business in my mind, and still do. For instance, the street number of the shop in Balham High Road was 182 and the shop rent was £825. The telephone number of East Ham was Grangewood 2124, and the rent was £1,725 a year. Much later, when we had over 500 shops at Carpetright, I could recall most of the addresses and the rents, and I could tell staff the price of a carpet before they could look it up. I might be a few pennies out because my mind rounds it up – for instance if it was £973 I'd round it up to £975 and so on – but I'd be close.

Every Saturday I jumped into my car and visited as many of the stores as I could, arriving unannounced and checking that the staff were ready and open for business. I also drove around the high streets looking for suitable properties and checking on the competition. I got to know just about every shop in every high street in south and east London and further out – what the rentals were, and which areas were growing fastest in the great building boom that was taking place as London repaired the scars of the Blitz and the V-bombs. The estate agents got to know me too and would increasingly come to me with proposals, even though they knew I drove a hard bargain.

Besides the tight management group around me, I relied heavily on the support of more experienced and specialist hands: David Bider-man helped with the buying, Mr Smith did the accounts, Ian Harris did all the legal work and David Stockwell designed the new stores and did the marketing.

The final member of the team came into my life in 1962, when I was looking to expand north of the river and into Essex. Harvey Spack, who was to become a great supporter and friend for nearly fifty years until he died in 2012, aged seventy-seven, liked to tell his own embroidered version of how we first met. According to Harvey, he came into our shop in Peckham one day to enquire about a shop that was for rent on the Walworth Road, and asked for Mr Harris.

> And there was this young sixteen-year-old boy, wearing a Fred Perry shirt, who was sweeping the floor. And I said: 'I want to speak to Mr Harris' and he said: 'I *am* Mr Harris.' So I said: 'Where's your father, son?' And he said: 'He has long since passed away – and I'm now the Mr Harris who is running this shop.'

I remember it slightly differently – and I wasn't sixteen, I was all of twenty, still too young to sign my own leases but old enough to be running twenty stores and on the hunt for more. Driving through Romford in Essex one day, I spotted a rental sign for a shop in South Street (number 104) with the phone number of an estate agent, Smith Melzack, in London's West End. I called and got through to a partner, who introduced himself as Harvey Spack. I explained that I wanted to rent the Romford property for a new carpet shop and a few days later I met his assistant there, who obviously reported back to the effect that he had encountered this pipsqueak of a boy who looked sixteen.

Harvey called me the next day. 'How old are you, son?' he asked suspiciously. When I told him I was twenty, he said dismissively: 'You're too young – you can't even sign a lease until you're twenty-one.'

But I persisted, explaining that my lawyer would sign on my behalf, and eventually he said he'd see what he could do but his client was looking for a lot in the way of collateral which he didn't believe I had (I did). I called him every day until eventually he gave in – or his client did – and I got the shop. David Stockwell then worked his particular form of design magic on it, Ron Poole got it ready and I invited Harvey to the opening. I was half-expecting a stiff, upper-class West End estate agent, but Harvey could not have been more different. He was in his late twenties, seven or eight years older than me, and was regarded as a star at Smith Melzack, where he was already one of their biggest fee earners. He wasn't a big man physically, but he had a huge personality that seemed to fill the room, and within minutes of his arrival he was the centre of the party, dropping a wise-crack there, telling a joke there, always smiling and laughing. I felt the mood of the whole room lighten – he had that effect on people. He certainly had it on me, and as we shook hands for the first time all my resentment drained away. This was a man I wanted on my side.

'This is the best shop in the world,' he boomed, looking around at my modest carpet emporium as if it were Harrods. I was proud of it and grateful to him for getting it for me, but I told him I wanted some more like it. 'How many?' he asked. 'Five or ten,' I replied nonchalantly. He gulped, nodded and went off to make some phone calls. Within days he called back to say he had found a shop in Ilford which was, yet again, 'the best shop in the world', a phrase I must have heard thousands of times afterwards. Every shop and every deal was always 'the best in the world' to Harvey.

I wasn't his only client of course and he had a close relationship with, among others, Ernest Jones, the jeweller, and Snob, the ladies fashion chain. But he gave me 100 per cent attention, and no one could have looked after us better. We used to drive around the high streets together and if I ever said, I want this or that shop, he would go out and try to get it. Within months of meeting him, I had seconded him onto the Harris team and over the next forty years we did literally thousands of transactions together (he once added them up to be over 4,500). And we had a lot of fun too. Harvey and his wife Jane became great friends, part of the family, and I still regularly see Jane, who Pauline and I are very fond of. We used to go on holidays together, too, where

I teased Harvey mercilessly. Poor Harvey was often the butt of my pranks, some of which I'm ashamed to admit were a bit childish, but for the most part he put up with them with good grace. He joined in when I took the lads for Chinese dinners that turned into bun-fights, or played the elaborate practical jokes of which I'm slightly – but only slightly – ashamed today.

When things were going well. I bought a second-hand Bentley, which Harvey borrowed to take Jane up to see his first horse – named Gold Prospect – race, and on the way back he called me from a garage to say he was running low on petrol and he didn't know how to get the petrol cap open. I had to confess I just taken delivery of the car and didn't know either and he was stuck for four hours before the AA rescued him. After that he was highly suspicious of my cars. A few years later, by which stage we had about fifty stores, I bought an Aston Martin, and I took him to a Chinese restaurant in Bushey to celebrate some deal or other. I never carried any money then – I still don't – and after we had eaten I told him that if he paid for it, I'd give him the money back. He was still grumbling about this on the way home when the red light came on indicating we were running out of petrol, which the thirsty Aston consumed in huge quantities. I pulled into a garage, filled it up, and had to borrow the money off an irate Harvey, who refused to speak to me for days.

He also came to boxing matches with me, which I still loved but never got the same enjoyment from without my father's expert commentary. I was a big fan of Dave Charnley, a local lad from south London known as the 'Dartford Destroyer', or, as the sports writers would have it, 'the finest British boxer never to win a world title'. I took some of the lads to Earls Court for the most memorable fight of Charnley's life (and mine) when he took on the reigning world lightweight champion, Joe 'Old Bones' Brown. This was a return bout after losing to Brown in Houston, Texas, because of a cut eye, and our hopes were high that he would now get his revenge. By rights he should have done, but he was robbed by the referee who, after fifteen closely fought rounds, narrowly awarded the fight to Brown on points. Charnley retired afterwards, allegedly with a fortune of £400,000, which he cleverly invested in hair salons and property, but he contested that decision for the rest of his life. I agreed with him.

And then there was Henry Cooper, known to all of us as 'Our 'Enery', probably the most popular British boxer of all time. He was another south Londoner, born in Lambeth, who, like Charnley, never quite made it to the top and is now best remembered for knocking down Mohammed Ali in a non-title bout at Wembley Stadium in 1963. I wasn't at that fight, when Ali (then called Cassius Clay) was saved by the bell and went on to beat 'Enery on points, but I took Pauline to Highbury Stadium a few years later to watch a return bout, this time for the world title. Henry was a big chap, 6ft 2in. and broadly built, but Ali, an inch taller, seemed to tower over him, a magnificent figure of a man who dominated the ring. Ali was a great champion but Cooper would have beaten him that night if Ali hadn't opened one of the many scars on his forehead, his big weakness as a boxer, and the fight was stopped with Henry ahead on points.

It was the only time I ever saw Ali in the flesh, but I never missed his fights, dragging my friends and team along to an East Ham cinema to watch them relayed live. He was a truly great boxer and champion. As for Our 'Enery, I got to know him well through his charity work and local causes. He was a lovely man who deserved to have been world champion.

* * *

It was through David Biderman that I first met Neville Cormack, a giant among carpet manufacturers and one of the first people to introduce tufted carpets, which revolutionised my business, into Britain. Originally a US development, tufted carpets, made from spun synthetic yarn and

manufactured on new super-fast machines, cut the cost of carpets dramatically and opened up the mass market of lower income households
for the first time. Every manufacturer in the country eventually piled
in, but Neville was the pioneer, a true innovator, who imported the first
tufting machines from the US in 1956 and founded Cormar Carpets in
the Rossendale Valley, where, he liked to say, the Industrial Revolution
began. I was one of the first retailers to stock them.

He was a Baptist, as straight as a die, and took huge pride in the
quality and service he provided, which was not true of all the manufacturers. He always took a patrician interest in me, looking for feedback
on what I thought would sell and what wouldn't. I learned a lot from
him but he learned something from me too.

Neville died, aged eighty-three, in 2013, and I gave the address at his
funeral in his native Cumbria. His company lives on, however, and is
now one of the largest private companies in the country, one of the few
successful British carpet manufacturers that remain.

Every year seemed to bring a new innovation in carpet manufacturing, including increasingly sophisticated forms of synthetic fibres such
as acrylic and nylon, and improved chemical technology for dyeing.
In 1960, the first wool (80 per cent) and nylon (20 per cent) mixture
emerged and a few years later screen-printed tufted carpets arrived.
We retailers had to move fast to keep pace with manufacturing developments and changing consumer tastes, and one of the big mistakes I
made early on was to ignore Beurstel, the Yorkshire-based manufacturer that David Biderman had introduced me to, when they offered
us nine-foot-wide rolls of hard-wearing tufted carpet. Our practice for
years had been to sell two lengths of 54-inch-wide carpet plus some
tape to put them together, and that seemed to work well enough. So,
when the wider measure came in, I was dismissive and said it would
never sell. David Biderman agreed with me, and we were both wrong.
It became a bestseller and we had to reverse track very quickly.

Then the manufacturers, including Cormar, began producing cheap three-colour tufted carpets in 12ft widths, which could be cut down to fit most average rooms, and the market really took off as people began putting carpets in every room. But it was the arrival of the cheap, fitted 'wall-to-wall' carpet a few years later that really transformed our business. The man who introduced it was Cyril Lord, who in the late 1950s built a massive, state-of-the-art factory in Donaghadee, which was largely paid for by Northern Ireland government grants, and began producing cheap, printed, synthetic tufted carpet. Before he emerged on the scene, maybe 10 per cent of carpets were fitted wall-to-wall. Within a decade it was 90 per cent.

I met him once and remember him as a pint-sized, flamboyant showman, no more than 5ft 3in., who came from a working-class Lancashire family and made his first fortune in textiles. The newspapers were full of his flashy lifestyle, his houses in Belgravia and the Bahamas as well as his three wives (not all at the same time), but he was a really clever, innovative man who spotted a real opportunity and went for it.

He might have made it, too, if he had been less extravagant and stuck to manufacturing, but, not content with Donaghadee, he went into the retail business and began opening carpet shops all over the country, spending a fortune on promotion. In the early 1960s, he and John Bloom, who introduced cheap washing machines at around the same time, were hailed as 'the working-class housewife's favourites', almost folk heroes for the way they were changing the lives of the emerging consumer classes. Lord got carried away by his own publicity (as did Bloom) and went on opening more and more shops, which seemed to me madness – and so it proved. At his peak in the mid-1960s, he had a chain of very expensive shops, and I went into several of them to see what he'd got that we hadn't. They were very well fitted out, with good lighting and an impressive display of carpet samples, but I could see at a glance he was no retailer and he would never make any money from retailing. His carpets were pretty, but the choice was limited to his own products, which meant there were basically two designs, a scroll and a pattern. We were already selling similar carpets, displaying them in the windows at 28s 6d a yard, undercutting his prices (we were buying from the manufacturers at 18s a yard). We bought from more than a dozen manufacturers, while he bought only from his Donaghadee factory, which was set up in such a way that it could only make a limited range, some of which were already out of fashion.

He spent more than £600,000 a year on TV advertising and for a time everyone, including my own staff, were singing his jingle: '*This is luxury you can afford – from Cyril Lord.*'

But really all it did was open up the market for me and others to provide a wider range of fitted carpets at more competitive prices with a better service. When the other carpet manufacturers got their act together and installed highly sophisticated rotary printers, which ran three times as fast as Lord's more mechanical process, he was doomed. There was no way he could re-equip his factory and by 1967 he was in financial trouble.

His final denouement was the introduction of 'Cyrilawn', a tufted form of Astroturf launched with great publicity to a packed audience in the ballroom of the London Hilton in April 1967. As with many of his products, he had not properly test-marketed it and he became a standing joke when it changed colour from green to blue and developed a slime, which made it unusable. He had produced 100,000 square feet of it as an initial run and couldn't even give it away. In 1968, he went bankrupt and retired, a broken man, to the Bahamas, where he died in 1984.

The closure of Donaghadee, which employed 1,200 people, was a massive blow for the Northern Irish economy, which had the highest unemployment rate in the UK and where Lord had provided not only jobs but hope for a brighter future. A few years later, the province exploded into violence which would last for two generations.

*   *   *

One day in 1970, Mr Smith, who was well into his seventies by then, shocked me by announcing it was time for him to retire, and strongly advised me that I should use the opportunity to create a proper management structure. He was a wise man, who had worked for my father and had been my financial backbone for the past ten years, but we had never really discussed my strategic direction or how the business should be managed as it got bigger. He obviously decided this was the time to do that.

'Phil, you are at a crossroads,' he told me. 'You can either continue as a family-run business, in which case you have to stop expanding and consolidate. Or you go on to become a really big business, in which case you need help. You must get a managing director to take over the day-to-day running of the business, while you concentrate on what you are really good at, which is buying, finding new stores with Harvey and opening them. You're the one with the ideas and the drive – now concentrate on that.'

I thought about this for a time and then rang David Stockwell's number. He wasn't home yet but I got Valerie, his wife, on the phone. I wanted her on my side, so I told her, even before I talked to David, that I was going to offer her husband a full-time job helping me to run the company. 'He knows the business almost as well as I do,' I said. 'He knows every shop and he knows all the people, and he has a big influence on them. I have to change the way I work now, and I want David to come and help me do it. He and I work really well together – we're a team.'

A few minutes later David came in and I could hear her tell him in shocked tones: 'Phil's on the phone. He wants you to work for him!'

David was equally taken aback when I talked to him, protesting that his design business was thriving, and that he had a partner and staff and responsibilities that he couldn't just walk away from. But I could tell he was intrigued and over the next few weeks I went on pressing him until he gave in. His partner, as it turned out, was not in the least put out and continued the business until he sold it to a bigger company for a hefty profit. David still complains that he missed out on that one, although he made up for it on his shares in the business after we floated. Sometime later, Mr Smith remarked: 'You realise that David earned more money working for himself than he did working for us this past twelve months.' When I told that to David, he replied cheerily: 'I'm aware of that, Phil – but I see this as just the beginning.'

He joined with the title of sales director and, within days of arriving, he was already making a difference. We started work together to create a proper structure with clear sales incentives – mine had been a bit ad hoc, decided on the hoof – and lines of reporting, promoting some of our best sales managers to area supervisors, each still based in their own store but with additional responsibility for a group of shops. That allowed us to open new stores, using trained staff from existing units to complement new recruits.

It was David who persuaded me to hold regular meetings wiht the team where we could discuss our expansion plans. It was also David who persuaded me we should no longer be C. W. Harris Linoleum Limited, but plain and simple Harris Carpets, which more closely represented what we had evolved into.

Within a year we were ready to take on my biggest challenge yet.

CHAPTER 8

KEITH ROYLE

In the mid-1960s, Pauline and I sold the house in Gibson's Hill and bought a very pretty house in Stapleford Abbotts, near Romford, in Essex. It was closer to the new shops we were opening, but I still got home late and worked six days a week, including a long Saturday. Pauline, bless her heart, never complained, and bore the burden of running the family more or less on her own. By that stage we had three children, daughter Susan and our twin boys, Charles and Peter, who were born in St Margaret's Hospital, Epping, on 8 April 1963. Pauline also had her horses to occupy her and had inherited from her mother a skill at dressmaking, which she continued to employ up to the time we began getting invitations to royal events and dinners in Downing Street or Chequers. By then we could afford couture.

But we never really settled in Essex and within a few years we moved back to Kent, initially renting a house in Beckenham before we bought Farley's in Farnborough Park, near Orpington, for which we paid the hefty sum then of £17,500. We would be there for the next eighteen years. The Orpington area is one I have always had an affinity with, and over the years we owned several homes there. It was the site of our first real headquarters and my office is in Orpington today. Pauline redecorated and furnished the new house stylishly, one of many houses she would transform, and we settled in happily with our three children (our fourth, Martin, came along in 1968, when we were both twenty-six). We had not been long in Farley's when, as I was walking down the garden one day, a head came over the fence and introduced itself as our neighbour. It was thus that Ernest Burrington and his wife Nancy, with whom we would have so much fun over the next forty years, entered our lives.

Ernest was an old-fashioned Fleet Street journalist – or 'hack', as he preferred – who had worked for the popular newspapers for years, and when I got to know him he was deputy editor of the *Sunday People*, part of the Mirror Group. He was one of the funniest men I ever met, with a wonderful, droll sense of humour, always with a witty remark to make on any topic that came up, delivered with perfect timing. I think I had more laughs with him than anyone else in my life. He was a professional editor to his fingertips, and would later become managing director of the Mirror Group after it was taken over by Robert Maxwell. His stories about Maxwell were hilarious but turned more serious when Maxwell fell off his yacht and drowned in 1991. Ernest had to take over as chairman and hold the place together, which he did with remarkable calm and fortitude. In Maxwell's office, he discovered an elaborate system of hidden microphones that his old boss had used to eavesdrop on conversations among his executives, including Ernest. 'I always used to wonder how he knew what we were going to say,' he told me ruefully.

Sunday was always a precious day for me with the children who were growing up rapidly. Charles, Peter and I used to play cricket in the garden, using a tree as the wicket, and I invited Ernest to join in, which he did with enthusiasm. He turned out to be a mean spin bowler and a half-decent bat, and he thoroughly enjoyed it. The next Sunday I invited him to play badminton on the lawn and I heard Nancy over the fence ask him why he was going around again. 'He wants me to play badminton,' he replied plaintively, as if he was being coerced into it. He was also a decent tennis player and over the years we had many good games together, often with Harvey and Peter Holmes.

Ernest and Nancy were at dinner at home with us one Sunday evening in 1974 when I received a phone call from Murray Gordon, the chairman of Combined English Stores, a sizeable retailing conglomerate that owned a carpet retailer called Keith Royle, which, like us, had twenty-three shops, mostly in the London area. It was rumoured to be for sale, and I wanted to buy it. I had visited all its twenty-three outlets except for the branch in Northampton, which was of no interest to me. The staff didn't know me, and I would go in, look around, examine their prices and note how the carpets were displayed (badly). It was obvious to me that the salesmen were not on commission because they would be sitting in a corner and wouldn't even get up. The group was making losses but I could clearly see what was wrong and reckoned I could turn it around in no time – if I could get my hands on it.

Besides Keith Royle, combined English Stores owned a ragbag portfolio of chemist and camping shops, a couple of jewellery chains, including Zales, Salisbury luggage, travel shops and goodness knows what else. It had been put together by Gordon, an old-fashioned wheeler-dealer who liked to buy run-down shopping groups, strip out some of the properties, close unprofitable outlets, rationalise and merge chains and then sell them on, usually at a good profit. He had well over 1,000 high street properties at one point. I was hoping he would sell Keith Royle before it was too late.

I had been introduced to Gordon a year before by Harvey Spack, who knew everyone in the Jewish community, and told him of my interest in buying the group. He agreed to meet me in Green Lane, East Ham, where he had a big shop selling everything from carpets to men's clothes and which he said he sometimes used as an office when he was in the area. I tried to persuade him that Keith Royle did not fit into his group, and I would give him a fair price for it. I could see him appraising me, wondering what this young man could see in it that he couldn't, and considering whether he should pursue it or show me the door.

In the end he neither said yes nor no but left me hanging. I persisted in so far as I could, leaving messages for him that he didn't return and letting him know I was still in the market. In the meantime, the Keith

Royle shops looked more run-down every time I passed one or went inside, but there seemed to be an awful lot of stock lying around that could quickly be turned into cash.

So, I persevered, and in the end Gordon presented me with some fairly rudimentary financial figures, basically turnover of the branches, details of the leases and a valuation of the stock. That was about it, but it was all I really wanted. He reckoned there was £1 million worth of assets in the group but I had no intention of paying that and he knew it. We never discussed price and I had no idea what he wanted for it.

Things went cool again after that and I began to assume that there would be no deal. Then, out of the blue, in the summer of 1974, came that Sunday night call when we were dining with the Burringtons. He was a civil man and after a few pleasantries and enquiries about the family, he asked: 'Do you still want to buy Keith Royle?' I responded yes, trying to keep the excitement out of my voice.

'I want to concentrate on my other businesses,' he said, 'and I've decided to sell it. But there's one price – £750,000. Cash. You take everything, including the staff. No negotiation. If you can come up with that, it's yours.'

After a few questions about stock valuations, which was critical to me, he wished me a pleasant evening and rang off. I went back into dinner with Ernest and Nancy who, without the slightest idea of the significance of my phone call, could see I was elated and joined in the celebration. Ernest was genuinely pleased for me, which I found very endearing. It was the beginning of a very close friendship.

Thinking about it later, I think there were other factors that persuaded Gordon to sell. Shortly after I first approached him in 1973 the Middle East exploded in what became known as the Yom Kippur War, oil prices rose four-fold in a few months, the British coal miners went on strike and Britain was forced onto a three-day week as electricity supplies were cut off. The Conservative Prime Minister, Edward Heath, called an election for February 1974, lost, and Harold Wilson returned to power with a minority Labour government. Interest rates soared from 7.5 per cent to 13 per cent and inflation hit 25 per cent a year later.

The result was the biggest fall in share prices and property values seen in Britain since the Great Crash of 1929, in turn leading to a full-blown banking crisis which was arguably worse than the one we witnessed in 2008/09. Through the spring and summer of 1974, the financial pages of the newspapers carried almost daily stories of yet another 'fringe' bank that had lent too much money to property spivs, went bust or was rescued by the Bank of England. I heard afterwards that Murray Gordon had been caught up in it, finding himself exposed on some properties he owned. He needed to raise cash urgently and decided to sell Keith Royle to me.

Finding £750,000 in the middle of a banking crisis was my next problem and I went to bed thinking about where I was going to get it. My business was generating cash but not enough, and I needed it for working capital and for opening new stores, each of which usually took a year or so to become profitable. So I'd have to borrow it. I knew that if I asked David Biderman, who had sold his business and built himself a wonderful house in Caesarea next to Lord Sieff, he would lend it to me. There were several others who I thought would back me too but I was determined to do it on my own.

My father had banked with Westminster Bank (which later became NatWest) since he left the army and I had carried on the relationship (I still do), but I had never asked the bank for anything because I didn't need it. I called the Tooting manager, a Mr Jones as I recall, the next morning and asked to see him. I think I had just one sheet of paper with a few, hastily put-together figures on it to present to him, but they were good figures, showing the business making a healthy profit and growing rapidly, which banks always like. He listened attentively and then said this would have to go higher up the bank, at least to regional level and probably to head office in the City, and he would call me. A few days later I was invited for lunch in the NatWest tower in the City, then the tallest building in Europe, to meet the top brass. The prospect terrified me: not only had I never met a banker other than Mr Jones, but I hated heights, and the dining rooms, I was told, were on the forty-second floor. I called David Stockwell in a panic and told him he had to come with me and we put on our best suits and even wore ties – one of the rare occasions when I did in those days.

David insisted we travel on the London Underground – 'No parking there,' he said knowledgably, 'and Bank Station's just up the road' – which was one of the only times I have ever been on a tube in my life. We arrived at the Old Broad Street building, and then took a lift to the top floor, which had a fantastic, panoramic view right across London, the first time I had seen it from this angle. We were greeted by waiters offering sherry and by several senior bankers who, I was later told, were several layers up from Mr Jones but several layers down from the chairman. This lunch is memorable to me for reasons other than for the £750,000 I'd come to borrow. The first course was whitebait, which I have always hated, but I had to pretend to eat it. So, I fiddled with my knife and fork (silver of course), sipped my white wine cautiously (cut glass), surreptitiously cut the heads and tails off the little fish and, when I thought the others were distracted, whipped the rest of them into my handkerchief and stuffed it into my jacket pocket. No one seemed to notice.

I did most of the talking during lunch, explaining my philosophy for the business and how we actually did better in recessions than in good times, which they found difficult to get their heads around. I thought I was really doing well until, at the end of lunch, the most senior man present said he regretted that NatWest itself was not in a position to make a 'term loan' of this size. Later I understood why: NatWest itself, Britain's second biggest bank, was in trouble too because of the banking crisis and managers had orders to put the shutters up. Later histories have told how close the bank was to a serious crisis.

But all was not lost. As David Stockwell and I were digesting this bombshell, this senior banker added that, although they couldn't lend themselves, they had decided to recommend me to their merchant banking subsidiary, County NatWest Bank, which looked after its bigger corporate customers.

One of the people in the room, more elegant than the others in what I assumed was a Savile Row suit (I was right), now took charge. Speaking in an unmistakably upper-class English accent, he introduced himself as Charles Villiers, executive director of County, and said that he thought he might be able to help us. He suggested that we meet again soon at his office a few hundred yards away in Bishopsgate, which we did the next day, entering for the first time a building in which I was destined to spend many hours and days, often locked in meetings that went on all night.

Villiers was elaborately courteous and friendly and despite our very different backgrounds, we immediately took to each other. He came from one of England's oldest aristocratic families, which included knights, earls and even a couple of dukes among its ranks, and his connections were impeccable: his wife had been a private secretary to Edward Heath when he was in Downing Street. He was also very sharp, scrutinising my figures and gently probing for any weaknesses in my argument. I remember one of the questions he asked was why I was paying full asset value. 'It is customary in these cases to offer a discount on asset values,' he said pointedly. I replied that asset value was actually £1 million, and we were paying £250,000 less than that. More importantly, I had agreed that figure with Murray Gordon after months of on-off discussions and I knew if I went back and tried to change the terms he would walk away – and I really wanted Keith Royle.

I had done my preparation very thoroughly and had a very clear picture of what I wanted to do with Keith Royle, and I outlined my plans for turning it around. The head office would go for a start – we would bring everything together under one roof, with immediate savings. With forty-six stores rather than twenty-three, we could centralise the cutting into a new warehouse which I was already planning, and take all the stock out of the shops, as I had done with our existing business, saving at least £200,000 and maybe more (it turned out to be a lot more). It would also give us greater leverage with the manufacturers and therefore we could negotiate lower prices. I thought the Keith Royle staff were good but needed to be motivated and if we brought them up to our own level of performance, we would double the sales per shop.

'There is no real competition,' I concluded. 'Just two other chains, Allied Carpets and Eastern, and they're both in decline.'

I must have convinced him because, at the end of the meeting, Villiers announced that he was prepared to make a 'term loan' of £750,000, repayable over three years. Bank Rate, or Minimum Lending Rate as it was called then, was 11.75 per cent, and we would have to pay a couple of percentage points above that. It was expensive money and the interest alone would cost me, I quickly calculated, over £100,000 a year or almost £9,000 a month – to buy a loss-making business. I left the bank determined to repay it well before its term was up.

And that's pretty well how it worked out. County did some superficial due diligence, poked around in the shops, kicked the tyres so to speak, and liked what it saw. We sent a team in to Keith Royle to do a stock-take, which took just two days, to satisfy ourselves that the stock we were promised was in fact there (it was). I reassured the management that we would look after them and that I wanted them to stay – which most of them did. There would be bonuses and incentives for those who did well, I said, and I could feel them respond. Clearly no one had promised them much in the past.

I have always hated owing money to the banks and I was determined to get County off my back as soon as possible. The Keith Royle deal was agreed in July 1974, completed by the first week of September – and the loan was fully repaid by the end of December. Those four months were among the most exhilarating of my business life.

CHAPTER 9

INTO THE BIG TIME

The day after we had completed the Keith Royle deal in September 1974, I gathered the team around me and set out our campaign of action. 'Look, we're going to take our time with this,' I told them, 'because we've got to get the stock out and centralise the warehousing and cutting, and that's not going to be easy. We'll do one shop at a time, get it right, and then move onto the next one.'

Everyone was assigned a role: David Stockwell would take charge of redesigning the stores with new facades and signage, which my cousin Ron would take responsibility for opening; Kingsley Elton and Ted Wright, by now seasoned managers, got the job of converting the stock into cash and motivating the staff to increase sales. There were some excellent people at Keith Royle, too, who I had high hopes for. I liked the look of a young man called Tony Behar, who was five years younger than me, and after getting the measure of him, I promoted him to the top team where he proved invaluable. Fred Fancy, in his mid-fifties, was one of the most experienced managers at Keith Royle and knew where the bodies – and the stock – were buried, and I needed him by my side. His son David also joined us. Alan Short-land was also a valuable addition. This was the team that would work around the clock for the rest of the year to get the job done. Everyone responded superbly.

There was about £25,000 worth of stock in each shop, which was really the key to the deal, and the first task was to monetise that, which we did through a series of bargain sales. We replaced it with my patent system of dummy carpet rolls, which were just cardboard drums wrapped in four feet of carpet and dressed up to look like full rolls.

We took down the Keith Royle name and replaced it with Harris Carpets and reconfigured the drab stores to our own formula, putting in better lighting, painting out the premises and greatly improving the window displays.

I continually went around the Keith Royle shops, trying to inspire the staff with the work culture we had at Harris. Many of them were very good, just demotivated – they had had no leadership for years and most of them joined in enthusiastically when they saw what we were trying to do. On average, they were probably a generation older than the Harris managers, in their forties and fifties when ours were in their twenties and thirties, and they knew their trade. I put them onto our commission system, and personally demonstrated how I wanted them to greet customers as they entered the shop, even taking orders – which I could never resist doing (I still can't).

My long-term aim was to sell more carpets made specifically to our own design and quality requirements, which David Biderman had helped me achieve, and I now had the scale to do it. At Harris, we were already selling a range of about fifty carpets, each available in seven designs or colours, at prices between £1.99 and £9.99 a yard, and that became the norm across the enlarged group.

The result of all this was that when we reopened the first revamped store, which was in Hounslow, trade doubled in the first two weeks. That set the pattern for the others, which achieved similar improvements as we reopened them at a rate of two a week through November and December. By Christmas time 1974, we were done, much to the delight of the Keith Royle staff, who had never had such a jolly time in their lives, particularly when I invited them and their wives to our annual Christmas party, a riotous occassion.

I watched the cash position day by day and, after a highly successful Christmas sales period, I called Charles Villiers just before the end of the year to tell him I was sending him back his £750,000. He could scarcely believe it. 'How can you do that?' he exclaimed. 'That was three-year money.' In this case, I replied, it was just four-month money.

* * *

The Keith Royle acquisition, which took us to forty-six shops, gave me the critical mass to do what I had been planning for some time: create a central warehouse which would fulfil the orders for all of the shops. I found suitable premises in Orpington where we installed high-speed automated machines that cut to a tolerance of 1 per cent and minimised waste. The system we had before the Keith Royle takeover was that East Ham would cut for Romford and Ilford, Balham would cut for Penge and Peckham in its basement, and so on. It was never a satisfactory system, and we used to have to work late on Saturday cutting carpets for delivery on Monday before staggering across to the pub for a well-earned pint of beer. Orders were now channelled through Orpington, where all the stock was stored, and the carpet was delivered direct to the customer within two days. Virtually overnight, we went from a stocking business to a non-stocking business, which freed up cash from both companies. That by itself paid for the entire Keith Royle transaction.

When I first started in business, people bought carpets for a lifetime, but by the 1970s a growing population of more prosperous and house-proud home-owners were prepared to refurnish their houses much more often. Every time a family moved house, they tended to change the wallpaper, which meant also changing the carpets, and this was a time of record house sales. The DIY boom resulted in working-class households doing up their own homes and entering the carpet market for the first time, which was great for me.

By 1975, we were shifting huge quantities of carpet as the orders poured in: an average of 1,000–1,200 a day. We brought cutting down to a fine art, with our two fully automated Darwen cutting machines making 60–70 cuts an hour, getting the most out of each roll. The warehouse operated seventeen hours a day, seven days a week, with eighteen men on in the day and twelve at night.

Before the Keith Royle deal, our twenty-three stores made a pre-tax profit of £335,000. In 1974, the year we bought Keith Royle, profits nearly doubled to £605,000. And, as we got our hands on our new acquisition and extracted the benefits I knew were there, we really started motoring: in 1975, the first full year of trading for the enlarged company, profits jumped to £1.2 million and to £1.7 million the year after.

For years afterwards, every time I ran into Murray Gordon he always said: 'I sold it to you too cheap!' And he was right: the Keith Royle deal was probably the best I ever did, the watershed of my career, providing the engine for the meteoric growth that drove Harris Carpets forward for the next decade.

CHAPTER 10

QUEENSWAY

U p to the time we listed the company on the stock market in 1978, we paid no dividends, ploughing all the cash we generated back into the business. I went on opening new stores and, as we outgrew Orpington, we planned a new 157,000 square foot carpet-cutting ware-house near Swanley in Kent, on the junction of the new M25 and the future site of the M20. In total, including the £750,000 we paid for Keith Royle in 1974 and the cost of the new warehouse, we invested more than £15 million back into the business in four years, all of it generated from cash flow.

We took virtually nothing out. Even in 1978, by which stage we were making profits of over £5 million a year, David Stockwell and I were on salaries of only £25,000 each and we received no bonuses. The first dividend we ever paid was in 1979, when we distributed £2.1 million to shareholders, and the first money the Harris family took out was when Pauline sold £3 million worth of shares on the flotation. I passed on my dividend that first year.

In these years, everything went my way, including the technology that was developing all the time. After wall-to-wall broadloom, in-troduced by Cyril Lord, we had printed pile, cut pile, looped pile, multi-coloured designs, tonal and patterned weaves and foam-backed carpets. The big US chemical company Monsanto, which became one of our major showjumping sponsors later on, introduced Acrilan, a revolutionary fibre that made carpets cheaper, softer and allowed better use of colour and patterns. Its rival, Dupont, whisked David Stockwell and me over to the US on Concorde to try out their new Antron carpet fibre, which they claimed offered 'virtually unlimited styling options and performance benefits', and we imported it in the UK before anyone else did. Wool by that stage had become too expensive to use for the mass market and was not as hard-wearing as the synthetics, which dealt a fatal blow to many of the traditional Axminster and Wilton carpet factories based around Kidderminster.

Earnest debate with David Stockwell at a stylish store opening.

Increasingly I thought of carpets as a fashion business, and I introduced new designs into our shops each year, often in the vibrant colours that were being paraded by models on the catwalks in Milan or Paris. I didn't go to the fashion shows of course, but I could often detect subconsciously the colours that were becoming fashionable that year and try to replicate them. I had been in the business so long by that stage that I had developed a sixth sense for what would sell and what wouldn't. I was sometimes wrong, but more times than not I was right and the manufacturers made us their testing ground, using our shops to try new colours and new materials, which kept us ahead of the game. It meant we got priority when the new bestsellers came off the production lines. Both Monsanto and Dupont, the world leaders in new affordable fibres, told us they had chosen us to lead the way because of our influence on the British carpet manufacturers as well as the consumer. The staff loved it, reckoning the new materials and designs lifted the whole sales appeal of the shops – and their commission with it.

Our basic formula was low prices, quick delivery and easy fitting, aimed at customers whose own lifestyles were changing. I always emphasised service and insisted that all the managers, however senior, regularly worked in the shops serving customers, and all the directors spent every Saturday visiting them. I also placed a lot of importance on display and ticketing, which David Stockwell first introduced me to in East Ham, and insisted on clear, bold tickets that were changed regularly to match our promotional activity.

One of my innovations was a ready-reckoner, attached to each carpet stand, which customers could use to estimate the approximate cost of carpeting a room. That also helped the sales staff, who could quickly work out what the customers needed and give them a price on the spot. We did very little advertising: we tried TV but it didn't work for us, and nor did the national newspapers, and what little we did spend went to the two London evening papers, the *Evening Standard* and *News*. We had some success with local radio, particularly Capitol and LBC, but when they jacked up their rates we dropped them. Basically, our shops were our advertisement: bright, colourful, attractive, with strong window promotions that shoppers couldn't miss.

*   *   *

I always went to as many carpet fairs as I had the time for and never missed out on the big one, which was held in Harrogate every year and which everyone in the industry turned up for. The big manufacturers all took stands, which I enjoyed visiting, and on my rounds one year, I stopped off at Lancaster Carpets, where I was greeted by a salesman I knew called Edwards. Lancaster had recently been taken over by the big textile company Nottingham Manufacturing, which had bought Cyril Lord's factory in Donaghadee after he went bust, and by the mid-1970s had built up a substantial base in the carpet industry.

Edwards was standing beside a striking-looking, handsome man, with big bushy eyebrows and a strong chin, whom he introduced as his boss, Harry Djanogly. Like everyone else in the industry, I had heard a lot about him but had never met him before. I instantly warmed to him as he greeted me with the broad smile that would later become so familiar to me and a firm handshake that almost crushed my fingers. Although he was only four years older than me, he was already one of Britain's leading industrialists, running probably the most successful textile company in the country. Nottingham Manufacturing was the biggest supplier of underwear, knitwear and other clothing to Marks & Spencer, with whom the Djanogly family, Russian-born Jewish immigrants from Nazi Germany, had a relationship that went all the way back to the founders, Simon Marks and Israel Sieff, in the 1920s.

We chatted for a while, and then he said: 'Mr Harris, I know you've got business to do and I am going to have a look round the fair, but I'd love to come and look at one of your shops.' I think he was probably just being polite but I took him at his word and called him the next day. His secretary clearly had no idea who I was and I think he had already forgotten, but I didn't mind and asked him: 'Mr Djanogly, when do you want to come and see the shops?'

A few days later I took him on a tour of our best shops, many of them old Keith Royle outlets that were now doing at least twice the business they used to. Harry knew Murray Gordon, who, he said, was already regretting selling me the shops. 'But he would never have made a success of them,' he said. 'And I can see that you already have.'

Like me, he was an Arsenal fan, and we talked football, carpets and trading, and agreed to meet again with our wives, Carole and Pauline. Over the next few years our friendship blossomed and today I'm proud

to count Harry among my dearest friends. At those times in my life
when I have most needed clear-headed and wise advice, it is to Harry
I have usually turned first – and he has never let me down. We meet
often, sometimes in the directors dining room at Arsenal where we
can grouse about Arsène Wenger and our performance in the Premier League, or in the House of Lords for dinner (his son Jonathan
is the Conservative MP for Huntington). He is also one of the most
generous-spirited and charitable men I have ever known, giving away
millions to charities, often anonymously.

*　*　*

The mid-1970s, leading up to the Thatcher era, were the worst political and economic times of my lifetime – at least up to the present
shambles. In September 1975, sterling collapsed, the Bank of England
pushed interest rates up from 10 per cent to 12 per cent, and the Labour
government was forced to call in the IMF. A few months later, in
April 1976, Harold Wilson, having successfully orchestrated Britain's
first referendum on European membership (which had a two-thirds
majority in favour), suddenly resigned as Prime Minister, making way
for Jim Callaghan, who was to spend the next three unhappy years
hopelessly battling the trade unions, inflation, balance of payments
and budget deficits and the virtual collapse of the British manufacturing industry. It was a good time to be a buyer of retail companies, if you
could afford it. And I could.

My takeover target was an out-of-town furniture retailer, Queensway Discount Warehouses, which was suggested to us by Charles
Villiers of County, whose parent bank, National Westminster, had
a shareholding in it. Its founder and chairman was a man called
Gerry Parish whom Charles described to me as a 'bit of an oddball
and maverick entrepreneur'. Parish was one of the pioneers of out-
of-town discount warehouses which Harvey Spack, who also knew

Parish, was urging me to expand into. Parish had moved to the US in the 1960s and was greatly taken with the brash, cut-price home furnishing warehouses which he thought would work in Britain where there was no equivalent. In 1967, he rented a disused warehouse near Norwich and, allegedly with just £50, set up the country's first out-of-town discount store, initially concentrating on selling carpets. By the mid-1970s, he had expanded into beds and furniture, spending millions on TV and newspaper advertising. You couldn't watch TV without seeing one of his ads offering furniture and carpets at such low prices he could almost justify his catchy slogan: 'Save More than You Spend'.

He grew the business to twenty-three discount stores but then, according to Harvey, he had a nervous breakdown, suffering from crazy mood swings, memory loss and fatigue, which no one could explain. He was also a bit of a musician, playing blues and folk harmonica in a local band, and had even appeared on *Opportunity Knocks* with Hughie Green. We had a lot in common: like me, he was dyslexic, left school at fourteen, started his career in the carpet industry and created a retail chain that would have become one of the biggest of its day if he'd been able to control it. Unfortunately, I only met him once and that, as we shall see, was not in circumstances in which we could form strong bonds of friendship.

I was told that Parish had hoped to raise more capital from the stock market before he encountered his health problems and was now a forced seller. Charles Villiers disclosed he was heavily in debt to NatWest, which had negotiated a swap of its debt for equity, giving County a 15 per cent stake. 'It's what we call a "recovery investment",' Charles told me ruefully. 'Only it's not recovering very well.'

I went through the figures that County gave me and immediately understood why Parish had to abandon his public offering. The profit record was erratic to say the least, leaping from a loss in the early 1970s to a profit of £1.1 million in 1975, then back into losses again. Parish might have been a gifted salesman but he could not manage his stock, and he had negative cash flow. When County offered it to me, Queensway was headed for a loss of over £1 million and Parish was facing bankruptcy.

It was risky, but it was also a great opportunity for me, and my team, having sorted out Keith Royle in record time, was ready for a new challenge. Harvey had been looking for suitable out-of-town sites for some time, but had never found anything as tempting as this. The traditional high street I had grown up with was already changing by the mid-1970s, with shopping centres beginning to replace the traditional shops, and the big department stores, which had dominated the retail industry for over a century, were clearly on the way out. The Arndale Centre in Wandsworth, when it opened in 1971, was the largest indoor shopping space in Europe and even bigger and more modern ones were on the way. I still loved the old high streets and continued to do well in them for many years, but I was also determined to expand out of town where I would have the space to move into furniture, the logical progression from carpets. Some of the supermarket groups were putting up French-style hypermarkets, and so were groups such as the B&Q do-it-yourself chain and Comet Warehouses, selling electricals. Most shoppers now had cars and were prepared to drive considerable distances in search of cheaper prices and convenience, particularly if there was easy parking available. But there were problems, too: local authorities were reluctant to give planning permission for fear of damaging their own high streets, there was a lot of opposition to the warehouses which were not exactly things of beauty, and late-night and Sunday trading were still concepts of the future.

I went to see a number of Queensway stores, including their biggest two in Biggleswade and Bedford. There was another Queensway on my own doorstep in Orpington which I spent hours prowling around, looking at every detail, and Pauline also went in to give me her views. The store in Edmonton was taking about £6 million a year, and that

got my attention – that was a serious store. On average, my stores took
£8,000 a week, or around £400,000 a year. Although it was always
packed, I thought Edmonton could have been doing even better: the
warehouse was on the ground floor but you had to walk up two flights
of stairs to get to the showroom, which I didn't think was the best way
to do it. I flew up to Aberdeen to take a look at a new discount warehouse they were opening there and travelled on to see several others
in Scotland, most of them in the 30,000–50,000 square foot range.
An impressive new discount warehouse was about to open in New
Malden.

Carpets were about 25 per cent of the business but I quickly concluded they had nobody in the company who knew much about them,
either how to buy or sell, and some of the salesmen told me they were
constantly running out of stock, or they had the wrong stock, or it was
in the wrong place. They were much better at furniture and had good
lines of beds, bedroom and lounge furniture and kitchens, well laid
out on one floor in modern buildings, with plenty of parking and easy
access. They were doing well but David Stockwell and I felt we could
do a lot more with them.

Harvey appointed himself principal negotiator and arranged for me
to meet Parish in Norwich, where he was said to live in flamboyant
style in a twelve-bedroom Georgian-style house on the outskirts of
the town. We stayed in a hotel overnight, and over breakfast the next
morning discussed our negotiating strategy.

'Whatever you do, don't rush,' Harvey cautioned, concerned by my
legendary impatience and impetuousness. 'Just take your time and let
me do the talking. Let's see if we can negotiate a good deal here. But
leave it to me!' Suitably admonished, I agreed, acknowledging that
Harvey's negotiating skills were superior to mine.

The arrangement was that Parish would pick us up at the hotel at
8.30 and take us to his Norwich store, show us around, and then we
would go on to his office to discuss terms. We were outside at the

appointed time when Parish drove up, not in the big car we had been expecting, but in a Mini with stuff in the back. Harvey refused to get into it and we had to get our own car out of the hotel carpark and follow him. We drove around Norwich, Parish's home city, for what seemed an age before I noticed we were going in circles.

'Harvey, I don't think he knows where his store is!' I exclaimed. 'He's lost.'

Harvey was furious with me. 'Don't be stupid – he knows where all his shops are.'

A few minutes later, it became apparent that he didn't. He stopped the car and came back and said: 'I'm sorry, I can't find the store. Do either of you know where it is?'

As it happened, I had a rough idea and eventually, with us now leading the way, we found it, went in and he showed us around. In this one big store, the manager told us, they had about 100 suites of lounge furniture and thirty models of beds. Three-piece suites were stocked at prices ranging from under £200 up to £700, and the stores provided credit, something I was not keen on – Harris was essentially a cash business, although we could arrange credit through one of the hire purchase companies if people insisted.

After a while I had seen enough, nodded my approval to Parish, and said: 'Yes, it's OK – let's go.' I was just keen to get on with the negotiation and outside my impatience overcame my good intentions and the promise I'd made to Harvey.

'How much d'you want for it?' I blurted out, ignoring Harvey's furious look.

'Three million,' he replied.

'Oh no, that's far too much,' I responded instantly. 'The most I'll pay is a million and a half.'

After a few minutes of to-and-froing, Harvey could no longer contain himself and, elbowing me aside, burst out exasperatedly: 'OK – let's do a deal at two million.'

If we'd rehearsed it, we couldn't have done it better. Parish looked from one face to the other, assumed Harvey was the softer touch, and said: 'OK – that's a deal.'

The whole negotiation took less than ten minutes.

But there was another surprise in store for us. Parish, looking anguished and diffident, suddenly asked if we would go with him to his head office. 'My directors are waiting for me there and I haven't told them I'm selling. Would you mind coming along and telling them?'

He gave us the address and we went into the boardroom where he had assembled his directors to brief them on the latest stage of what they thought was just another board meeting. He briefly introduced me and I had to tell them I was the new owner and these were the terms of the deal we had negotiated. I still remember the shock on their faces – they had known nothing about it. It seemed a strange way to run a business.

I thought it was a done deal but we weren't finished yet. County, which was handling the nuts and bolts of the transaction for me, discovered a snag: Parish didn't actually own the company, or at least not all of it. Over the years he had distributed shares widely among his executives and family members, several of whom were unhappy with the terms. The lawyers informed us that, because of the nature of Queensway's share structure, we would not be able to exercise Section 109 of the Companies Act, which gives a purchaser the right to buy any outstanding shares once it has gone above 90 per cent. Under the company's articles, every single shareholder would have to sign simultaneously, in the same room – without exception.

'That's not going to be easy,' said Charles Villiers when we realised this. 'I'll have to bring this to John Padovan.' He took me downstairs to meet Padovan, nominally his boss, who was even more patrician than Charles, a very correct gentleman who gave me the impression it was not really his job or inclination to get involved in such minor matters of detail. He listened to us, shook his head portentously and then called in his assistant, Andrew Deacon, and told him to 'get on with the job'.

After that, Charles took a back seat, explaining that he felt too close to Queensway to oversee the deal, but Andrew, who took over from him, proved a brilliant replacement. He was a serious go-getter, just twenty-five years old, and a really creative thinker. He soon established that, besides Parish, there were about thirty other shareholders in Queensway and began tracking them down, bullying and cajoling them to attend a meeting in Old Broad Street where they would all have to sign the papers. If just one of them reneged, he told them, there would be no deal and none of them would get their money. 'They're not all singing from the same hymn sheet,' he warned me when I asked for a progress report – which I did several times a day. 'Some of them don't understand why they should sell the company to an unknown retailer from south London who is smaller than Queensway.'

It was quite a feat but Andrew did eventually get all of them, or their representatives, together in the County boardroom in Old Broad Street on the appointed evening. I waited anxiously in another room with Charles, who was just as nervous as I was, until Andrew emerged triumphantly to say we had done it – everyone had signed. Queensway was ours.

There is an amusing little sequel to this that Andrew recently reminded me of. After the deal, I was so impressed with the job he had done that I went to see John Padovan and told him I wanted to give Andrew a present. How much could I spend on it? Every gift, he replied, had to be registered with the bank and the maximum value should be no more than £50. I thought, after a £2 million deal that Andrew had pulled out of the fire for me, this was a bit mean, and bought a gold watch which was probably worth ten times that and presented it to him with my sincere thanks. He immediately showed it to Padovan, and asked him what value they should put on it. '£50, I would say,' said Padovan, after examining it. 'Gold-plated, obviously.'

Only years later, when he saw the same watch in a jeweller's shop, did Deacon realise it was solid gold.

Parish, poor chap, had a tough time after he sold us his business. He converted his house into a health club, another idea ahead of its time, but then sold it and went back to the US where he tried to recreate Queensway in Florida. He lost all his money and returned to the UK where a doctor magically found a cure for his illness, which turned out to be the result of exposure to chemicals used in a dry-cleaning shop he'd been working in forty years before. He made a complete recovery and sued the manufacturers, ICI, as well as Roche, makers of Valium, which he had taken in large quantities. He didn't win, but his campaign helped enormously towards greater understanding of so-called Gulf War Syndrome, which was apparently also related to the effect of drugs soldiers were given. He had no formal qualifications so he was not taken seriously until his findings were published in the journal *Medical Hypotheses*. By that stage he had died, aged seventy.

*   *   *

For the first year or so after the Queensway acquisition, I spent four days a week in Norwich, working late into the evening to turn around my new acquisition, which was big enough to sink me if I got it wrong. On top of the £2 million purchase price, I had to find another £1.5 million in capital investment to bring the stores up to the standards I planned. There were 800 staff when I bought it, which was way too many, and we reduced that to 560. I moved the head office from Norwich to the Harris Carpets building in Orpington, not far from my home, bringing down the key managers I wanted to keep.

Queensway's carpet side, which was losing most of the money, was the easiest to fix. I did what I always did – took the stock out, moved in my carpet-covered cardboard drums and sample books, widened the ranges to include the carpets we sold through our high street shops, sold off several surplus warehouses (at a profit of £500,000, thanks to Harvey and his partner Russell Field), and centralised the cutting and delivery systems at our newly opened warehouse in Swanley. Queensway had never employed specialist carpet staff and it was a simple matter to put in some of our best store managers and watch the proceeds rise.

There was an enormous amount to be done. Although he was still very young, I appointed Kingsley Elton to run the Queensway business, but I still needed David Stockwell, who I wanted to take charge of the Harris Carpets high street operations, to redesign the stores for me. They looked like what they were, inside and outside: warehouses. I didn't want that, and David cleverly managed to make them much more welcoming and intimate inside, creating carpet display areas and what he called 'room-sets' to show bedroom, dining room and kitchen furniture as they might look in the home. That's standard stuff now, but quite new, at least in Britain, in those days. By the time he had finished they still looked like warehouses, but only on the outside – on the inside they were bright, cheerful and customer friendly. Queensway had spent £1.4 million in the last year on advertising, which was about 5 per cent of its turnover and I cut that back to 2 per cent, which saved us £840,000 a year – and sales still went up.

The impact of all this on profits was instantaneous, taking even me by surprise. Queensway was losing about £50,000 a week when we bought it in the summer of 1977, but in the final three months of that year we made a profit of £300,000, a turnaround of nearly £1 million in one quarter. The next year, 1978, started out even more strongly and we delivered a profit of £550,000 in the first three months alone. By that stage revenues of Queensway were running at £28 million a year, which was more than our existing carpet business, and we were expanding again, looking for more sites for a business that was on a roll.

I had one more acquisition to make that year (1978), which was J Ross, a Scottish group with twenty-nine carpet shops, which County offered me. It was yet another loss-maker, but after Keith Royle and Queensway that was almost an incentive. I flew up to Scotland with Harvey, Russell, Ron Poole and David Stockwell to take a look, and bought it there and then for £480,000 in cash. We got that back in a few months. The logistics of delivering the carpets to Scotland were solved by transporting them in container lorries from Swanley to our depot in Glasgow and delivering them to the customers in our own vans. I added it to the growing managerial portfolio of Tony Behar, who had developed into a gifted retailer (I later put Alan Shortland in charge).

We now had a business with annual revenues running at more than £50 million, against £3 million in 1973, and profits before tax heading for £5 million, compared with £340,000 five years before.

It was time to take it to the next stage – a public listing on the London Stock Exchange.

CHAPTER 11

IN THE PUBLIC EYE

For as long as I could remember, I had always wanted to run a company whose share price appeared in the newspapers every day. It dated back to my father's time, when one of our suppliers was Associated Weavers, then a giant carpet manufacturer whose share price was listed in the textiles section of the financial pages. Someone showed it to me when I was about fourteen years old and after that I used to look at it every day. The shares, I can still remember, traded at 2s 6d for a long time and then dropped to 1s 11d, and fluctuated between those two levels for several years. I never bought them, but there was something mystical for a young teenager about following them and dreaming that one day maybe I might see my shares in the newspapers too. I had no idea how you got there and but I did know it had something to do with the stock market.

As we grew larger, the prospect of becoming a public company quoted on the London Stock Exchange began to become a real possibility. Our biggest competitor, Allied Carpets, was listed, as were some of our suppliers, and I felt it was time for us to play in a bigger league. By the late 1970s we had a number of people working for us, including David Stockwell, Ron Poole, Kingsley Elton, Tony Behar, Ted Wright and Howard Ellis, who had been with me for some time but had never had a chance to take any real money out of the company. We paid no bonuses and people lived on their basic salaries, which were heavily taxed – the top rate in the 1970s was 83 per cent, which was paid on anything above £20,000 a year; my salary was £25,000. Dividends were even more highly taxed, but that didn't affect us because we never paid any. After twenty years of hard work for not much reward in cash terms, Pauline and I felt it was time to cash in some of our shares and get some capital into the hands of the family and our little team. The Harris family owned 95 per cent of the company after distributing the other 5 per cent among the senior staff, but none of us had any idea what our shares were worth. The best way to find out was to get a market listing.

When I discussed the possibility with Charles Villiers and Andrew Deacon at County Bank, I found they had been thinking along the same lines. They would have come forward earlier, Charles said, but the market conditions had not been right and there had been almost no new issues for the past few years. Andrew had been doing some analysis and concluded that Harris Queensway was something special and its time had come: house prices, after a dip in the mid-1970s, had recovered strongly and were now rising at an annual rate of nearly 30 per cent, house ownership had grown from 50 per cent to 57 per cent since 1970, and consumer spending was also rising fast – all of them, admittedly, fuelled by inflation. This was a healthy background for selling carpets and furniture, and we were witnessing stronger demand than I had ever known. County, eager to establish itself among the front rank of City banks such as Warburg's, Rothschild's, Schroders or Hambros, was keen to push the button, and so we began working on a plan to prepare the company for our stock market debut within a year.

The first stage was to get Queensway into good financial shape, and that was going really well, even better than my most optimistic hopes. The loss of £1 million was replaced by an annualised profit of £2 million in 1978; then we bought Ross, which gave us critical mass, a presence in Scotland and a third strand to the company; and we continued to grow the core business, Harris Carpets, which powered ahead right through the economic turmoil of the late 1970s when half the country seemed to be on strike and the Labour government of Jim Callaghan hung on by its fingernails.

Andrew Deacon, who was also preparing Saga for a public issue, two of only a handful of new issues that year, tested opinion among a small group of potential investors and reported back that there was a keen appetite for our shares. 'The combination of Queensway with Harris Carpets makes it an eminently floatable company,' Andrew told me. 'People are interested in out-of-town shopping and no one else combines that with the high street – that's unique. You also have an ideal combination of furniture and carpets, and you have a proven record of turning companies around. The City will love all that.'

The downside of going public was that I would lose the anonymity and independence of running a private, family-owned company, basically answerable only to myself and my board. But the benefits, as set out by County, outweighed that: access to a wider pool of capital to support further acquisitions and growth; an enhanced profile in the City and financial community; the ability to issue shares instead of cash to take over other companies; free publicity surrounding the brands, Harris and Queensway; and the realisation of some capital for the senior executives as well as the Harris family.

5,000,000 Ordinary shares of 20p each at 155p per share
payable in full on application

The shares now offered rank in full for all dividends hereafter declared or
paid on the Ordinary share capital of the Company.

Authorised £3,600,000	Share Capital in 18,000,000 Ordinary shares of 20p each	Issued and now being issued fully paid £3,000,000

● The Group's trading results for the five financial years ended 24th December, 1977 were as follows:—

Year ended December	Turnover £'000	Profit before taxation £'000
1973	2,951	335
1974	4,857	605
1975	9,265	1,147
1976	14,694	1,696
1977	29,822	1,585*

*The profit before taxation for the financial year ended 24th December, 1977, which included approximately £192,000 attributable to the disposal of property, was adversely affected by the acquisition in July, 1977 of Queensway Discount Warehouses Limited which was not at that time trading profitably.

Our five-year profit record as we prepared to list the company, capitalising it at £23.5 million. Profits the next year more than tripled to £5.5 million.

Every company listed on the London Stock Exchange had to show a five-year profit record, and ours looked good: £335,000 in 1973, then £605,000, £1.15 million, £1.7 million and a small drop in 1977 as we absorbed the costs of restructuring Queensway. In the first six months of 1978 we made pre-tax profits of £1.6 million and I was confident that, with our engines firing on all cylinders, we could exceed £5 million for the full year. Not many companies could better that in the 1970s, and County said they had never seen a record like it.

This was my first real exposure to the City, which had always intrigued me. Initially I found it a forbidding, private and exclusive world, full of upper-class toffs who didn't want anything to do with the likes of me. But as I got to know it, and it got to know me, I discovered that many of the people there *were* like me, from middle-class backgrounds in Essex or Kent, except not so fortunate – they travelled up on crowded trains every day to work in Dickensian offices for not very much money, which I had never had to do. In the pre-Big Bang era, it was still basically a village, literally a square mile, where everyone seemed to know everyone else. There was still a strict class culture, with the state school boys doing the less exciting jobs as clerks or 'blue buttons' on the floor of the Stock Exchange. At the partner level it operated as a privileged Old Boys' club, which Charles was part of, and he could not walk down the road or go into a wine bar without being greeted by someone he knew. Other than secretaries and receptionists, there were almost no women.

To make the issue more attractive to outside shareholders, County insisted on making some changes to the board. Pauline had been a director from the early days, as had my cousin Ron Poole, but Charles Villiers and Andrew Deacon insisted that was not right for a public company and they would have to come off the board. I should replace them, he insisted, with at least one outside 'independent' director, neither a relative nor a friend, with a good reputation in the City. Charles gave Pauline the news himself and he did so graciously, holding a

My father (*above left*) joined the British Army as a private
in September 1939, was commissioned an officer in April 1945
and ended up as an acting-major. *Above right*: with his fellow
officers in Lemgo, Germany, on Waterloo Day, June 1945.

With Every Good Wish
for
Christmas and the New Year
from
Charlie

Middle East Forces
Christmas 1945

1939	December	Saar.
1940	May	Flanders.
1940	June	Dunkirk.
1944	June 6th	"D" Day. Queen Beach White ("H" Hour 07 30).
1944	June 9th–July 16th	Gazelle, La Londel.
1944	July	Sannerville, Banneville, R. Orne.
1944	August	Vire.
1944	September	Seine, Escault Canal.
1944	October	Overloon, Venray.
1944	Nov. Dec. Jan.	R. Maas.
1945	February	Goch, Kevvenhcim.
1945	March	R. Rhine, Wessel, Haldern.
1945	April	Enschede, Lingen, Wildeshausen.
1945	May	Bremen.
1945	August–September	Belgium
1945	October	Ismailia (Egypt).

Field Marshal Montgomery awards my father the Military Cross
for 'exemplary gallantry' in an action outside Bremen in April
1945. *Right*: a Christmas card sent from Ismailia in 1945 on the
way to Palestine. *Above right*: my parents on a rare holiday after the
war and (*middle*) Dad, in white shoes, with my cousin Denny and
his brother Tom.

Above left: my father's first lino shop in Peckham High Street, which he opened in 1947. Me (*left*) in front of the ruins of St Luke's Church and (*above right*) training for junior Wimbledon.

Engagement to Pauline Chumley (*above left*) and our wedding day in December 1960; we were both aged eighteen. *Left*: with baby Susan, born the day before my mother died of cancer on 27 June 1961, less than four years after my father. *Right*: I inherited the family house and eight carpet shops after both my parents passed away.

Lino firm woman chief left £12,000

Mrs. RUTH HARRIS, of 27 Gibons-hill, Norbury, of C. W. Harris Ltd., linoleum and carpet dealers, High-st., Penge, Rye-lane, Peckham, Peckham High-st., and Balham High-rd., who died last June, left £12,655 net (duty paid £643), in her will published this week.

The team that built Harris Carpets: my cousin Ron Poole (*left*), Ted Wright (*centre*) and Kingsley Elton (*right*) all joined me in their teens and stayed for nearly thirty years.

Three of my great mentors: Harvey Spack (*left*), with whom I did over 4,000 property transactions; Neville Cormack (*centre*), one of Britain's greatest carpet manufacturers; and David Biderman (*right*) who taught me the art of buying carpets and even how to dress properly.

The Harris Queensway executive team in 1978. *Back row*: Peter Davis, Ian Horwood, deputy chairman Hugh Sykes, Tony Behar and Howard Ellis. *Front row*: Kingsley Elton (*left*) and David Stockwell, my managing director and right-hand man.

Pauline examines a silver bowl presented to her by Charles Villiers of County Bank for agreeing to come off the Harris Queensway board. *Right*: County Bank's prospectus in November 1978 valued Harris Queensway at £23.5 million; ten years later, I sold it for £450 million.

HARRIS QUEENSWAY GROUP LIMITED

Offer for Sale
by
COUNTY BANK
LIMITED

Below: the team celebrates after the shares soar when trading begins on the London Stock Exchange. My daughter Susan and sons Charles and Martin (*extreme right*) joined us.

Honours time: (Lord) Jeffrey Sterling (*top left*) presents me with the Businessman of the Year Award in 1983; (*top right*) I became Sir Philip Harris in 1985 and (*above left*) Lord Harris of Peckham in 1996; (*above right*) one of my thirteen honorary doctorates; accepting an award from Princess Anne for supporting the Queen Mother Hospital for Animals in Potters Bar; and Pauline receives her DBE from the Queen.

In our central warehouse, where we stored and cut carpets for our shops across the country. In 1985, we opened our first fully automated carpet-cutting centre in Swanley, Kent, which delivered huge savings and cut delivery times in half. *Below left*: in 1986, I bought Hamleys Toys for £30 million – and gained a giant friend.

Chairing an early annual general meeting of Harris Queensway. David Stockwell is right behind me – as he always was.

Top left: Pauline and I escort Prince Philip around the genetic unit of Guy's Hospital, where I became chairman in 1990. *Top right*: Mrs Thatcher opens the MRI scanner I donated. *Right*: with Mrs Thatcher in later years. *Below*: my portrait replaces Thomas Guy's in the hospital he founded in 1721.

VICE CHAIRMAN

EDWARD G. SLESINGER ESQ. 1948
AUBREY E. ORCHARD-LISLE ESQ. 1964

SUPERINTENDENTS

JOHN CHARLES STEELE 1853
SIR EDWIN COOPER PERRY 1892
HERBERT LIGHTFOOT EASON 1920
PROFESSOR THOMAS BAILLIE JOHNSTON 1937
WILLIAM DAVID DOHERTY 1948
JOHN BARNARD BLAIKLEY 1958
PHILIP JOHN HELLIWELL 1967

THE GUY'S AND LEWISHAM NHS TRUST

CHAIRMAN: SIR PHILIP HARRIS
CHIEF EXECUTIVE: PETER GRIFFITHS

In the 1980s, Sir George Pinker, the Queen's surgeon-gynaecologist (*right*) introduced us to the women's charity Birthright, Princess Diana's favourite. *Above*: accompanied by Sir Evelyn de Rothschild, she opens one of our Harris Birthright centres; and (*right*), unveiling a plaque at the opening of the Sheffield unit.

Above left: with Sir Victor and Lady Sylvia Blank at the 30th anniversary dinner of Birthright, now Wellbeing of Women; in all, we have supported six Harris Birthright centres, all but the last opened by Princess Diana.

With the Majors at Chequers, where Pauline helped
Norma raise more than £7 million for charities.
Left: at home with the Majors and Djanoglys.
Below: playing an elegant on-drive and (*bottom left*)
two veteran cricket fans.

Some old friends: (*left*) Ernest Burrington, the Fleet Street editor who lived next door; (*centre*) Sir Hugh Sykes, my first non-executive director, and his wife Ruby; and (*right*) (Lord) Basil and Gita Feldman, who introduced me to Mrs Thatcher.

Left: with the Ronsons, Gerald and Gail. *Right*: with Peter Holmes, my oldest friend, and his wife Jenny.

With Sir Harry and Carole Djanogly. It was Harry who advised me to accept a £450 million offer for Harris Queensway in 1988 and served as a non-exec at both Carpetright and Tapi Carpets.

David Broome, Britain's greatest-ever showjumper, rides my two most famous horses, Sportsman (*left*) and Philco (*below right*). They were household names in the 1970s when everyone watched the Horse of the Year Show on primetime TV.

Left: Scott Brash, riding a triumphant Hello Sanctos, after winning gold for Britain in the 2012 Olympics (Copyright: Telegraph.co.uk). *Below*: with (Lord) Graham Kirkham and Scott. *Right*: the two Paulines, Kirkham and Harris, Sanctos's proud co-owners.

Left: with Sir Dan Moynihan, chief executive of the Harris Federation, which now runs forty-four academy schools. *Above*: with (Lord) Andrew Adonis, the Labour minister who drove the academy school initiative.

I love visiting the schools and meeting the students, who come from a wide variety of London society and ethnic backgrounds. Many of them qualify for school meals. *Above*: with the kids on sports day, my most enjoyable day of the year. They love it almost as much as I do.

(Lord) Jeffrey Sterling (*back*) arranged for some of our prize-winning students to learn to row and crew *Gloriana*, the Queen's barge. *Below left*: two of our star graduates, the rap artist Stormzy, who studied at Harris Academy South Norwood; and Louisa Johnson, the youngest-ever winner of *The X Factor*, who went to Chafford Hundred School in Thurrock.

Above: James Hanscombe, principal of the Harris Westminster sixth form college, who aims to get half his students into Oxbridge within ten years.

My father's bronze statue now stands in the quadrangle in Harris Manchester College, Oxford. The principal, Dr Ralph Waller (*middle*), and (*right*) Peter and I with my beloved uncle Fred after receiving honorary degrees.

To mark the occasion of her Diamond Jubilee, the Queen posed for just one official portrait, by the Australian painter Ralph Heimans. I presented it to Westminster Abbey, where it will form the centrepiece of the new Jubilee Galleries. It had to be repaired after a Fathers4Justice campaigner sprayed the word 'help' across it.

Restoring Westminster Abbey: Hawksmoor's glorious towers after cleaning; and (*right*) the three central windows in the King Henry VII Chapel that I commissioned. Pauline and I pray on our knees in the bottom left-hand corner.

Above: the dean, Dr John Hall, ushers the Queen into the Abbey. *Pictures © Dean and Chapter of Westminster*

Well-earned rest: Pauline and I relax at our home near Edenbridge, in Kent, with our dog Maxwell. *Below left*: Martin and Zoe on their wedding day.

With our three boys: the twins, Peter and Charles, flank Martin. *Inset*: daughter Susan.

dinner in her honour and presenting her with a silver dish, which, she says, 'still sticks in my throat every time I look at it!'

Charles then came up with the names of several people I should consider as a non-executive director. I didn't know any of them but agreed to meet the man he most strongly recommended for the role, Hugh Sykes, who he said was both an industrialist and a financial man, well regarded in the City. They knew each other slightly from County's connections with the cement company Bath & Portland (later Blue Circle), where Sykes was a non-exec. His CV was impressive. It recorded his profession as chartered accountant, but he was also a Cambridge-educated lawyer, who had been joint managing director of Steetley, the refractories group, but had stepped down several years before. He now ran his own financial consultancy.

I was instinctively opposed to non-executive directors – I still am – and was a bit wary of him and his potential impact on the informal way I ran the company. We didn't really have board meetings in the formal sense – they were more gatherings of our little team where we discussed the latest sales, exchanged information (and industry gossip), decided on what we were going to do next and went out and did it. These meetings were also fun, where we swapped jokes and anecdotes, talked about football and our families, and I didn't want them to become too stuffy just to suit a City-appointed non-executive. Mostly we didn't even keep minutes and there was no schedule of future dates – we had a meeting whenever we needed to, sometimes twice a week, sometimes every three months, often called by me at a day's notice. My office was wherever I happened to be, and that was usually in my car or in one of the shops. David Stockwell always said I was a telephone junkie but that's how I ran the business, calling the other directors several times a day to discuss the sales or some other issue, ending each conversation with the question: 'Anything else?' There invariably was.

With some reluctance, I agreed to meet Hugh Sykes, and a few

weeks later, Pauline and I took him and his wife Ruby to a horse show
in Wales, where one of our horses was jumping. They turned out to be
lovely people, and I warmed to them instantly, as did Pauline. Ruby
was a pretty, vivacious and intelligent lady who spoke her mind, and
Hugh, ten years older than me, was charming, affable and witty, and
clearly very informed about what was going on in the business world.
By the end of the day I had made up my mind – and so, I think, had
Hugh, who also, he confided later, had his reservations before we met.
He remarked that it was the only interview he'd ever had where he was
not asked a single question.

He joined our board in August 1977 and initially worked for us for
three days a week, helping me sort out the Queensway acquisition. He
rented a house in Norwich, which was freezing in the winter, where
I often stayed on my frequent visits. I found Hugh's observations remarkably astute and it was very useful having him there. I made him
deputy chairman in 1978, just before the listing. He and Ruby became
great friends and in later years we often visited them in their lovely
home in Sheffield, where Hugh rose to the dizzy heights of Master
Cutler and Ruby became the High Sheriff.

Hugh introduced a degree of formality into our board meetings,
insisting on an agenda which we roughly adhered to, as well as minutes
and a schedule of future meetings. I still remember his face when he
attended his first board meeting and listened in amazement at the
ribald banter between David, Elton and me. 'There wasn't even a
proper agenda,' he said later. 'And the first third of the meeting was
spent with everyone, including me, doubled up with laughter and the
second two-thirds getting down to serious, intense work.' At Steetley,
where he was on the board for years, it was a cardinal sin to crack a
smile, let alone tell a joke.

I suppose you could say Hugh taught me how to chair the board of a
public company, which I had to do many times afterwards, sometimes
with unfriendly non-execs looking balefully at me. He had a great

sense of humour and joined in the general leg-pulling and repartee and made a perfect foil for me from the beginning.

Hugh wrote his memoirs a few years ago and was generous in his comments about me. Modesty forbids me quoting them all, but I will include one passage:

> Phil was a fast thinker and a fast actor and I quickly learned I would have to change a mental gear to keep up whenever I was with him. It was refreshing working for him. He was a superb leader with an infectious enthusiasm and the ability to bring humour and fun to his business without endangering discipline. I was supposed to be teaching him the mechanics of public companies but he had something much more valuable to teach me about how to get discipline, fun and commitment from a team. I watched him carefully.

I just behaved as I always did, working on the principle that if I enjoyed the job there was a fair chance the rest of the band might too. And I have always liked a joke. Working with me must have been a bit trying at times, although most people gave back as good as they got. Hugh soon learned that, just as Harvey Spack and Andrew Deacon (and David Broome, of whom more later) had to, but I think they all had a good time.

I do remember Hugh looking a bit shocked at his first company dinner, which we held at a Greek club where everyone wore national costume. It was the usual raucous affair with the entertainment provided by a juggler performing with plates, every so often pretending to drop one, which smashed on the stage. I was dressed up as a Greek waiter and decided to join in, taking a plate from the table and dancing on the stage where I smashed it – which is what I had seen Greek dancers do. Everybody else took my lead and soon the stage was littered with broken plates. The management rushed out and pleaded with us, pointing out that the plates we were breaking were expensive ones whereas the juggler used his own cheap earthenware.

We all went back to our seats, but I couldn't resist the temptation and a few minutes later I threw another plate, which was the signal for a shower of the management's best crockery landing on the stage. This time the manager threatened to throw us out and I had a big bill to pay the next day. We were never allowed in that club again. I think Hugh wondered what kind of madhouse he had joined (although someone said they did see him discreetly hurl a plate himself).

A few weeks later at one of our board meetings, Hugh joined in the laughter when Kingsley Elton complained that his fiancée had been woken in the middle of the night by a man claiming to be a recruiting sergeant for the French Foreign Legion and had been told Kingsley wanted to join. Or when I arranged for a goat to be delivered to Kingsley as a birthday present – he lived on the second floor of an apartment block.

These were in the days before corporate governance entered our lives, and we wouldn't tick many boxes today. I was executive chairman, combining the roles of chairman and chief executive, which was still fairly common in the 1970s but broke the rules later on. We still didn't have a full-time finance director so, at Charles's insistence, we employed a head-hunter and hired Graham Povoas, who was a nice man but, although he bravely soldiered on, never got the hang of our informal way of doing business. Charles also insisted we move to a bigger firm of auditors, so we took on Price Waterhouse (or, I suppose you would say, they took us on), where the partner looking after us was Peter Davis, a brilliant accountant whose boast was that he came sixth in the country in his accountancy exams. He later joined us as finance director. I also promoted Howard Ellis to the role of company secretary. Messels, one of the City's most august stockbrokers, agreed to act for us.

It was Andrew Deacon, I think, who came up with the suggestion that we change our name in anticipation of our listing. I wanted to keep us as Harris Carpets but had to acknowledge that carpets were only half the business and did not have such a glamorous ring to it in the

City. Alastair Campbell-Harris, our PR man, and Charles Coode-Adams, our stockbroker from Messels, wanted to call it, grandly, House of Harris, but we settled for Harris Queensway as best representing what the company now stood for.

In the build-up to the issue, I spent more and more time in the City where Coode-Adams took me round to meet potential institutional investors: the big fund managers, insurance companies, investment houses and pension funds. The Messels brokers had this wonderful sign-off line after we had finished our presentation: 'This is a compelling business and you'll have to buy!' With that we would pack our bags and move on to the next meeting, often doing seven or eight a day.

The first mention of our plans for a public issue appeared in the *Sunday Telegraph* in June 1978, my first exposure to the world of financial journalism. In this case it was a pleasant one. The journalist, Ivan Fallon who helped me write this book, arranged to meet me in Orpington but I had German measles and wasn't in the office, so he came to my home and we talked in the garden on a lovely day. The following Sunday the article appeared under the headline 'Harris's magic carpets' and neatly set out our history and recent performance, adding: 'Later this year, Harris will probably go public, joining the group of new issues which are gradually building up after a four-year hiatus.' I was amazed at how many people read the financial pages of the Sunday papers, particularly the *Telegraph*, and for weeks afterwards wherever I went people commented on it, mostly because they wanted to know if they should buy shares.

I had a stroke of luck shortly before we went public when Associated Dairies, a major supermarket group (now called Asda), took over my one true competitor on the high street, Allied Carpets. It had been a decent company when it was run by its founder, Harold Plotnek, who started from modest beginnings in Birmingham in the 1950s and built it into the biggest carpet retailer in the country, many times bigger than Harris. I had a lot of respect for him, but by the late 1970s he was past his prime and eventually decided to sell up and retire to Bethesda in the US (where he died in 2008). Andrew Deacon was delighted when we heard the Asda news. 'Harris will now be the only quoted specialist carpet retailer,' he exclaimed. Allied shareholders, he reckoned, might well use the proceeds of the sale to buy our shares.

Asda was good at selling groceries but it didn't know what to make of its new acquisition and it proved a disaster for them. Some years later, Archie Norman, Asda's chairman (he's now chairman of Marks & Spencer), confided to me that he wished he'd never got into carpets. I eventually bought out what remained of Allied, just a few shops at that point – all that was left of a wonderful company at its height.

*   *   *

The Queensway and Ross acquisitions had given us terrific momentum and by October I was confident we would beat our profit forecast of £5 million by a handsome margin. That was well ahead of the figure we had given to County when we first talked of going public. The balance sheet looked healthy, too: Harvey Spack had revalued all the properties for the offer document, throwing up a surplus of £743,000 over book value, which was a nice surprise. We had cash in the bank of £1.4 million and total borrowings of only £258,000. The proceeds of the offer for sale, after Pauline and the family had taken out £6 million, would add another £1.2 million to the company cash pile. I intended to use it for the next acquisition, which I already had my eye on.

County proposed that we offer 5 million shares to the public at a price of 155p a share, capitalising the company at £23.5 million. The Harris family, after selling nearly 4 million shares, would end up owning 8.5 million shares, or 57 per cent of the company, worth over £13 million, which in 1978 put me among the richest people in the country, something I had never even dreamed of when I had set out twenty years before. David Stockwell had shares worth over £500,000 and Kingsley and the rest of the team also did well out of it. I had tried to spread the shareholdings as far down the ranks as possible. The shares would be worth a lot more a few months later, making some of these boys, who had joined me in their teens, wealthy men. I was delighted by that – they deserved every penny.

The flotation created a lot of interest in the press, setting the scene, as County and the advisers intended, for a favourable reception in a market that was still flat. Under the headline, 'Harris issue times it nicely,' David Brewerton in the Questor column in the *Daily Telegraph*, reckoned it was 'probably the right time to buy a share such as Harris'. He had a few caveats, however: 'The mere size and speed of the profits recovery at Queensway is as much a cause for worry as celebration, for it does demonstrate the volatility of the furniture business, particularly as the Harris management have not yet had the misfortune to steer Queensway through a consumer recession.'

My response to that was that I had weathered at least three consumer recessions in the past twenty years and had steered Harris Carpets through perhaps the most turbulent economic decade in Britain's history. I had no fear of recessions. In fact, I liked recessions.

The date set for the issue, the end of November 1978, was scarcely an auspicious time. We were still trading well but the rest of the country was heading into the so-called Winter of Discontent, when industrial strife, particularly among lorry drivers and British Rail, almost brought the country to a standstill. Ports and refineries were picketed and motorists, including me, had to queue for hours at the few petrol stations that were open. Even the grave diggers in Liverpool went on strike, causing the authorities to consider burying their dead at sea. It was probably the worst time in Britain's economic history since the war, but what worried County as much as anything was the prices and incomes policy, which Jim Callaghan had introduced in a desperate and ill-fated attempt to control inflation. Callaghan, now in the death throes of his government's tenuous hold on power, had tried to impose a 'social contract' on the unions, who would be forced to accept smaller wage increases of no more than 5 per cent. Business, including the retail industry, was prohibited from putting prices up even though inflation was eroding profit margins almost to nothing.

But, by the autumn of 1978, the prices and incomes policy was in tatters, breached first by Ford, which settled with the unions for a pay increase above the 5 per cent limit. Others followed, and in a wave of strikes and rising prices, the policy collapsed. From that time on, I was an admirer of Margaret Thatcher, the Leader of the Opposition, who contemptuously dismissed Callaghan's futile efforts to bring down inflation through state controls. She made some powerful speeches, which I thoroughly approved of, attacking the state 'watchdogs', particularly the Price Commission, who still tried to stem the breach. 'People like Freddie Laker with Skytrain, and Marks & Spencer, and British Home Stores and the supermarkets', she wrote in a memorable article in *The Sun*, 'have been responsible for better value in keeping prices down than the Price Commission. Our policy is really effective competition.' That reflected precisely my own philosophy: the more competitive my prices, the more carpets I sold and, contrary to what County and the City expected, price controls never worried me. Competition was the way to go, not state controls. After that I was a big fan of Thatcher's.

We had our own brush with the unions during this period, which could so easily have disrupted our public issue. Although we had moved most of the warehousing to Swanley, we continued to use a smaller warehouse in Barking, which was conveniently situated near the tunnels under the Thames. But it was also close to the giant Ford Motor factory at Dagenham, a hotbed of industrial unrest, which seemed to rub off on our staff.

The manager I had appointed to Barking was not up to the job, and I put another manager in over his head and demoted him to number two. What I hadn't realised is that he had the support of the van drivers who went on a one-day strike and picketed the building. We were non-unionised but that didn't matter: no one was brave enough to cross the picket line and our orders were now trapped inside the warehouse.

My wife Pauline saved the day. For years she had been driving horseboxes around the country and had an HGV licence, fully up to date. Driving a delivery truck was a mere trifle to her, and she clambered into the cab and set off determinedly for Barking. The pickets were too astonished to stop her driving in, and inside the delighted warehousemen, who were not part of the strike, quickly loaded up the truck. On the way out she performed an expert double-declutch, roaring the engine briefly, to show the picketing drivers she knew what she was doing, and drove on. When she went back for more, the pickets parted like a wave, and again she drove out with another load.

The industrial action, such as it was, petered out after that and we resumed normal deliveries.

* * *

Andrew Deacon got the Harris Queensway board together for dinner in the County boardroom on the eve of the float, and gave us all a lecture on the responsibilities we would have as directors of a public company. We all felt a bit downcast by that, sensing that the days of our freestyle, spontaneous and often very creative meetings were becoming a thing of the past. Corporate governance had not reached the ridiculous levels it would a few years later and I was determined to keep the entrepreneurial spirit – as well as the humour – alive in the boardroom. But we were now a grown-up company, responsible to outside shareholders with a different set of rules and regulations, and we knew he was right.

Within hours of Messels sending out the formal offer document, they were receiving requests for far more shares than were available and we were several-times oversubscribed. A few days later we were allowed onto the Stock Exchange floor as our shares traded for the first time. I remember the excitement of seeing the opening price, which was 182p, come up on the board (no screens in those days), quickly calculating that I had made £2.5 million in about five minutes.

The next day, 30 November 1978, I opened the *Financial Times* to see the name Harris Queensway, with a price of 175p next to it, listed under Retail, in the same column as Marks & Spencer, House of Fraser, Burton Group, General Universal Stores, British Homes Stores and Debenhams, all giants of the high street. It had taken me twenty years, but I had fulfilled my boyhood dream.

CHAPTER 12

JUMPING FOR JOY

When we first listed on the Stock Exchange in 1978, I was probably best known to the general public as the owner of two of the greatest jumpers of all time, Philco and Sportsman. Showjumping in the 1960s and 1970s, like boxing in the 1940s and 1950s, had a huge following and big events such as the Horse of the Year Show, which took place at Wembley, or the King George V Gold Cup, staged at either Wembley or White City, were shown live on prime-time BBC1 television after the 9 o'clock news, six days in a row from 9.15 p.m. to 10.45 p.m. Only Manchester United playing Liverpool could match its audience, and riders and horses were as famous as movie stars. The BBC's main commentator, Dorian Williams, known as 'the voice of showjumping', was as familiar in most living rooms as a member of the family.

After I started work I didn't have much time for riding but Pauline never lost her enthusiasm and in 1968, when the company was making a bit of money, I bought her a young horse called Warlord to compete on and she did really well. She used to drive to horse shows with her father and three children (Martin wasn't yet born) and sit them down beside the ring, ride in the tournament, and then put them all back in the lorry and drive home again. Her energy was phenomenal. She was a first-class rider, prepared to take on anything, even race horses, but after a number of increasingly tough events she decided she wasn't quite up to international showjumping standards, which required full-time commitment. I think if she'd done nothing else she could have been up there with the best of them, but she had her children and a selfish husband to look after – not that she ever complained.

When she decided she couldn't ride any more at the top level, we offered Warlord to George Hobbs, a member of the British show-jumping team who was looking for an international-class horse. My enthusiasm for the sport was rekindled when we went to Hickstead in April 1969 to see him jump, and when he was picked for the British team we flew to Barcelona to see him compete in the Nations Cup.

Also jumping with the British team that day was David Broome, a beautiful rider renowned for his fine balance and his uncanny ability to clip precious seconds off a round without seeming to hurry. He was twenty-nine then and had already ridden in three Olympics in which he won two bronzes. He had also won gold three times for Britain in the European championships and finished first in two King George V Gold Cups, one of the most prestigious events in the showjumping calendar. He had been voted winner of the BBC Sports Personality of the Year award when he was only twenty, an amazing achievement in a sport not highly rated by sports writers generally.

In other words, he was the best, and watching him jump in Barcelona I said to Pauline that we should buy a really top-class horse and get him to ride for us. From boyhood, I had nurtured a secret ambition to win an Olympic gold medal and here was a way I could achieve it. George Hobbs was nearing retirement and was never going to make it, particularly on Warlord, but David Broome had already come close twice and on the right horse had a good chance of pulling it off. So, I decided to approach David with a proposition. He didn't know me well and I had to chase him about for several days before I got him to myself. 'Would you like to ride one of my horses?' I asked him outright. 'Can I buy you a horse that could win a gold medal in the Olympics?'

He already had some very good horses: Mister Softee (named after a brand of ice cream), Sunsalve and Beethoven were already top of the tree. But they were past their best and I could see he was interested.

We agreed that he would look for a suitable horse and I re-emphasised I wanted only the best – a horse that would win us a gold medal.

Only later, after I got to know him well, did I realise that an Olympic gold meant more to David even than it did to me. As a boy, he had been brought up on the legend of Harry Llewellyn, a fellow Welshman who won Britain's only gold medal in the 1952 Olympics in Helsinki – yes, we won just one that year, our worst Olympics performance ever – on Foxhunter. 'That gave the sport a real boost,' David told me. 'And Harry – or Sir Harry as he became – lived off that the rest of his life.' One of David's proudest memories was of meeting Llewellyn and seeing Foxhunter jump.

David's father was a greengrocer in Cardiff who moved to a large farm in St Arvans, near Chepstow racecourse, where he had a dairy herd and dealt in horses, mostly Welsh ponies, later selling the farm and moving six miles down the road to Mount Ballan Manor in Crick, which David eventually inherited (and where he still lives). 'When I was very young, I used to be the jockey who used to get on them,' David likes to relate, 'and I was bucked off them so many times that by the time I was six I got fed up and retired.' Then his father gave him a little pony that he liked the look of. 'So, I decided to have another ride and it sort of kicked in from there.' Ten years later, he was picked for the British team and won his first King's Cup on Sunsalve.

After that he won just about everything, but an Olympic gold medal eluded him. He won a bronze in the 1960 Olympics in Rome on Sunsalve, losing narrowly to the Italian brothers Raimondo and Piero d'Inzio, who competed in their Italian army uniforms. He did poorly in Tokyo in 1964, but, riding Mr Softee in the Mexico Olympics in 1968, he won bronze in the individual competition and, riding with Harvey Smith and Marion Coakes, came within a whisker of a team gold. They were leading by nearly thirty faults after the first round but then Coakes was eliminated and they had to settle for bronze. 'We went from hero to zero,' David told me, still crushed, many years later.

'We were heartbroken. It could have made a big difference, that gold medal. And it would have been good for Harvey too – two old boys, you know.'

My approach could not have come at a better time for him. That year he published his autobiography, *Jump Off*, which ended with this:

> We are beginning to run very thin on top-class jumpers; the champions
> of the 1960s – Stroller, Mister Softee, Firecrest, O'Malley and Mere-
> ly-a-Monarch – are slowly reaching the end of their show-jumping days
> and I think we'll be hard-pressed to find another bunch as good. I'd very
> much like to find another Mister Softee, or another Sunsalve, myself.

By a magical run of luck and opportunity, I was able to provide him with a couple of horses that were even better.

But it took some time for us to get going. After our conversation in Barcelona the months went by and nothing happened, until one day, in early 1970, I spotted an advertisement in the Horse & Hound for a horse in Essex which looked promising. I called David and told him he must go and see him and he rang a few days later to say he 'quite liked' the horse and he thought we should buy him. We got the Olympics vet to examine him and, based on his clean bill of health and David's recommendation, I bought him. His name was Cranham King – and he was a disaster. We took him to Hickstead in April and he seemed to fly over the first eight or nine fences, then hit everything after that. After a couple of rounds David said: 'I think there's something wrong with this horse. He goes clear until about fence nine then he becomes a mowing machine. He just goes like lead under me.'

We looked up his record – too late – to find he had done exactly the same thing the previous year, going clear for ten fences and knocking down everything after that. David took him home and had his own vet look at him, and he was diagnosed with a chronic heart condition which he had had for several years. So much for the Olympic vet!

The great British showjumper – possibly the greatest – relaxes.

David called me with the bad news and I told him to get rid of him as soon as he could and find another horse. I think he eventually swapped him for some younger horses in Ireland.

Towards the end of the 1970 season, another triumphant one for him during which he became the first British rider ever to win an individual gold medal at the World Championship (riding Beethoven at La Baule), David went to visit an old friend of his in Ireland, Frank Kernan. Kernan, one of the biggest and most successful horse-breeders in the world, lived on a farm near Crossmaglen, just north of the Irish border – known as 'bandit country' by the British forces trying to contain the IRA. Kernan had already bred several Olympic medal-winners and David and other big names in showjumping had great respect for his judgement and integrity.

David was shown five or six horses but nothing he saw interested him. The next morning, as he was eating a good hearty Irish breakfast, he watched through the kitchen window as the horses worked out on Kernan's practice area. One of them, coming in to jump a 2ft 6in. high pole, immediately caught his eye. 'Well, if I told you the bells rang and the lights flashed when he jumped that pole, you'll have some idea what it meant to me,' he said later. 'Everything was right about him.

Even young Ned Cash, who was riding him, came over and told me he didn't understand why they were selling him and said he was one of the best horses he had ever sat on. And when I got on him, I knew exactly what he meant. I had to have him.'

But he was very careful not to reveal his hand, so he took his time, pretending to be interested in several of the others. 'My problem was trying to buy him without Frank really knowing that he was the one I wanted! It took me all day to do the business,' he reported. He flew back to London where that evening someone took him to a casino – he never gambled so it was a pure chance – called the Sportsman's Club. 'I knew then the horse I had just bought was going to be called Sportsman,' he told an interviewer.

I first watched Sportsman jump at Hickstead in April 1971 and I thought he was one of the most beautiful horses I had ever seen. As David himself later said: 'He has a natural balance and perfect rhythm. He's the sort of horse everyone dreams about.' I wanted to buy him but David was reluctant to sell, and for the rest of the season he rode him at various events where, although he jumped well, he was disappointing. He hurt his mouth badly at a show in Bridgewater when he somehow twisted his bridle in a lorry and a few days later, at an event in Hickstead, where David's sister Mary rode him, he seemed fine, starting with three clear rounds. Then, racing against the clock, Mary, turning sharply, naturally pulled hard on one side of his mouth which must still have been sore, and he swerved into the side of the arena and jumped the rails from a sideways position. 'I don't know how he did it but if he had touched those rails they would have had one hell of a fall,' David said afterwards. Mary was eliminated but was just happy to survive.

Sportsman had a string of seconds after that but David never lost his faith in him, reckoning he just needed another season to find his proper form. I watched him jump a couple of times and kept telling David I'd love to buy him and let him ride him for me. At the end of the season, he finally agreed, partly I think to make up for the previous horse, which he still felt guilty about. David Biderman had become keen to buy a horse and I shared Sportsman with him.

David Broome and I agreed that, if I was really going to compete seriously at an international level, I needed more than one horse, and he called me one day to say we should go to America to look at a promising chestnut that Frank Kernan had told him about. We flew to Florida, hired a car and drove to the yard of Harry Gill, one of the top owners in the US, who was waiting for us with Rodney Jenkins, the top professional jockey in America. We watched the chestnut, which was called Number One Spy, jump and neither David nor I were particularly taken with him. He was certainly not a patch on Sportsman. As we were walking around the yard, we suddenly noticed a grey horse that was being expertly ridden by a very pretty girl wearing a tiny tube top, doing a sitting trot. I'm still not sure whether it was the girl or the horse that caught our attention but I do remember both of us quickly losing interest in the chestnut.

Gill told us that the grey had been a racehorse that he'd discovered a few days before as he was walking across the racetrack in Jacksonville and he had just arrived in the yard. He was only starting his training and was not for sale. 'He's very green, just a novice.'

But when we watched him jump, with the pretty trainer in the saddle, I heard David mutter 'phenomenal' beneath his breath. I wasn't sure if he was referring to the girl or the horse – both looked pretty good to me. But we had come this far to buy a grand prix horse, not a novice, so we went on to see other horses suggested by Frank. After a week of this, when we had still not bought anything, David called Frank, who had gone back to Ireland, to tell him where we were at. 'Look, you should be buying that grey,' Kernan urged. 'There's a future for that horse.'

I agreed. 'Come on, let's buy him,' I said to David.

Right from the first time I saw him, I had a feeling about this grey, but David thought we were being asked a ridiculously large amount of money for him. I insisted we went back to the yard for another look and David had to admit he was worth whatever we – or I – had to pay. Harry Gill, although I offered him a handsome profit, was genuinely reluctant to part with him, but eventually we settled on a figure of $100,000 (about £42,000), the highest price paid for a young show-jumper up to that point. David complained that he didn't sleep for two nights because he was worrying so much about my money.

Our new horse didn't have a name but, as we were driving down to Disneyworld for a few days' relaxation, I noticed a billboard on the side of the road advertising Philco electrics. That looked like an omen. 'That's a great name for him,' I told David. 'We'll call him Philco.' So, contrary to what people may have thought over the years, Brit-ain's best-known showjumper wasn't named after me but after an electric razor.

David took him back to his stables in Wales and two months later he jumped at Badminton, the first time I saw him compete. He was sensational, out-jumping the opposition by a huge margin and ending the competition with two clear rounds and the beginnings of a big reputation. 'It was incredible,' David wrote in his memoirs. 'And of course Phil was delighted with what the horse had done. After all, he had made the final decision about buying him and he had a right to feel pleased with himself.'

Rodney Jenkins came over from the US to compete in the World Professional Championship, held at the castle in Cardiff that year, riding Number One Spy, the horse we had turned down in Florida. He made no secret of his determination to thrash the 'dud grey' we had been foolish enough to buy off him. David rode Sportsman for the first two nights, and then Philco on the last, when he handsomely outjumped Jenkins (who, to give him his due, had a fall) to win the championship. Jenkins took it in good spirit, proud that he had rescued Philco from an undistinguished racing career to become a champion.

* * *

Sportsman and Philco turned into two of the best and most loved horses of all time, winning event after event. Sportsman won the King George V Gold Cup, a very special event for me, in 1972 and Philco won it five years later. David won it again in 1981 with another of our horses, Mr Ross, to give me a hat-trick and David his sixth victory, a record that still stands (I've won the cup six times on six different horses with three different riders: Michael Whitaker and Nick Skelton both rode for me after David retired). In those days, you could take the cup home as long as you brought it back the next year, and it had pride of place in our home, Farleys, year after year. It had a big lance that stuck out of it and we had a scare when Martin, aged about four, took it out to play George and the Dragon and lost it. We couldn't find it for ages.

As my friendship with David deepened, so did our professional relationship, and by the mid-1970s David rode only my horses and I used him as my only rider. It was a fairy-tale partnership for me and I think for him too. I loved to watch him wherever he was jumping and at one stage he even bought a caravan for me so that I could be close to the action.

David won five Volvo World Cups on Philco (each time getting a new Volvo car), the most ever won by one horse. I shall never forget the Horse of the Year Show in Wembley in 1975 when he rode Sportsman, Philco and another of my horses, Heatwave, to win seven out of eleven events. I told Pauline that if he made it eight I would buy her a mink coat and she never forgave him when he clipped a fence and came in second. I saved a lot of money but she always accused David of doing it on purpose.

Of all the hundreds of times I watched David compete, often travelling abroad to countries such as the US, Germany, Holland, Ireland and even South Africa, the most memorable was the World

Championship at Aachen in 1978, where David led the British team that included Caroline Bradley, Malcolm Pyrah and Derek Ricketts. Britain had never won a team world championship but with Philco jumping brilliantly, we won that night. It was one of the most exciting moments in all the years I owned horses.

Our two star horses attracted so much publicity that from 1975 onwards they became a medium for promoting the Harris Queensway brands, a trend that was on the rise in showjumping as TV audiences grew and grew. The Horse of the Year Show was watched by millions of housewives, the audience we most wanted to reach, but the BBC didn't allow direct advertising, so companies got publicity by sponsoring events or displaying their brand names prominently – or by giving their horses commercial names. Volvo, which had a managing director who loved showjumping, were big sponsors, as were Longines, Norwich Union, Courvoisier, Radio Rentals, Whitbread and Butlins; Everest Double Glazing supported Nick Skelton and the Whitaker brothers, as well as Liz Edgar, David's sister. It was an expensive sport and without sponsorship it could not have endured.

I think we used it to good effect. We would take up to three boxes at Olympia, complete with dining and bar service, and offer it as a Christmas treat to our suppliers, bankers, staff and friends, including their spouses. To make more of an occasion out of it, we made it evening dress, which most of the boxes did. When David Stockwell was told this, he assumed it was yet another of my little jokes designed to embarrass him, and he turned up in an ordinary suit and tie. His wife Valerie didn't speak to him all evening.

David Broome would come into the box afterwards and charm everyone, and Pauline or I often made an appearance in the show-ring in front of the prime-time TV cameras. Our staff loved it and when I went around the shops over the next few weeks they would greet me as if I was a celebrity.

Our main disappointment was that neither Sportsman nor Philco ever got to compete in the Olympics, where either of them would have been among the favourites to win gold. That would have capped everything, particularly for David, for whom the Olympics had an almost mystical significance. 'The Olympics are terribly, terribly special,' he said once. 'They are the one-off, they are the one that the sports editors judge you by, they're the yardstick. You've got the world at the window.'

David rode in his first Olympics when he was twenty, and his last when he was forty-eight, and he should have ridden another one in Barcelona in 1992 until he was unfortunately dropped from the team, as I shall relate.

Sportsman wasn't quite ready for the 1972 Olympics in Munich so he rode Manhattan, serving as flag-bearer for Team Great Britain, a considerable honour. But that was David's last Olympics until 1988, and Sportsman and Philco, who would have been at their peak for the 1976 and 1980 games, never got a chance to jump at the Olympics.

The reason for that is because, in 1973, the British Showjumping Association shocked us all by announcing that David was a 'professional' and could therefore not compete in the Olympics, which was still, totally hypocritically, claiming to be an amateur event. The barrier between professionals and amateurs, blurred at the best of times, was coming down in many sports, including tennis and cricket (rugby took another twenty years), and many expected showjumping to go the same way. The British authorities believed if they led the way other countries would follow, but they didn't and for the next three Olympics Britain's greatest riders could not compete. When the jumping authorities sent David a form to fill in, asking if he wanted an amateur licence or a professional permit, he simply enclosed £1 and sent it back unsigned. A couple of weeks later it was returned with a professional rider's licence with the registration number 003. And that was that – we were out of the Olympics.

David and Harvey Smith, the two biggest names – and earners – in

the sport were the most affected. I was furious with the pompous officials whom I felt were doing great damage to the sport in Britain
by singling them out, but David was amazingly philosophical. 'To be
perfectly honest, it was on the cards a long time before,' he said later
in an interview. 'Harvey and I had talked it over a lot of times and had
decided we would eventually turn professional.' The cost of keeping his
string of showjumpers was £50,000 a year and without his winnings
he couldn't afford it. As a way of getting him some earnings outside
showjumping, I helped him and his brother Fred to start a carpet business, but he was still dependent on what he made in the arena.

The rules finally changed in time for the 1988 games in Seoul, but
by that stage both our great horses were past it. David rode my horse
Countryman and finished fourth, which was a pretty good result in the
circumstances, although Pauline and I were disappointed for him. But
he was determined he would end his career on a high at the Olympics
in Barcelona in 1992, when he would be fifty-two years old, and trained
hard for them. He was to ride Countryman again but on the way to
Barcelona with the British squad he rode another good horse of mine,
Lanagan, in an evening contest in Royan, France. It was intended
that this would be a final work-out for the team before Barcelona but
David rode out immediately after the floodlights had been switched
on, and before the horse's eyes could adjust, he refused – which he had
never done before – and sent David tumbling over his head in a heavy
fall, hurting his back.

He arrived in Barcelona almost doubled up in pain and when I
got there he was barely able to walk, although he was still hopeful of
making the team. 'The back is quietly getting better,' he told me, 'and
the horse is jumping well.' In the warm-up round the next day, he went
clear and our hopes were high that he would still be picked. I had two
horses and riders in the team, David on Countryman and Michael
Whitaker on Monsanto, and realistically there was only room for one.
I begged the officials to put Countryman in instead of Monsanto,

knowing it would be David's last chance for a gold medal. But the team manager, Ronnie Massarella, wouldn't listen and announced on Sunday night, 2 August 1992, that he was going with the Whitaker brothers, Michael and John, as well as Nick Skelton and a young rider, Tim Grubb, who lived in the US. David was confined to the benches, asked by Massarella to 'stay and support the team' as reserve.

To give him his due, Massarella had agonised over his decision, telling reporters the next day that 'it was very difficult leaving David out. He's been a good friend for thirty years and he's a fantastic rider.' He had made his decision, he said, based on 'form', and David's back injury was not the deciding factor. 'It would have been easier for me if I'd made the decision a week ago, just after David was injured, because no one would have questioned it then.'

But people did question it, and I raised it with Princess Anne, who told me tartly: 'Ronnie Massarella picks the team and you've got to stick with that.' I thought it was so unfair on David who, after his 32-year record in the Olympics, deserved his last chance for a gold medal. Typically, David put a brave face on it but I could see he was bitterly disappointed, for me as much as anything else. 'It's Ronnie's call and he's left me out, and that's that,' he said fatalistically.

The next day Grubb stopped at the fourth fence and had a disastrous round, contributing to a poor performance by the whole team which was well out of the medals. 'David would never have done that,' I said to Massarella. I had booked a fortnight in Barcelona but left after a few days, thoroughly fed up with the whole thing and deeply disillusioned with the way the greatest British rider of his day, who had given so much for his country, had been treated.

David later acknowledged that his fall at Royan had shaken him more than he admitted and he retired a year later. In retrospect, as he admitted himself, he probably should have done so earlier and not waited to be dropped. But I lost some of my enthusiasm after that, particularly for the national team and the way it was run. My horses continued to win events, including another King George V Cup, but it was not the same once David had gone.

It was not quite the same without my beloved Philco either, long retired by then. One day, on the way to Gothenburg to compete, David noticed he wasn't well and had a vet look him over after he landed. He pronounced he had a bad heart. 'You better have him checked out when you get home,' he said. David's own vet confirmed that his heart was missing beats and we agreed to retire him on the spot. We expected him to keel over at any moment but he recovered and in fact lived for another sixteen years, dying peacefully on David's farm aged thirty-two. He was a very special horse and I felt as if I had lost a close friend or relative.

For a long time, I thought that Barcelona had marked the end of my Olympic hopes but then, one day in 2011, David called to ask me if I would consider buying a horse for a young man called Scott Brash, who he and Nick Skelton reckoned could win gold for Britain. How could I say no? As David always said: 'Once you've had horses in your blood, you've got them for ever.' But that's for later.

CHAPTER 13

BATTLING FOR HARDY'S

After its stock market listing in November 1978, Harris Queensway was a substantial company, with 129 carpet shops, twenty-three Queensway Discount Warehouses and 1,314 employees, nearly 1,000 of whom worked in the shops. We still had three warehouses, but the big one at Swanley was coming on stream and beginning to produce the savings and efficiencies I hoped for. We designed it with a view of acquiring even more shops, and it was a giant, with a storage capacity of 2 million square yards of carpet, capable of processing 22,000 orders a week. It was fully automated, using the latest computerised technology available, and really gave us an edge over the competition in terms of providing a quick and certain delivery date. No one else had anything like it.

I had been thinking a lot about my management style and mode of operation. I have always been a hands-on manager, in every sense of the word, as happy in a shop – perhaps happier – taking a customer's order as I was in a boardroom. I knew every aspect of the carpet business because I had done it all: bought, sold, cut and laid carpets, rented or bought new shops, and had built around me a team of keen young managers from backgrounds similar to my own. I was confident that the formula on which we had grown the carpet business would also work for furniture, and there were other revenue streams I wanted to look at: electricals, for instance, and the do-it-yourself market, which was growing very rapidly. B&Q, Homebase and Comet were all attracting a lot of interest in the City, which was already beginning to ask what I would do when the carpet business reached maturity – which inevitably it would.

My days spent in the City working on the Harris Queensway listing had made me realise that running a big public company involved a different set of disciplines. From now on, I would have to publish detailed statements twice a year, which the City analysts and financial journalists would pore over. I would have to do presentations to existing or potential shareholders, meetings with the press, and learn the art of 'managing' City expectations of future profits, making sure I didn't disappoint on the downside. Above all, I had to accept that from now on I had to delegate more and take time to think strategically.

It required a different kind of organisation and, advised by Hugh Sykes, I began putting the structure in place. I moved my headquarters from Sevenoaks Way to a modern four-story building in the centre of Orpington, which we called Harris House, where we concentrated our administrative staff and our state-of-the-art computer operations that we integrated with Queensway's. I had picked Orpington carefully for several reasons. Besides being close to our home, it was a pleasant, commuter town, with fast railway connections into London, and it was easy to attract high-quality people to work for us, particularly women whose husbands commuted to the City. The car park filled up with upmarket cars in the mornings, as the wives, often highly qualified people who had stopped working to have children, dropped their husbands at the railway station and came on to us. Part-time work and flexi-time suited us fine.

I closed the Queensway office in Norwich and moved the people we wanted to keep to Orpington. Gerry Parish had a super personal assistant, Liz Chaplin, who had taken more and more of a senior role as his health deteriorated, and I persuaded her to come down to Orpington as my personal assistant. She had a wonderful, natural charm, always enthusiastic and able to deal with the hundreds of different tasks I asked of her – and I was a demanding boss. She dealt brilliantly with the manufacturers, bankers, City advisers, journalists and my family and friends. I was increasingly taking on new projects outside the business – hospitals, charities, schools and politics, which I shall talk about later – and I could not have done so without her enthusiastic support.

My key executive team remained unchanged, but I assigned them clear areas of responsibility, allowing them more autonomy. David Stockwell, probably my closest confidante and counsel in the company, ran the carpets business; Kingsley Elton ran Queensway; and I put Tony Behar in charge of developing the high street furniture operation I was planning. I had a new finance director, Ian Horwood, and Harvey Spack, who I spoke to several times a day, was my property arm and also adviser on acquisitions. The City bankers Charles Villiers and Andrew Deacon, who I also talked to most days, were effectively on the team. And Hugh Sykes, my deputy chairman and still the sole non-exec, was my friend and mentor on whom I relied for sage advice.

In February 1979, four months after the flotation, I was on the takeover trail again, making my first bid outside the carpet and furniture industry. We teamed with another group, London & Midland, to launch a hostile bid for Caledonian Holdings, which owned a small chain of DIY stores called Timberland, which we wanted to buy out. It was a messy, drawn-out battle that I found frustrating, particularly when Comet made a counter-bid and our deal fell apart. The Timberland management, however, didn't like their new owners and came across to me, forming the kernel of our new DIY arm which we called Harris Homecare DIY. It was not the ideal start to our move into the business – and unfortunately, as time went on, it didn't get any better.

In May, six months into our new public company status and with the bid for Timberland still undecided, we got to the big one – probably the biggest acquisition I ever made. It began with Harvey Spack, who one day asked me what I would give to get control of Hardy's (Furnishers). Quite a lot, I replied, knowing he had a reason for asking. It was a much bigger company than we were, with about 350 high street properties and sold carpets as well as furnishings. Harvey and I, on our trips around the country looking for properties, had often wondered whether we could buy them, never thinking that it would be available. The properties hadn't been revalued for years and he reckoned they were worth many times the balance sheet values. The company, quoted on the Stock Exchange, was a loss-maker and a bid would really be a property play.

It was controlled by two inter-related families through one of those old-fashioned voting structures that family-owned companies often employed, with a small block of voting shares controlling the company (they are more unusual today). Harvey had heard on the Jewish grapevine that the two families, the Slotovers and the Datnows, had fallen out and might be open to an approach. 'I reckon I can get the Slotovers to sell,' he said confidently. 'They want to get out.' So, we went along to see them and came away with an option to buy 41.5 per cent of the ordinary (voting) shares and 23 per cent of the (non-voting) 'A' shares. So far so good.

But when we approached the Datnows, who owned 45.6 per cent of the voting shares, we hit a brick wall. They refused even to see me, and County, who loved the deal, advised me that without their approval it was very unlikely we could get control. Andrew Deacon, however, was a very determined fellow and was not put off by that.

'We've got to get over 50 per cent before we can launch a bid for the rest and there are only 10 per cent of the voting shares available in the market,' he told me. 'But as soon as we announce, the voting shares will go beyond any price we can afford, and we won't be able to buy any in the market. However, I think there's a way of doing this.'

He then unveiled his cunning plan. The first step involved getting the Slotovers to give us irrevocable acceptances on their shareholding, which meant we would own the shares with the dangerous possibility of being stuck in as an expensive minority. But I was prepared to take that risk – the prize was big enough to justify it. Andrew went to see the Slotover lawyer, the legendary Stanley Berwin, who told him: 'We'll give you the irrevocables, of course, but I have to tell you, Andrew, I don't think your bid is going to succeed.'

He came back rather shaken by that, but still believed we could win.

Now we had to find the other 8.5 per cent of the votes we needed to get us control. A careful search of the register revealed some of the voting shares were held by distant relatives of the Datnows, former employees, trusts and so forth, but some were also held by City investment funds. So, Charles Coode-Adams, our broker from Messels, and Andrew set off on a trek around the City to persuade them to part with them. The voting shares had been 34p earlier in the year and we offered 115p, which was at the top end of what they were worth, and I didn't want to go any higher.

At each stop, Charles and Giles made the same pitch: 'Look, you hold some voters and some non-voters, and we are going to make a very generous offer for the non-voters – but we won't, unless you first commit to selling your voting shares to us.' One institution, the Pearl Insurance company, refused and, by the end of the day Andrew had only managed to get our acceptances up to 47 per cent, still short of control. One of the shareholders was our old friend Murray Gordon, who I thought might still be smarting from the Keith Royle deal but he accepted the offer and we bought his shares – or so we thought.

The news of our interest leaked of course: the next day's *Daily Mail* reported that Hardy's had been one of the best performing shares of the week 'and have doubled since January to 74p on gossip of a big holding being built up. Harris Queensway are tipped as bidders'. We could only respond that we were 'interested in anybody in that market but are not looking at the moment', but of course we were and now the markets and the press knew it. Clearly, we were not going to be able to hold the line for long.

Back in the County offices, Andrew, clearly disappointed that we had not got above the 50 per cent mark, asked me what I wanted to do. 'We've got to go for it,' I told him.

The next day, 16 May 1979, we announced a bid worth £25.7 million in a mixture of shares and cash for Hardy's and I went along to see Edward

Datnow, the chairman, to deliver the offer personally. I was politely but firmly shown the door and by the time I got back to the County offices he had issued a statement announcing the Datnow family was rejecting the offer. Andrew reported that the Datnow brokers, Duff Stoop, were already in the market, bidding up the price of the voting shares to 182p a share, which was way beyond their real value. By mid-morning, they had taken their holding to 48 per cent, which meant that between us we had 95 per cent, leaving just 5 per cent available in the market.

We were now stuck, unable to buy shares because the market price was well above our offer, and I could see that Charles Villiers was getting concerned. My bid for Timberland had not been an outstanding success and if this bid failed I would be seen by the City as a loser, which would affect future bids. County was in a similar position.

But Andrew was not finished yet and had another ploy up his sleeve. He called in a journalist from the financial press agency Extel and persuaded him to write a story, which was quite correct, saying that if Harris could not get more than 50 per cent of the votes, the offer would lapse and the share price would fall all the way back to where it had started. But, he added, there was a way out: if shareholders of the non-voting shares, which were the overwhelming majority, bought voters and then accepted the offer, they would still come out ahead. That story was well followed up by the rest of the press.

It worked. A man from Monte Carlo called me the next day to say he had been reading about me in the financial press and he'd bought enough Hardy's voting shares to take us over the top. I could have them – at a price. He also held some non-voters, and if I raised my bid even by a small amount, giving him a reasonable profit, he would sell me the crucial voting shares.

Jubilantly, I called County to give them the news, but found them surprisingly frosty.

'Who is he? How well do you know him?' Charles Villiers asked suspiciously. Clearly he half-thought I might have put him up to it, which would have got us – particularly him – into deep trouble with the Stock Exchange and City Takeover Panel.

'I don't know him at all,' I replied. 'I only heard of him for the first time today.' But he had told me he lived in Keston Park, only a mile from me, which made it look even more suspicious.

They assured me they believed me, but others, they said, might be less generous. So, Andrew went to the Takeover Panel, told them the story, and said: 'I want you to satisfy yourselves, before we agree this deal, that this man is not a concert party and is acting independently.' He gave them the number in Monaco and they called and questioned this poor fellow for over an hour before deciding he was genuine.

Once Andrew got the Panel's go-ahead we raised our bid marginally to £27 million and announced that we had over 50 per cent acceptances. The Datnows of course cried foul and the next day's *Times* reported that 'the Hardy camp views the sudden emergence of this stake with suspicion'. The Panel, however, revealed that it knew all about it and were satisfied there was 'no concert party'.

There was one final twist to the Hardy's story. Although Murray Gordon had pledged to accept our offer for his voting shares, he now reneged, causing great embarrassment for both Messels and County, who had publicly announced the number of shares we thought we'd bought. When Andrew called him at home he put the phone down. He did the same thing when Andrew called back, so he got his wife to phone and this time got through. Gordon was unrepentant and continued to hold out, even when Messels threatened to sue him.

But it didn't matter. The Datnows, having extracted another couple of million from me – as well as a handsome pay-off and pension package for Edward and his brother – finally threw in the towel and recommended the deal. I had won my first hostile bid battle. But it had been a close-run thing.

* * *

To the City, Hardy's was an old-fashioned, badly run, loss-making furniture chain that had seen better days. To me it was a gold mine. While
all the shenanigans with the Datnows had been going on, Harvey Spack
had been out with his measuring tape and slide rule, revaluing the shops
and sounding out potential buyers for those we didn't want. In July 1979,
when the deal was completed, we acquired 198 town centre shops and
by the end of the year only eighty-five were still trading as furniture
units. Harvey sold eight freehold properties, which had a book value of
£500,000, to the Burton Group, for £5.8 million. We received an offer
of £1.5 million for the headquarters, which we no longer needed, and
was an awkward building to do anything with. I wanted to accept the
offer but Harvey said we should hang on as the site could be developed
and would be worth much more. 'If you want to buy it, you can have it,'
I told him. 'But I'm selling.' Harvey's fees for the bid and revaluation
came to £500,000, so I said: 'Waive your fees and you can have it for £1
million.' So Harvey bought it, but couldn't get planning permission and
eventually sold it on at a loss – one of the few times he ever misread the
property market. I never let him forget it.

I also sold the credit business to Tricity Finance, a hire purchase
company that was part of NatWest Bank, for another £14 million
which, including the property sales, got me nearly all my money back.

Trading was going well too and in October I announced that Harris
Queensway group profits in the first six months of 1979 had doubled
to £4 million and for the full year we made £8.8 million, well ahead of
the market's expectations.

The markets reacted well, and the shares rose to 242p, compared to
the issue price of 155p a year earlier.

In April 1980, we acquired another sixty-nine high street furniture shops
and two discount warehouses when we took over Henderson-Kenton for
£15.4 million, and, a month later, we bought ten UKAY out-of-town furniture warehouses from ADG Group for £3.8 million. There would be a few
more add-on deals, but that basically was the furniture division.

CHAPTER 14

TAKEOVER FEVER

In September 1982, I gave a lunch at the Inn on the Park to celebrate my 40th birthday and to mark my twenty-five years with Harris Carpets. I invited everyone: deliverymen, carpet-layers, salesmen, managers, directors and bankers (not necessarily in that order). In my speech, I thanked those who had stayed with me for most of that time – quite a few had known me since my teenage years – and I was very moved when I was presented with an engraved silver bowl, paid for by a whip-round among the staff. It was a milepost in my life, a quarter-century of hard work, risk-taking and endeavour, but also of exhilaration and enjoyment. I got a lot of satisfaction from that day.

We now had over 400 stores and I was working on plans that would add quite a few more. If the past twenty-five years had been hectic, the early and mid-1980s were to prove probably the peak of my business career, the period when most things I tried seemed to work, the company went on expanding, and my standing and reputation in the retail and financial communities were established.

I never consciously set out to cultivate an image or establish a reputation, and basically carried on as I had always done, working six days a week, minding my stores, watching the cash flow and looking out for new acquisitions. But, as time went on, I couldn't but be aware that my reputation went before me, and there was hardly a week when my name wasn't in the newspapers.

I had to get used to embarrassingly effusive descriptions, including 'the greatest retailer since Isaac Wolfson' (*Evening Standard*), 'the

Picasso of retailing' (Tiny Rowland, quoted in the *Sunday Times*), 'highly talented' (*Sunday Telegraph*), 'carpet king' (dozens of references), 'Orpington's most successful and wealthiest businessman' (*Kentish Times*), 'boy supremo' (*Daily Express*), and 'whizzkid of furnishing' (various). The *Sunday Telegraph* said I was 'the best retailer in the business today' and (Baroness) Patience Wheatcroft wrote in *The Times* that I was 'one of the most astute retailers around'. The *Sunday Express* even called me 'the David Broome of discount furnishing', which I took – as it was intended – as a major accolade. The *Evening Standard* said my 'astounding success story is a model for every young entrepreneur'. There were a few epithets too: 'carpet bagger' cropped up a lot, as did 'magic carpet' and 'carpet tycoon'. It was all very flattering, but I knew it wouldn't last for ever and that the first time I faltered the City and press would turn on me, as they always do.

Fortunately, the company grew in leaps and bounds, and kept on growing. We became a serious retailer not just in carpets, but also in furniture, electricals and discount stores. In our first five years as a public company, we made fourteen separate acquisitions and acquired 492 stores – by July 1985 I had 679 outlets, and the following year I added another 300. Ten years before that it had been just thirty-six shops and it didn't seem so long ago that we were in single figures.

My name was now mentioned in connection with just about every potential takeover on the high street: I was confidently said to be about to bid for Debenhams or Woolworths and I was rumoured to be interested in Harrods, Burton and others, some of which I had considered, others didn't even figure on my radar. Some commentators even mentioned Harris Queensway itself as a target and I had to keep my eye on my back as well as the front.

The mid-1980s were the years of a crazy takeover boom that spread from Wall Street to London and affected just about every company quoted on the Stock Exchange. I knew most of the major players, some better than others. James Hanson and Gordon White built Hanson

Trust into the fifth biggest company in Britain through a series of the most dazzling takeovers of their generation; David Alliance was mopping up the textile industry as he created Coats Viyella, at one stage the biggest pure textile company in the world (I bought carpets off him); Stanley Kalms, one of the best retailers I ever met, dominated the world of electrical retailing. Then there was Tiny Rowland, the colourful chief executive of Lonrho, who tried to get me involved in his attempt to take over Harrods (owned by House of Fraser, in which he had a 30 per cent stake), Ralph Halpern, who revolutionised Burton Group, Jeffrey Sterling of P&O and many others: Sir Hector Laing, Terence Conran, Lord King of British Airways, Nigel Broackes of Trafalgar House (which owned the Ritz, Cunard and the *Daily Express*), Rupert Murdoch and others.

I used to meet most of them at dinners or drinks parties, sometimes in 10 Downing Street where the Prime Minister, Margaret Thatcher, liked to entertain her favourite businessmen. Gerald Ronson was often there and we became friends, frequently going out together for dinner with Pauline and Gail, Gerald's beautiful wife. I ran across some more controversial characters too (although not in Downing Street): Robert Maxwell and Ernest Saunders, for instance, both disgraced in one way or another in later years.

During these years, I tried to keep my feet on the ground and get on with running a business that was becoming increasingly large and complex. The company had long outgrown the original management structure, where I had basically promoted my old East End gang from selling carpets over the counter to managing one of the biggest retailers in the land. They had done a fantastic job but, as the '80s wore on, I had to accept some of them were getting out of their comfort zones and I was forced, often against my better judgement, to recruit new managers from outside – which didn't always work.

A brokers' report written in 1985 gives an interesting outsider's view of how I was seen at the time in the City:

The management style of the much larger company still reflects strongly that of the much smaller organisation from which it originated. This style is best characterised as having all the merits of the successful owner-run business – major concentration on selling, close identification with store management, payments geared to results, simplicity of operation with little bureaucracy, rapid decision making, detailed up-to-the-minute knowledge of essential trading data and highly visible senior management.

This approach, the report went on, 'has been successfully orchestrated by the chairman, in conjunction with key directors and senior managers steeped in the business and in very frequent personal contact'. But I needed to widen the experience and skills in the company and brought in Peter Davis from our auditors Price Waterhouse and made him deputy chairman (alongside Hugh), responsible for corporate finance and acquisition policy – although in truth I handled most of the acquisitions myself. I also recruited James Cook from Reed Publishing to support Ian Horwood in the finance portfolio, and we were big enough to need a personnel director, William Beattie, who joined in 1984.

These new managers, all with big company or accounting backgrounds, were the forerunner of further management changes that the City insisted on and which were designed to free me from day-to-day decision-making and allow me to concentrate on the longer-term strategy of the company. Maybe I'm just not a big company man, but I stopped enjoying our more formal board meetings so much and missed the creative spark the old team always seemed to be able to ignite in the earlier days. By the mid-to-late '80s, the spirit that had guided the company and driven it for nearly thirty years was still there, but it was dimmed, and I regretted that. It would flicker and die in the stormy times that lay ahead, but I didn't know that as I stepped up my plans to expand even faster.

* * *

My first significant deal of the 1980s was the acquisition of a 50 per cent stake in a little discount trader in Yorkshire, which brought Stephen Fearnley into my life, a major addition to my management team for the next seven years. He was a natural trader, who could buy and sell anything to anyone, and we saw in each other kindred spirits from the start. He had done his apprenticeship at Marks & Spencer, one of the best training schools in the retail industry, then joined his family retailing business, which was sold to Great Universal Stores (GUS) a few years later. Among the many assets GUS had collected in the time of its founder, Sir Isaac Wolfson, was a discount chain called Thoms, which Stephen was put in to run and which he built into a forty-store division, making £1.5 million a year. But he hated working for somebody else and after a few years he and his colleague, Paul Appell, left to form their own rival chain, which they called Pennywise. They sold that to Cope Sportswear but then, in 1978, Cope went bust, leaving them high and dry.

Pennywise was what was called a 'close out' retailer, which meant selling leftover stock from the end of production lines or unsold goods of another retailer – basically anything that could be bought cheaply and offered to customers at a fraction of the normal price (Poundland works on the same principle today). It was probably the only profitable business in Cope and was bought out of receivership by Stylo Shoes, which was seeking to diversify out of shoe shops. Fearnley and Appell were asked to continue running it, but they had more ambitious ideas than that. Stephen reckoned they had hit on a successful formula, they had all the contacts to make it grow, and they did not want to work for Arnold Ziff, Stylo's austere and autocratic chairman. They were looking for a partner to start again when Hugh Sykes met them – and immediately thought of me. A week later, David Stockwell and I met them in a village pub in Yorkshire.

'We've got this situation,' said Fearnley, who was clearly the senior of the two, 'where our parent company has gone bust, and we have a wonderful formula that's proven and it's making money. We're being sold to Stylo, but we don't want to work for Stylo. We want to go on our own. We need a partner – and we need some shops. And you've got the shops.'

When David and I asked them how their business worked, they made it sound simple and straightforward, which of course it wasn't. 'We take all the stuff off the mail order companies that they can't sell,' Paul explained. 'All the manufacturers and stores groups have got lots of broken stock, or it's the wrong colour, or slightly damaged, or it's out of date and they can't sell it – and we take that too, sometimes for a few pennies in the pound. We sometimes buy it by weight, literally by the ton, and we sort it, we put it in bins and we sell it at more than half the normal price.'

'Paul here – he's a real trader,' Stephen interjected admiringly, gesturing to his partner. 'I heard him on the phone last week talking to Mars down in Slough and he bought all their old Christmas stockings, full of Mars bars – four lorry loads of it, which they'd been left with. So, we'll just slit the bags open, dump the bars into bins and sell them at half price.'

'Or d'you want an *A–Z*?' Paul chimed in. 'I've just bought seven-and-a-half tons of them.' When we asked how on earth he was going to get rid of those, he waved his hand dismissively. 'I've already sold them on,' he said, 'and never even looked in the lorry. Doubled my money.'

So, what did they want from us? I asked them.

'You've got all these surplus units and we could do something together with them. We also need some funding, and if you back us, we could make a lot of money for us both,' said Stephen earnestly. 'But I don't want to work for you,' he added, in case I had any misconceptions. 'I want a joint venture in which we both have equity, linked to the performance of the business.'

He was right about the surplus shops. I had quite a few of them, left over from the Hardy's and Henderson-Kenton acquisitions. The good ones, occupying prime sites, had already been converted into Harris Carpet shops, leaving a bunch of less attractive stores in poor positions which I was trying to sell. They were no good for carpets – but they would be just right for this kind of down-market discount business. It was a perfect fit.

'Where do you want to start?' I asked him. 'Newcastle,' he replied immediately, and we began to work our way down the list of our surplus shops.

After a while, he suddenly stopped. 'Hang on,' he said, 'we haven't done the deal yet!' In fact, I'd done the deal in my mind half an hour before. 'Let's not worry about the detail,' I responded. 'Peter Davis will sort all that out.'

A couple of days later, Stephen took the train down to London, met Peter Davis and we all ended up having lunch at the Drones restaurant in Pont Street. None of us had any paper, so Stephen wrote it down on his table napkin, which later he rolled up and took away (he says he's still got it). We agreed to start from the basis of a 50/50 deal, but we would have the option to buy out half of his shares at a price linked to performance, giving us 75 per cent, with the option to buy more. 'The better we do, the better you do,' he said, 'because you can consolidate the full 100 per cent.' I heartily agreed – I wanted us both to do well.

The business still didn't have a name but a few days later, Stephen saw a British Airways advertisement for its new 'poundstretcher' air fares. BA hadn't registered it as a brand name so we purloined it (and Stephen, cheeky chap that he was, later tried to stop BA using it).

Four weeks after that Yorkshire dinner, Harvey Spack, David Stockwell and I caught a train to Newcastle for the opening of the first Poundstretcher store. I had been opening carpet and furniture shops all my life, but had never seen anything like this. It was a Thursday morning and already there were hundreds of people outside, and when the doors opened the place was heaving within minutes.

Harvey and I fought our way inside and found Stephen and Paul Appell on the floor working along with the rest of the frenzied staff. 'Can't talk to you now,' Stephen shouted above the din. 'If you want to do something, you can help pack at the tills.' We rolled up our sleeves and went to work.

Newcastle was the first of many Poundstretcher stores. We started on 1 April 1981, and by the end of the year we had nineteen what we called 'variety discount' stores, selling a wide range of clothing, toiletries, household goods, toys and confectionery – whatever Stephen and Paul could buy cheaply. We injected our (loss-making) home textiles unit into it and over the next few years we would add Bakers, a family-controlled retailer which we bought for £6.3 million, Pennywise, which the boys had worked for, and Thoms, the discount business owned by GUS. By 1987, we had 150 Poundstretchers, with a turnover topping £100 million, a fifth of the entire Harris Queensway group.

We all profited from it. When the time came to pay Stephen his first cheque for deferred consideration, I gave a dinner for him and then made a little speech, saying: 'I'd like to give you more – this is not enough. The better it is for you, the better it is for me.' In fact, as I now owned 75 per cent of the business by then, for every pound he made, I made three.

CHAPTER 15

WIN SOME, LOSE SOME

At the end of 1983, I was made Businessman of the Year at a lunch in the Savoy in front of 400 captains of industry. It was a great honour, which I shared with Peter Thompson, chairman of the National Freight Corporation, a former state-owned business that he had successfully privatised. We did a lot of business together, delivering furniture and carpets, and I was delighted we had both been chosen.

When it was my turn to speak, I said I was particularly honoured to be the first retailer to receive the award since 1976, when it was presented to Marcus Sieff of Marks & Spencer, one of the greatest British retailers of all time. 'What a man to follow,' I said to a roar of approval. Sieff, who I had met through Harvey Spack, was a god in this room.

The past year, when I had been able to announce profits up by 56 per cent, had certainly been a good one for me, but even as I left the lunch, I was already thinking ahead to 1984, which I intended to make my biggest year yet. I had not made a serious acquisition since Hardy's, although many were offered to me, and I felt I needed to move urgently or I would be left out of the massive reshaping of British retail business which was now taking place. James Hanson had captured United Drapery Stores, one of the largest of all the retailers, hotly contested by my friend Gerald Ronson, Tiny Rowland was still battling to get his hands on Harrods, Terence Conran's Habitat bought Mothercare (and later merged it with British Home Stores) and Burton, under Ralph Halpern, seemed to be buying up half the high street, creating the empire which was later acquired by Philip Green after all the hard work had been done (mostly by Stuart Rose, who had to sort out Halpern's mess).

My one failure in this period was DIY, which I had never been able to make a go of. The management I took over from Timberland was a disappointment and the business ran away with itself. It was a much more complex business than the carpet trade, where we dealt with about eight major suppliers, whereas in DIY we had literally thousands. We had fourteen DIY stores at the start of 1980 and built up the chain to twenty-eight, but they were mostly in the wrong places and the losses just kept on rising. I quietly folded it, my first defeat, taking a write-off of a couple of million on the £10 million we had invested.

Thankfully it wasn't a train wreck but I decided to pick my next target for expansion more carefully. For some time, I had had my eye on Comet, one of the pioneers of out-of-town shopping, which I thought would make an ideal fit with our Queensway stores. Towards the end of 1983, I arranged a meeting with its chairman and biggest shareholder, Michael Hollingbery, who I knew and liked. We came from fairly similar backgrounds: he had inherited a small electrical retailing business from his father at the age of twenty-five, floated it on the Stock Exchange in 1981, and now headed up one of the most successful electrical retailers in the country. He had been a great entrepreneur in his day but was now in poor health and his business seemed to have gone off the boil. There were rumours that he wanted to sell and I got him to promise me that he would let me know when he was ready. As the months went by with no word, I began to look at other targets. One came my way very quickly, although not in the electrical market.

Stylo Shoes, which I had already encountered before with the Poundstretcher people, was a smaller version of Hardy's Furnishers, an old-fashioned high street retailer that had not revalued its properties for decades. The chairman, Arnold Ziff, had inherited the business from his father, a Russian Jew who ended up in Leeds in the early part of the century and built a very good business there. Like Hardy's, it was controlled through an archaic voting structure with a majority of the votes held by the family: six Ziffs owned 480,000 shares, each of them with sixteen votes, adding up to 52.5 per cent of the total between them. If the family stuck together, they were unassailable. But dislodge just one of the them, and we could win.

The shares were trading at around 150p (where they had been stuck for about four years) but Harvey Spack, who knew the Ziffs, calculated the assets were worth at least twice that. In January 1984, I went along to see Arnold Ziff at his office in Leeds to tell him that I intended to make an offer for his company, conditional on the family accepting. I indicated my offer would be in the region of 275p a share, which I thought was generous but was still well below what I believed the break-up value of the business was.

Ziff listened to me politely and then equally politely showed me the door. It was an uncanny replay of my experience with the Datnows of Hardy's, who also showed me the door. That afternoon the Stylo share price began to move up and there were deals at 162p, 165p, 167p and 170p, so the news was clearly leaking. I gave the nod to Messels, our City brokers, who then swept into the market and bought 5 per cent of the company at an average of 175p.

We had still not declared our hand when Ziff issued a statement the next morning, saying I had informed him that we were intending to buy a 10 per cent stake (I had never mentioned that figure) with a view to making a bid, and the shares rocketed to 250p. The press that weekend was on my side. 'If Harris does decide to put a bid on the table,' wrote the *Sunday Telegraph*, 'Ziff is going to find it difficult to defend, even with his voting structure. Harris is perhaps the best retailer in the country today and the Stylo management is at the other end of the spectrum. A bid of, say, 275p, would start an interesting battle.'

In fact, I offered 325p a share, or £35 million, which I hoped would be a knockout blow. I tried to call Ziff in advance of the announcement and urge him to accept, only to be told that 'Mr Ziff is too busy to

talk to you'. I called him again the next morning, half an hour before
the bid was due to be announced, and again got no response. We got
acceptances of 53 per cent of the non-voting shares but only 32 per
cent of the voters and my bid lapsed. I sold my shares at a decent profit
but the Ziffs must have regretted not taking my offer: in 2008, the
company went into receivership.

*   *   *

It was around this time that Harry Djanogly called to ask me what I
thought of Harrods. He said he had been to a meeting at Hambros
with its senior partner Christopher Sporborg, one of the smartest and
most highly regarded merchant bankers in the City. Sporborg, he told
me, said that Tiny Rowland was trying to sell his 29.9 per cent shareholding in House of Fraser and he had been asked to find a buyer. It
had to be done very discreetly, or Rowland would get spooked and
back off.

Like everyone else, I knew a lot about Rowland and his dream of
taking over Harrods. Whole books have been written about the long,
drawn-out saga, which engaged the City and financial press for years.
Rowland, a wily German-born Rhodesian, had famously provoked
Edward Heath, then the Prime Minister, to brand him 'an unaccept-
able face of capitalism' after a boardroom row that involved members of
the royal family as well as Lord Duncan Sandys, a former Foreign Secretary and Winston Churchill's son-in-law. The establishment hated
him and found a hundred different ways of frustrating his attempt
to gain control of House of Fraser, with its crown jewel, Harrods. He
fought back by buying *The Observer* newspaper and waging his own
campaign against his many enemies.

I had met him several times, once when he asked me to dinner
in The Berkeley hotel. He was a handsome man, very tanned, with
a vulture-like grin and piercing blue eyes that fixed on me like a cat

about to pounce on its prey. He wore a beautifully tailored suit and, although he had been interned as a German citizen during the war (and was said to have served in the Hitler Youth in his teenage years), he had been educated in England and spoke with a posh English accent as he imperiously ordered the waiters about. He began talking about some of the African dictators he did business with and, seeing I had no interest in this, spent the rest of the dinner telling me what a brilliant retailer I was, before finally he got to the point. Would I lead a consortium bid for Fraser, which he would support with his 29.9 per cent shareholding? He had taken advice and reckoned I could not be stopped by the Monopolies Commission, which had thwarted him twice already. He would keep Harrods and I would get the rest of the Fraser stores, including Army and Navy, Barkers and a chain of other department stores.

I said I would think about it, but in fact I had no intention of taking it further. It was a very messy situation, highly political and contentious and I wanted no part of it. He obviously hoped to cajole me into it because that weekend he told the *Sunday Telegraph*'s City Editor that I was 'the Picasso of retailing – he knows where to put the last dot on the picture which turns it into a masterpiece'.

Now, according to Sporborg, he had accepted defeat and wanted out. He had come to Harry because Nottingham Manufacturing, the Djanogly family company, was stuffed with cash, over £100 million of it, which was an enormous sum in 1983. Harry sensibly said he wasn't a retailer – but had a good friend who was. So I was brought into it. So was Gerald Ronson, who, according to Sporborg, was 'also sniffing around' Fraser and maybe should be part of our consortium too.

Sporborg, Harry, Gerald and I held a meeting in Gerald's office in Marylebone Road but none of us could see how we could make it work. Harry later told me that Rowland tried to acquire a stake in Nottingham, offering to inject his loss-making Brentford Nylons company into it in return for shares. Harry turned him down flat and Rowland then offered Brentford to me, with the condition that I would have to take the manufacturing side as well as the shops it owned. I rejected it on the basis that I didn't want to get into manufacturing.

Eventually, in June 1984, Rowland sold his 29.9 per cent shareholding to Mohamed Al Fayed, who he then claimed double-crossed him and waged a savage campaign against him for the rest of his life, mostly through *The Observer*. However, Rowland's Lonrho empire unravelled in the early 1990s, hit by debt and declining metal prices, and in 1993 he was ousted. He died in 1998, a bitter and disappointed man. As for Al Fayed, he later sold Harrods to the Qataris in 2010 for £1.5 billion, a profit of well over £1 billion.

I might possibly have pursued Fraser and Harrods more energetically but for the fact that I now had another fish to fry. My approach to Michael Hollingbery was finally getting somewhere. At the end of March 1984, he called me to ask whether I was still interested in buying Comet. Of course I was, and Hollingbery, whose family owned 30 per cent of the shares, and I agreed on a price of £155 million, to be paid in a mixture of two-thirds cash and one-third shares. I assembled my advisory team, led by Andrew Deacon, and for two weeks we worked day and night in the County offices to get all the documentation ready. Then, on Monday 9 April 1984, with everything on course for signing, the story leaked and Comet rushed out a statement saying it was in merger talks with an unidentified party. It didn't take the press long to work out it was me and we issued our own statement, acknowledging our intention to make a full-scale bid.

Two days later I took the whole team, including our lawyers, up to the Comet offices in Hull, ready to sign. We were shown into a room and asked to wait. Hollingbery, we were told, was holding a meeting with his family trustees but he wouldn't be long. So we waited – and waited. Finally, after an hour and a half, Hollingbery's lawyer came in to tell us the deal was off. Comet, he said, had been sold for a higher price to another bidder, Woolworths, and an announcement was already going out to the stock exchange.

For a long moment, I couldn't believe my ears. Why had they asked us to come up to Hull, ready to sign, when all the time they were doing a deal with someone else? Indignantly, I protested that we had an agreement with Hollingbery and we had not even had the chance to respond to the other bid. Woolworth, I was told, had learned of our interest from the press and had instantly leapt in with a higher offer – £30 million more than us – and it had been accepted. 'You made it very clear that you were not going any higher,' the lawyer pointed out, which was true.

It was a crushing disappointment, my worst so far. Asked that weekend by an *Observer* journalist how I felt, I replied: 'Sick. Fed up. But what could I do? My price was enough and it would have been stupid to go higher. My heart said yes, but my mind said no. You know, I'd earlier lost Timberland to Comet. And I don't like losing.'

Only after the dust had settled did I discover there was more to it than had been revealed at the time. In an interview with Ian Watson of the *Sunday Telegraph*, John Beckett said that he had been stalking Comet for some time and my move had caught him 'on the hop'.

'I have a great admiration for Phil Harris,' he said, 'but it does not extend to letting him walk off with a company which last autumn we identified as the most efficient electrical goods retailer in the business, and one we wanted.' I hadn't even known he was interested.

I couldn't blame Hollingbery for accepting the higher offer but I did blame him for not telling us he was talking to a third party. In the end, it would probably have made no difference as I could never have matched the Woolworth price. But he was wrong not to have told us.

So, I'd lost again, twice within a matter of months, although the City, far from holding it against me, was impressed that I'd walked away rather than get into a fight I would be unlikely to win. 'Only a fool would try to outbid Woolworth Holdings,' commented the *Daily*

Telegraph's Questor column, 'and Harris is no fool.' At that moment, I wasn't so sure.

Beckett rubbed salt in my wounds a few weeks later when he came to see me with a proposition. Why didn't we merge Woolworth with Harris Queensway and create a retailing conglomerate which would dominate the out-of-town market, he suggested? It would be highly popular in the City, which liked both our companies, and a combined B&Q, Comet and Queensway would be superbly placed to get the benefit of Sunday and late-night trading which was beginning to come in. Would I be interested in talking?

No, I wasn't, I told him. But if he was ever interested in selling Woolworth to us, I would be very interested in buying it. A merger would have to be on my terms, not his, I said. In fact, it was a bit of bravado on my part, because Woolworth, particularly after the Comet and B&Q deals, was a good deal bigger than Harris Queensway. He had an ambitious management, headed by Geoff Mulcahy and Nigel Whittaker, and I didn't see much room for me and my team in that structure – or them in mine. We agreed to go our own separate ways.

My next plan to get into the electrical business took a more roundabout route. A friendly journalist arranged for me to meet Bob Thornton, then the chairman of Debenhams, Britain's biggest department stores group with sixty-seven stores, including Harvey Nichols on Knightsbridge, a massive 4.5 million square feet of selling space. Thornton had long accepted that department stores were, as he said, 'jacks of all merchandise and masters of not very much', and in their existing form were destined for extinction. His answer was 'specialisation', granting concessions to established retailers such as Benetton, the Italian fashion franchise, and Topshop, which took space within his stores. That was what I was after – space to sell my carpets and furniture. It was a big prize, if I could land it.

We had an agreeable lunch at the Savoy where I suggested to Thornton that we took over the management and operation of his carpet and furniture departments. These were usually housed in the basement of his department stores, badly laid out and run by people who were not specialists, and my idea was that we would set up a joint company which would work on the 'shops-within-a-shop' principle. We would run them as if they were our own, dramatically improving the look and feel of the selling space and tailoring our range of carpets and furniture to suit the more upmarket Debenhams customers. We would pay Debenhams a rental for the space, and we would split the profits 50/50 after all costs.

I made my case over the first course of our Savoy lunch, but he was a bit sniffy about the prospect of a discount retailer, as he regarded us, selling carpets and furniture in his stores and wasn't sure it would improve his profitability. He pointed out that 35 per cent of Debenhams' sales were made on credit, and its in-house finance company, Welbeck, made most of its money on carpets, furniture and electricals. We, on the other hand, would want to push the non-credit sales, which would hurt Welbeck (which actually accounted for 50 per cent of Debenhams' total profits). Finally, as we finished the main course, he said that he was happy with his existing arrangements and would continue with them.

That, I thought, was that, so I went on chatting in my usual way about the business and what was going on. Debenhams and I both used some of the same furniture manufacturers and as it happened I had talked to one of them that morning. He told me he sold the same dining-room suite, under different brand names, to both Debenhams and Harris Furnishings. 'Do you know how many you sold last week?' the manufacturer asked me. 'Over a hundred,' I replied. 'And do you know how many Debenham sold? None.' The reason, he said, was because they were selling them at £999 a time, displayed them badly and didn't promote them. We priced them at £599, displayed them well and promoted them hard. 'They have no idea what they're doing,' he said. 'They're not really interested in furniture.'

I couldn't resist telling Thornton this over our coffee, and went on to mention other items where we were outselling him at least ten to one. He looked more and more bemused, and I could see he knew nothing about this whole side of his business, while I seemed to have every fact at my fingertips. By the time we reached the coffee stage, he had changed his mind. 'He knows he can't live with you,' remarked my journalist friend, who had followed this conversation with great interest. 'He wants you on his side.'

We started off negotiating to take on Debenhams' furniture and carpet business, but within weeks Thornton asked us to include electricals as well – which I had not even asked for. Debenhams, some years earlier, had bought an electrical chain called Greens and opened branches in its stores, where they floundered. 'They haven't made a profit since 1976,' Thornton told me gloomily. He hoped I might fix that.

In March 1984, we signed a deal, creating a new joint company which gave us a 51 per cent interest in Greens and a 65 per cent stake in the Debenhams furniture and carpet business. Together they accounted for 20 per cent of Debenhams' total selling space, a huge addition to our total at that time. Concerned by the rumours whirling around a Debenhams takeover – House of Fraser were said to be thinking about making a bid, as were Ralph Halpern of Burton Group, James Hanson and Gerald Ronson (to name just a few of the interested parties) – I insisted on ten-year leases protected from change of ownership. That turned out to be very important.

I knew the joint venture was going to need a lot of work, but I confess I was wholly unprepared for the size of the task I had taken on. It was mammoth. The deal was finalised in June 1984, and I sent in every spare hand I had to get it up and running in time for the busy Christmas season. Carpets were easy: we cleared out all the old Debenhams stock with a 'sale-of-the-century', redesigned the drab selling space, and introduced a new range, sourced mostly from our own suppliers but pitched a notch or two above our usual high street customer. It paid off within weeks.

Furniture was trickier. Our autumn sale was disappointing and we had a poor Christmas, although 1985 looked better. Electricals got off to a terrible start when Stephen Fearnley told us about a computer company that had recently gone into liquidation. The receiver, he said, was selling off its stock of 100,000 Commodore home computers and we bought the lot for £30 each and put them into the Debenhams stores at £99.99. Home computers in those days were rare and there was a great demand for cheap ones. Alan Sugar was selling his early Amstrads faster than he could make them and ours just about walked off the shelves. We sold out before Christmas, complimenting ourselves on our first coup, but it didn't last long. The computers were a disaster, many didn't work and the complaints came pouring in – as did the offending machines. We didn't have a proper after-sales service or guarantees, so that was a tricky situation to handle.

But these were all teething problems and after that first six months, during which we learned a lot of lessons, things began to pick up.

CHAPTER 16

IN SICKNESS AND
IN HEALTH

One day in November 1984, as I was wrestling with the Debenhams issue, I got an urgent phone call from my daughter Susan to say Pauline had been involved in a riding accident and that they were on the way to hospital. They had been out hunting and she jumped a tall hedge and was thrown by her horse which then trampled over her. One of the other riders, a doctor, thought she might have ruptured her spleen and pancreas, which seemed to me pretty serious.

Pauline had ridden all her life and I had always been concerned at the risks she took, but I couldn't stop her even if I'd wanted to. She rode out for the trainer Toby Balding (the uncle of the commentator Clare Balding) three or four times a week and she hunted most weekends. Just a couple of days before, she had taken part in a two-mile charity race at Sandown Park to raise money for dyslexia, competing against professional jockeys, and was disappointed she had not won. I was just pleased she remained intact.

Susan told me that she and Pauline and a couple of other riders peeled off from the main group early to ride back to where they had left the horseboxes. They had to cross several fields to get to the road, but a farmer had unfortunately padlocked the gate and the only way out was to jump a hedge into the next field. Her horse landed awkwardly, tipping her over its head, and then ran over her, leaving a big hoof-print right in her middle. Game girl that she was, she got up and sat on a log, and insisted, against the doctor's advice, on taking the horses back to the yard. She and Susan then drove on to our little cottage where they left the horsebox and, finally, with Pauline bent over in agony, they set off for the hospital. On the way, she insisted on being taken to Bromley Hospital, which was near our home, 'where everyone can come and see me'.

I don't think the gravity of the situation had yet dawned on her because when I called them they were at the back of the queue in A&E in Bromley waiting to be seen. I immediately arranged for her to be taken to the emergency ward, where she finally collapsed and was put on life support. By the time I arrived she was unconscious and on a breathing machine, and from the looks on the doctors' faces I realised she was in serious danger.

She had a ruptured spleen and serious damage to her pancreas and underwent emergency surgery that night. It was touch and go for several weeks, during which she was in and out of consciousness, and I spent hours at the hospital, as did the children, willing her to live. I had been with her all my adult life, and we had shared every experience together: the loss of our parents, having children, building the business, as well as houses, horses, boats – everything. I would have been completely lost without her. She had always been by my side and I could not envisage a time when she wouldn't be.

It was a near thing, but she pulled through, causing chaos in the ward when she finally recovered enough to insist on washing the mud from her hair, upsetting the array of tubes and wires she was attached to. Her physical fitness probably saved her life, and by March, five months after the accident, she was back in the saddle again. Today she rides almost every day.

* * *

I was involved in all sort of deals at the time, but for weeks I could barely think about my business, which I think probably suffered in this time. The accident probably distracted me from the Debenhams partnership, which in its first six months lost £4.5 million, mostly because of writing off old stock. By the early part of 1985, however, we were getting on top of things and the joint venture turned in a profit of £500,000 in the first half of the year. Everything seemed to be going well, and I was starting to feel pleased with the deal.

The Debenham management, however, wasn't, and I began to see why joint ventures so seldom work. Early in 1985, I told Thornton that I'd like to buy him out and get 100 per cent of the joint venture, which I intended to integrate fully into my growing electrical business. But Thornton wouldn't have it. I was getting a lot of favourable publicity in the press which was often critical of him, and I think he felt I was trying to take advantage of the situation. All my efforts to talk him round simply made him more determined to carry on.

I was on the point of giving up when, in May 1985, Ralph Halpern appeared on the scene and changed everything.

CHAPTER 17

GOING FOR A BURTON

In the mid-1980s, Ralph Halpern was one of the big stars of the retail scene, a former Selfridges trainee who had worked his way to the top of the Burton Group and transformed it from a struggling, mid-market men's clothing chain into one of the most successful retailers in the country, with over a thousand shops including Topshop, Dorothy Perkins, Peter Robinson and Principles. Basically, he was the man who put together what became the Arcadia retailing empire of Philip Green, who took the credit for it – and stripped out the cash. But it was Halpern, with his intense, burning energy and drive (which later got him into trouble with the tabloids – but that's another story, not for a family readership like mine), who did all the real work.

I had met him on many occasions, usually at the social or charitable events we all seemed to attend in those days, and we got on well enough but we were not really friends as such. He was a fashion retailer, in which I had no interest, and for his part he had no designs on furniture or electricals. But we rubbed along.

On the other hand, I was very friendly with another player in the next stage of this saga. Gerald Ronson, with whom Halpern had crossed swords several times, was sometimes referred to in the financial press as 'the last of the great British tycoons', and who, like me, had left school at fifteen. His father, like mine, was briefly a professional boxer who fought (as a heavyweight) for the Jewish Lads' Brigade before the war, and then set up his own successful furniture business in the East End of London. Gerald, three years older than me, made his considerable fortune in property, but his real love was the Heron chain of petrol stations. 'If everything else goes wrong, I can always continue to live my lifestyle pumping petrol,' he liked to say.

I first met him at a Jewish charity dinner and we clicked at once, as did our wives. Gail Ronson was involved in raising money for the Royal Opera House and roped Pauline, who liked opera more than I did, into her fold. I did some business with Gerald, buying a couple of petrol stations off him and converting them into Harris Carpet shops, and found him a formidably tough person to deal with, but once we'd shaken hands, that was it – he always stuck to his word. Gerald liked to talk rough and look tough, but he was also an immensely charitable man, although you'd never know it because he never talked about it.

In 1983, Gerald made a bid for United Drapery Stores (UDS) but was beaten by the even cannier James Hanson, master of the takeover bid. He then set his eyes on Debenhams, by far the biggest prize left in the retail sector, and began acquiring shares. Early in 1985, as I was trying to buy out the Debenhams stake in my joint venture, he approached Bob Thornton to propose an agreed takeover, but the Debenhams chief executive turned him down. Gerald, however, had not lost interest and he quietly went on accumulating shares in the expectation that sooner or later someone else would bid. He didn't have long to wait.

For months, there were rumours in the press and the City that Ralph Halpern was looking at Debenhams, and it emerged later – we didn't know this at the time, or at least I didn't – that he had been to see Thornton to propose a merger, which was rejected. Terence Conran also approached Thornton and received a similar rebuttal. When news leaked that House of Fraser was buying shares, Gerald asked me how a takeover might affect my deal with Thornton. I replied that I had a ten-year agreement, but I was trying to buy Debenhams out of the joint venture and was making no progress. He suggested that I acquire some shares too with a view to having some influence over how the situation unfolded. I informed my board, explained my reasoning, and we began building a shareholding through the company. I didn't have any shares personally.

On 4 May 1985, by which stage Harris Queensway had about 2 per cent and Gerald had a bit more, Burton Group, in partnership with Conran's Habitat Mothercare group, launched a £450 million bid for Debenhams. Thornton and his board immediately turned it down, and so began what one newspaper called 'the most entertaining takeover battle the City has seen in years'.

Halpern had very cleverly cut Conran in for a 20 per cent stake and an agreement to redesign Debenhams' stores as 'gallerias', which went down well with the City. The bidders thought poor old Debenhams was a sitting target, but Thornton gave as good as he got. He succeeded in demolishing Conran's proposed 'galleria' concept which involved converting some of the old-fashioned Debenhams stores into big, modern spaces with lots of air, glass and rows of trendy shops. The concept, which initially played well with the press and City, rebounded when Debenhams calculated it would cost £400 million, almost the value of the bid, and Thornton joked that 'galleria' sounded more like a disease than a business plan.

Thornton found an unlikely ally in the shape of Mohamed Al Fayed, the Egyptian owner of House of Fraser, who came out against the Burton bid and continued buying Debenhams shares in the market. Because of my shareholding and my friendship with Gerald, I found myself in the middle of it all, alternately wooed and bullied by the various parties involved in this long, drawn-out bid battle that ran for sixty days. Thornton tried to put together a bizarre management buy-out, which he asked me to support, and I said no. Then Burton's aggressive director of mergers and acquisitions, Frederick Deitz, attempted to strong-arm me into supporting Halpern and again I refused. After that, stories reached me about disparaging remarks Conran made about the range of furniture we sold in the Debenham shops, which eventually appeared in *The Observer*, whose reporter, Stella Shamoon, had good contacts in the Burton boardroom. When I tried to see Halpern to discuss his intentions towards my joint venture, I was told he was too busy and I was referred to his finance director, John Coleman, who said he couldn't make any promises.

I was determined I was not going to be steamrollered, and reacted by buying more shares in Debenhams, as did Gerald. Overall, we spent about £40 million between us and took our joint stake to 8 per cent, effectively dealing ourselves a powerful hand in this giant game of poker. Professor Roland Smith, chairman of House of Fraser, then revealed that the Al Fayed camp had taken its shareholding past 10 per cent and was still buying.

All this activity inevitably drove the share price up well past Halpern's first offer, forcing him to raise it to £550 million. He eventually announced he had received acceptances of 38 per cent, but he got stuck there. House of Fraser raised its stake to 25 per cent and announced it was staying with Thornton. We were now sitting on a handsome profit but what I really wanted out of it at the end of the day was a commitment from the winning side to sell me the other half of my joint venture.

It all came to a head on Friday 2 August 1985. There was frenzied activity all day in the market, with House of Fraser and Burtons both buying, and at one point Burton announced it was putting back the closing deadline for the bid until Sunday, something that had never happened before. Halpern was calling Gerald, almost begging him to back him, and Thornton was calling me, pleading for my support. Gerald was far more used to this kind of pressure than I was and I let him do the negotiating on both our behalves. He called me just before the markets closed to say he had agreed to sell our stake to Halpern, who he thought would be more helpful to my ongoing relationship. That was enough to win the day for Halpern and within minutes, he had put out a statement claiming acceptances of more than 50 per cent, including our shareholding.

I felt sorry for Thornton, who had fought a good fight and achieved a very good price for his shareholders. House of Fraser held out for another few weeks, prompting rumours that they were preparing a counter-bid, but I don't think the Al Fayeds had either the stomach or the funds for it, and would probably have been referred to the Monopolies Commission in any case.

Gerald and I found ourselves briefly in the headlines again a few weeks later when the Stock Exchange announced it was investigating the share dealings in Debenhams shares in that last frenetic day of the bid. I still don't know what they were looking for, but we hadn't even been in the market that day. We had done everything openly and with full board approval, and our advisers were clear we had nothing to worry about. The Stock Exchange agreed, and we never heard any more about it.

* * *

There had been a big personal development for me during the course of the bid. When it had started in May 1985, Pauline and I were plain old Mr and Mrs Philip Harris. By the time it ended in August, we were Sir Philip and Lady Harris, ennobled in the Queen's Birthday Honours List in June for my contributions to charities. I confess I was very chuffed with the honour, as were Pauline and the rest of the family. Who would ever have expected it when I started out in Peckham at the age of fifteen? I certainly didn't and I don't suppose any of my teachers or childhood friends did either. I was still only forty-two, with my best years ahead of me, but this marked an important watershed in my life, a visible recognition that I was doing some good in the world. I insisted everyone still call me 'Phil', as they always had, but I couldn't help noticing that the 'Sir' bit caused me to be treated with a bit more deference in the City and, particularly, in restaurants.

A few weeks later, I took the whole family to Buckingham Palace for the investiture by the Queen, a memorable day in all our lives, and held a dinner afterwards for friends and family. How I wished my parents had lived to see that day – my father, if he had lived, would still have been only sixty-seven and my mother even younger.

*   *   *

After the closure of the Debenhams battle, I tried to contact Ralph Halpern to talk about buying him out of the joint venture. But he had become very grand, and I couldn't get near him, and once again I was referred to John Coleman, the finance director, who was more helpful. After some discussion, we agreed terms, which were actually very favourable to me, and one of the brokers, Laing & Cruickshank, did a calculation that even I hadn't thought of – and nor had Halpern, I'm sure.

'In June 1984 Harris Queensway paid only £7.8 million for their controlling stake in 20% of Debenham's selling area,' they said in a report. 'Under the Burton bid, Habitat have acquired the option of a 20% stake at approximately five times the cost. As we believe this is advantageous for Habitat at this price, Harris Queensway's deal now appears an outstanding bargain.'

It wasn't quite as good as they made it sound – our space was mostly on the upper floors or basement, whereas Conran got prime space on the ground and first floors. But it was still a good deal for us.

In June 1985, in order to give us some scale in electricals, I bought Rayford Supreme, which had thirty-two stores on the edge of major shopping centres, and we also launched our own out-of-town brand, Ultimate Electrical. Once I got control of Greens, I put all my electrical businesses into one division which gave us over 120 outlets across department stores, the high street and out-of-town locations. We dropped the Greens name and changed it to Supreme, integrated the buying and marketing functions in a new office in Camberley, and within a year we were doing £100 million of turnover in that division alone, about the same as carpets. Margins were not so good, but I was working on that.

*   *   *

We ended 1985 in good shape, with profits up 45 per cent to £39.6 million on revenues which almost touched £500 million. We also raised the dividend by 25 per cent, of which my share was £2 million, which I intended to use for a purpose. At the end of the year I announced I was making a personal donation of £1 million to help small businessmen in Britain by starting the Young Entrepreneurs Fund, which would invest amounts as small as £5,000 in fledgling businesses that might not otherwise get off the ground. I got my friend Norman Tebbit, then the chairman of the Conservative Party, to launch it, and I assembled a panel of senior industrialists and business people to advise the recipients.

'The way to create jobs is to encourage the entrepreneurial spirit and to help young people with good ideas, ambition and sound business sense to develop their companies,' I told the *Sunday Times* that weekend.

CHAPTER 18

GUSSIES

In May 1986, I joined the board of Great Universal Stores (GUS), one of the biggest, most secretive and admired of all the high street giants. I was very flattered to be invited. GUS, or Gussies as it was more familiarly known, was a British institution, one of the country's great retailers that sat on a wealth of undervalued assets in an array of subsidiaries acquired over the lifetime of its founder, Sir Isaac Wolfson, including the Burberry fashion company, makers of the world's most iconic raincoats. At one time, GUS was the biggest mail order company in Europe, and at its height had 2,200 shops on the British high streets.

I never met old Isaac, but I knew many people who had. Harry Djanogly knew him well and says he was one of the most charming and charismatic men he ever met, and that I would have loved him. The son of a Polish-born cabinet maker, he had grown up in the Gorbals, one of the roughest areas of Glasgow, where as a teenager he sold his father's cheap tables and chairs. He went on to become one of the great entrepreneurs of his day, a genius at making money from everything he touched in his long lifetime. By the time I joined the board, he was an old man (he died in 1991, aged ninety-four), living in Israel, and the company was run by his son Leonard.

The Wolfsons controlled the company through yet another of those non-voting structures I had become familiar with, but most of the family wealth was in the Wolfson Foundation, which in Sir Isaac's lifetime gave away more than £1 billion, and goes on giving. Old Isaac liked to boast that he was the only man since Jesus Christ to have a college named after him in both Oxford and Cambridge.

It was Poundstretcher, now expanding in leaps and bounds, that first brought me together with Leonard. In 1985, Poundstretcher was making profits of over £5 million and Stephen Fearnley, always on the lookout for further growth opportunities, had heard that GUS wanted to offload Thoms, which he had once run. He asked me if I would approach Leonard, who I knew from charity and industry events. He was a strange, painfully shy man, and had a reputation for being tricky and hard to deal with, and he certainly drove a hard bargain. Thoms was small fry for GUS but he still haggled over every detail, all of which he seemed to keep in his phenomenal memory. We reached an agreement at last: I would take over Thoms in return for giving him a 20 per cent stake in Poundstretcher.

That was just the beginning. A few years later, when GUS began to tidy up the many businesses it owned, I asked Leonard whether he would be interested in selling me some of his high street stores, which were looking a bit neglected and run-down. He was, but he said he didn't want cash for them (I think probably for tax reasons – they were in the books at almost nothing). That took some more tough negotiating but eventually we agreed to buy 341 Times Furnishing shops and 175 Home Charm decorating outlets, as well as GUS's 20 per cent stake in Pound-land. The acquisition, valued at £140 million, would be paid for in shares, which meant that GUS would end up owning 23 per cent of Harris Queensway – more than me. Cleverly, Leonard insisted on retaining the freeholds, for which I agreed to pay a rental of £12.5 million a year.

He appointed two representatives, Trevor Spittle and Eric Barnes, to the Harris Queensway board and in return asked me to join the GUS board. That prompted immediate speculation in the press that I was being 'groomed' as the next chairman, as the *Telegraph* put it. In fact, Leonard and I had not even discussed that and, as things worked out, we never did.

I attended my first GUS board meeting in June 1986 in an austere, 1950s building just off Tottenham Court Road. It could not have been more different to my board meetings where, even with the arrival of the non-execs, we liked to have a joke and a bit of a laugh in between the serious business. The GUS boardroom was as solemn and respectful as a church and the proceedings just as formal. We received no board papers in advance, and what we did get at the meeting was collected again and counted afterwards. No scrap of paper left that boardroom without Leonard's permission, and he never gave it in my time on the board. At my first meeting, Leonard unsettled me by suddenly asking me a question, causing me to protest that I'd only just seen the board papers half an hour before and was still trying to read them. I soon learned that he liked to demonstrate his skills at mental arithmetic, arriving at answers, always correct, before his finance director could even get his calculator out. When he discovered that I had a similar skill, he used to engage me in a contest which, fast as I was, he usually – but not always – won. I've never met anyone who could do sums faster in his head (although it was said that his father Isaac was even quicker).

Other than that, however, the meetings were deadly dull, nodding through lists of transactions that required board approval or budgets which had almost no detail attached to them, usually without comment or much in the way of discussion. I don't think I ever heard a single initiative or new idea proposed in all the time I sat on that board. Leonard could not have got away with it in today's climate of corporate governance, but it worked for GUS for more than fifty years, during which time shareholders benefited hugely. In my time, its market value was a few billion at most. Later, when its component parts were sold off under Victor Blank's chairmanship, the value to shareholders was £25 billion. Burberry alone is worth £6.5 billion today, and Experian, which also came out of GUS, is worth £15 billion.

GUS may not have been a barrel of laughs, but I was generating plenty of excitement in my own business. In June 1986, Ralph Halpern suddenly announced that he was putting Hamleys Toys, which he had acquired with Debenhams, up for sale. Hamleys was an iconic name, promoting itself as 'the greatest toyshop in the world', which it probably was. In 1947, as a small boy of five, my parents took me to the Regent Street shop as a treat and I have a clear memory of emerging, hours later, clutching a clockwork train-set. I even remember the price: 17 shillings and sixpence. I had it for years.

There were other bidders for Hamleys, including Woolworth, which had 10 per cent of the toy market through its high street stores, and I ended up paying £30 million for it. It was a pretty full price, particularly as Burton had stripped it of cash, but I had plans to expand it outside London through large out-of-town sites selling toys, children's wear and sportswear. I thought there might be potential for overseas franchises, and I also asked the GUS people about selling Hamleys Toys through their mail order business.

I completed the GUS deal in July 1986, Hamleys in August, and in October I made my final takeover in what had been a busy year. The last one – and it really was my last, at least as far as Harris Queensway was concerned – was Harveys Furnishing Group, for which I paid £9.5 million in cash for a 75 per cent stake. That added thirty-two curtain and soft furnishing shops to the group, taking us to 1,315 outlets, an increase of 75 per cent in a single year.

No matter how flush we were, I was always worried about cash and to be on the safe side, I raised £70 million through a rights issue at 225p a share, a small discount on the market price of 250p. The company was generating cash and, despite all the acquisitions, we ended the year with net cash of £50 million in the bank.

Profits in the year to 31 January 1986 hit £39.7 million, an increase of 47 per cent, and we raised the dividend by another 25 per cent. The following year, we topped £50 million and raised the dividend again, this time by 15 per cent. Turnover that year was £600 million, 20 per cent up on the previous year and my mental arithmetic worked that out to be £11.5 million a week, not all that far short of the £15 million a year we were doing in 1976, a decade earlier. Profits over that time had risen nearly thirtyfold.

I had no inkling at the time that this was to be Harris Queensway's last good trading year.

CHAPTER 19

FINANCIAL SCANDALS

Early in 1986, my friend Norman Tebbit, then the chairman of the Conservative Party, took me aside to tell me that the Prime Minister had become increasingly concerned that the City was out of control following a series of well-publicised financial scandals. An election was expected in 1987, Mrs Thatcher's third, and she didn't want a breath of scandal around her business and City friends, which would brush off on her and the party. 'We're going to go for the next one,' he said.

He meant it kindly, as a friend, and I took it to heart. I had inadvertently strayed into controversy when Gerald Ronson and I were allotted shares in the privatisation of BT a few years before, which we sold at a good profit. Our advisers were very clear we had done nothing wrong and we never heard anything from the authorities who were reported to be looking into it. An investigation into share dealings in Debenhams on the last day of the bid had also attracted headlines but again nothing came of that – basically because there was nothing in it. But I realised that my knighthood and success made me a target for the opposition and I would have to tread even more warily in a world where greed was triumphing over principle and even some of the most respected names in the City were being dragged into scandals.

Tebbit's words were still echoing in my head in February 1986 when I was approached by a stockbroker called Anthony Parnes, whom I had met with Gerald with a proposition. He was, he said, assisting some leading City figures in putting together a 'fan club' to support the share price of Guinness, which was in the middle of a £4 billion takeover battle for Distillers, Britain's biggest drinks company.

All I had to do was buy Guinness shares and the company would underwrite my losses if they fell, but if they went up, which was 'a near certainty', the profits would be for my account. On top of that, there would be a fee.

That sounded much too good to be true and I was immediately on the alert. Guinness, Parnes said, was losing the battle for Distillers because its rival bidder, Jimmy Gulliver, whose Argyll group was hotly contesting its offer, was playing dirty by mounting a bear offensive to force its share price down. Guinness had to hit back and Rothschilds, one of its advisory banks, was assembling a group of supporters to prop up its shares. Gerald, Parnes told me, was 'in', and he went on to name well-known firms, including Cazenove, Morgan Grenfell and other leading City banks and brokers, most of whom I knew, or at least knew of.

When I called Gerald, he told me he was indeed taking part in the support operation, and had taken advice which confirmed there was nothing illegal about it. To be on the safe side, he had also gone to see the Guinness chairman, Ernest Saunders, who assured him that the support operation had the full approval of his board as well as its City advisers. That was good enough for Gerald. 'Guinness was underwriting its fan-club members' losses because that's the way it worked in the City in those days,' he wrote later in his autobiography. 'There was never anything illegal or underhand about this.' He bought £25 million worth of shares and also received a 'success fee' of another £5 million.

But I didn't like it, and, with Tebbit's words ringing in my ears, politely declined. Over the next few weeks, however, I felt a bit foolish as everywhere I went people seemed to be 'in' on it, openly boasting about the killing they were making. I can remember Robert Maxwell, with a knowing wink, asking me if I'd had 'a glass of Guinness' and almost sneering when I told him no. That persuaded me I had made the right decision.

Guinness had been running behind in the titanic battle which dominated the financial headlines for weeks, but the support operation turned the tide. Its share price, which Gulliver had driven down, suddenly shot up and the value of its bid caught up with Argyll's – and then passed it. Gulliver, who complained bitterly to the authorities, later commented that if the Guinness share price had not been 'gunned up in the way they were, we would have won'.

But the drama had only begun. In December 1986, the Wall Street arbitrageur Ivan Boesky was arrested and charged with insider trading and fraud. In return for a promise from the federal officials to his jail sentence, he blew the whistle on a wide circle of inside traders, including some prominent names in London. The Department of Trade and Industry (DTI) launched an investigation into the Guinness 'support operation', which led to the arrest of Saunders in May. Then, on 1 October 1987, Anthony Parnes was stopped by the FBI as he was boarding a plane and charged with offences relating to the Guinness battle.

Then came the big shock, one of the biggest of my life. On 11 October, I heard the news that Gerald Ronson had been arrested and released on bail of £500,000. I called him immediately and he told me the story was not quite correct: his lawyer, Lord Mishcon, took him voluntarily to a police station where he was charged with eight offences (later reduced to four). He was furious, blaming Parnes for getting him into it, convinced he had done nothing illegal. Two days later, he and Saunders appeared at Bow Street Magistrates Court with half the world's press waiting outside, and charged with a variety of offences.

One after another, some of the City's top bankers and brokers were picked off. Roger Seelig, the Morgan Grenfell banker who was probably the leading takeover specialist of his day, was arrested and charged two days after Gerald, and in March 1988, Lord Spens of Ansbacher suffered a similar fate. To say the City was stunned would be an understatement – and no one was more stunned than me when the next man to have his collar felt, so to speak, was David Mayhew, the Old

Etonian senior partner of Cazenove, the Queen's stockbrokers, and one of the most establishment figures in the City.

The case took an age to come to court, and I tried to keep Gerald's spirits up during that time. We talked often on the phone, and he was really angry, believing, with some justification, that he had been chosen for a 'show trial' by the authorities who wanted a rich, well-known, preferably Jewish, businessman to make an example of.

After a trial involving seventy-five days of evidence, Gerald was found guilty of conspiracy, theft and false accounting, fined £5 million and sentenced to a year in Ford Open Prison, where he served eight months with remarkable forbearance and dignity. Even the judge acknowledged that 'the only person in this courtroom who has told the truth from the beginning of this affair was Mr Ronson', and he went on to speak of Gerald's frankness, honesty and helpfulness, describing his Guinness involvement as his 'one aberration'.

That remark still causes Gerald to explode. 'Bullshit,' he wrote. 'There was no aberration. I built up my business in a straight line. That is how I always work.' It's how he has always worked with me.

CHAPTER 20

BIRTHRIGHT

From the moment we had any real money, Pauline and I decided we would adopt the principle of giving away at least 20 per cent of our wealth to charities. In the early years, before Harris Queensway went public and freed up some capital, that wasn't much, but as the company did well and dividends flowed, we were able to make a meaningful contribution to causes that mattered to us. I have long lost count of how much I have contributed over the years, but Pauline has probably matched me pound for pound with her spectacularly successful fundraising events, and between us we have been responsible for charitable donations that probably run into the hundreds of millions.

Both of us have always taken the view that simply giving money is not enough – it's just as important to become involved, physically and emotionally, in the chosen charity. For instance, I think we helped put Birthright, a mother and baby organisation (now Wellbeing of Women), on the map with the contributions and efforts we put in; the impact of the money I have put into my schools has been multiplied many times over by the efforts of the Harris Federation, which I like to think has helped to improve the lives of some of the country's worst-off children.

I gave money to help restore Westminster Abbey, one of the grandest buildings in the country, but I raised even more and made a real difference there, as I shall relate in a later chapter. And my contribution to Manchester College, now Harris Manchester, enabled it to get full Oxford University status, which has transformed its whole position in the university and academic world. In the cases of both venerable institutions, and of Guy's Hospital, where I have also been a major donor, I did more than write a cheque, and I'm very proud of the results.

But, for all the effort, time and money I have invested, Pauline has transcended me. She does it the hard way, on one occasion driving 15,000 miles around South America in a classic Porsche to raise money for prostate cancer research, sending out her appeal in verse, including the memorable lines:

'Please give as generously as you can / To help the life of many a man
This dreaded disease is quite taboo / So come on, ladies, it's up to you.'

She may not be the world's greatest poet, but that appeal brought in £750,000.

She was one of the most successful fundraisers for the NSPCC, where, as chairman of the committee responsible for the Children's Royal Variety Performance, she took the annual takings from £80,000 to over £200,000, presenting its patron, Princess Margaret, with a bigger cheque each year. Organising that was almost a full-time task, but she still had enough energy to take charge of the Conservative Party Winter Ball and, when Norma Major asked her, she became involved with Mencap too. At the request of Princess Anne, who we often saw at showjumping events, she helped raise funds for the Queen Mother Hospital for Animals in Potters Bar.

Then there was Save the Baby at St Mary's Paddington, Chicken-shed and dozens of others, too numerous to mention. They even gave her an office at the Royal College of Obstetricians and Gynaecologists (RCOG) in Regent's Park, when she was chair of the appeals committee.

Given our family histories, cancer research was the most important cause for us, and we started with that. My mother died of breast cancer and when Pauline and I were approached by Hammersmith Hospital in the mid-1970s to make a donation for a new breast cancer unit, we agreed without hesitation. We also raised money for the first breast cancer scanner in Britain, which was installed at Paddington Hospital in 1974. They needed about £250,000, and we put in half and raised the rest from friends and other donors.

Then I felt we should do something for our local town, Orpington, where Harris Queensway was one of the biggest employers, and I contributed to a new hospice, Harris HospisCare, offering palliative care to terminally ill cancer patients. It has since merged with St Christopher's Hospice, but the Harris name survives.

After Harris Queensway floated in 1978, we had more money to give away and we enjoyed doing what we could for a variety of causes. Dyslexia, still basically unrecognised then, was high on our list. It tends to be mostly (although not exclusively) a male gene and our daughter Susan was fine, but our three sons, Peter, Charles and Martin, all took after me. I never knew I was dyslexic until Pauline realised there had to be a reason why all three of our boys, who anyone could see were fairly bright, were struggling at school.

Fortunately, we could afford to send them to special schools, where they got their A Levels and Peter went on to university. But that's not available to everyone, even now. Properly handled, dyslexia is not a big problem, and I insisted from the start that all our Harris schools have fully equipped dyslexia centres, with computer facilities and every other modern means to support people with learning difficulties. In 1990, I gave £1 million to a new dyslexia centre at Anerley in Kent, part of one of our City Technology Colleges, which was designed to take forty children with learning difficulties. All the children at the Harris academies have access to special needs education.

The charity that probably gave us most satisfaction was Birthright, which was focused mainly on premature pregnancies, one of the biggest women's issues in the mid-1980s. When we first became involved, Birthright was run out of the RCOG which had adopted it as its medical research arm, pioneering new treatments for women with pregnancy problems. Pauline and I first encountered it through Sir George Pinker, one of the most senior consultants at the Royal College, whom we had met when our daughter Susan had some gynaecological issues.

George was a lovely man, gentle and soft-spoken, who was recommended to us as the leading specialist in the country. He was the Queen's surgeon-gynaecologist and when Lady Diana Spencer married Prince Charles and began having babies, George, who later delivered both Princes William and Harry, asked her to become patron of Birthright. Diana made it her favourite charity for the rest of her life. But the real driving force behind Birthright's success was Vivienne Parry, its national organiser, whom I first met when she invited me to see the foetal unit at King's College London, where I was introduced to Professor Kypros Nicolaides. He and his colleagues, Professor Stuart Campbell and Mike Brudenell, were doing some brilliant things with ultrasound and other new technologies that could really make a difference to pregnant women and Pauline and I were blown away with what we saw. He was in desperate need of funds to build his new unit, so I agreed to contribute £250,000, Pauline raised more and in 1984 Princess Diana, then pregnant with Prince Harry, opened the first Harris Birthright Centre.

Over the years that we were involved, Birthright funded some amazing research. One of its early breakthroughs was the diagnosis of Down's syndrome in pregnant women, which helped make the amniocentesis test more accurate. It also identified a link between smoking and babies being born underweight, another important breakthrough. Later, its research projects laid down the ground rules which today enable many thousands of women to have safe laser treatment to treat cervical cancer.

Diana proved time and again how much Birthright meant to her. In one of her speeches at a Harris Birthright Centre opening, she said: 'To long for a baby and not to be able to have one must be devastating.

I don't know how I would cope with that. And if my work for Birthright can alleviate that suffering for just one couple, it will have been all worthwhile.' Just that made it all worthwhile for me – she had that effect on people. I would have done anything for her.

When Pauline took over as chairman of the Birthright appeals committee, she chose her friend Pamela Noble to be her vice chairman, and they made a formidable team. Working with Vivienne, they turned Birthright into the most fashionable charity of the 1980s, with major fundraising events to which everyone came and which were widely covered in the social columns. There was a wonderful ball at the Albert Hall, which was converted into a huge nightclub for the evening, and both Prince Charles and Princess Diana came to listen to the pop group Three Degrees (said to be Charles's favourites). In March 1989, 300 guests paid £500 a head to attend the Birthright Ball at the Savoy, where Pauline had arranged for can-can dancers to be flown in from the Moulin Rouge. Again, Charles and Diana came, as did half of London society – people like Geoffrey and Sylvia Leigh, Alistair and Romilly McAlpine, Basil and Gita Feldman and of course the ubiquitous Nicky Haslam. Diana attended the opening of The Mission to help raise funds, and Andrew Lloyd Webber donated the proceeds of the opening performance of *Evita* to Birthright. I remember an event called Lunch for Life in the Savoy, at which Princess Diana was also present, which was raising money for foetal medicine. The committee had set a target of £500,000 and when it only came to a disappointing £225,000, I couldn't resist announcing that I would make up the difference. That was an expensive lunch.

In 1986, Diana came up to Sheffield to open the Harris Birthright Research Centre for IVF Reproductive Medicine, which is now generally credited with providing the biggest stimulus to reproductive medicine in Britain, focusing on male as well as female infertility. The whole Harris family were there to greet her, and she was brilliant.

Princess Diana, accompanied by Sir Evelyn de Rothschild, arrives to open
a Birthright Centre. © PHOTOGRAPHERS INTERNATIONAL.

She went back to the Sheffield unit again in 1991 to review the progress
we had made, but by then her appearances were getting rarer and she
looked increasingly stressed. In May 1992, the whole sad story of her
marriage and her bulimia came out when the *Sunday Times* serialised
Andrew Morton's book, *Diana: Her True Story,* which I found very sad.
We got caught up in the media storm that followed when our friend
Richard Jarvis held a Birthright event in Garrard's jewellers in Regent
Street, which Diana had agreed to attend. The shop was surrounded
by photographers and TV cameras and I had to go out on the street to
greet her on the pavement. I will never forget the moment she stepped
out of the car, wearing a jewelled cross around her neck and a tightly
fitted velvet bodice with a high collar, looking sensational. That picture
appeared in all the newspapers the next day.

She and Charles parted soon after that and the rest is history.

Pauline later calculated that she raised between £15–20 million for
Birthright and I probably gave another £5 million. That went towards
building five Harris Birthright Centres, all specialising in different
areas of women's health. After five years with Birthright, Pauline stood

down as chairman and soon afterwards Vivienne Parry left to pursue a successful career as a radio journalist.

In 2012, Pauline and I were guests of honour when Sir Victor Blank, the chairman of Wellbeing of Women, gave a centenary dinner for me at the Royal College of Obstetricians. Victor has done a fantastic job with the charity, widening its scope considerably to include the whole gamut of women's problems relating to pregnancy. He has personally raised (with the late Sir David Frost) over £6 million for it from his annual cricket matches on his own ground near Oxford, one of the social events of the summer season. In his typically generous speech, Victor acknowledged our role in its earlier days, and I was so moved that I spontaneously announced I would endow one more centre, our sixth and last – and the only one that Princess Diana didn't open. We chose to put it in Liverpool Women's Hospital and the University of Liverpool, a leader in research into pre-term births (our twins were pre-term, so we are well aware of the trauma it can cause).

Despite the change of name to Wellbeing of Women, our centres are still called Harris Birthright and I hope they always will be. Many children are alive and healthy today because of them, and that is worth more than any amount of wealth. Pauline said it for both of us in an interview she gave about her charitable work: 'We do it because it gives us pleasure to help people less fortunate than ourselves. We are in a position where we can support research work that benefits a wide range of people. But you have to feel deep down that it is the right thing to do.'

CHAPTER 21

END GAME

The financial year 1987/88, my last full year as chairman of the company my father had founded forty years before, began well enough. In his spring Budget in 1987, Nigel Lawson, the Chancellor, fired the starting pistol for what the financial press and City analysts hailed as 'a new surge in high street spending', and there was much comment about 'the cash tills ringing merrily' and record sales figures. Taxes were cut, with the top rate coming down to 40 per cent against the 83 per cent I had been paying under the Labour government, interest rates and inflation fell and restrictions on credit eased, ushering in what became known as 'the Lawson boom'.

In the City, there was great excitement over retail shares, and the stockbroker Savory Milln forecast a 25 per cent increase in profits for the whole sector. We were a particular favourite and Phillips & Drew, one of the biggest broking houses, tipped Harris Queensway as a 'strong buy', as did others.

In the boardroom, buoyed up by all this optimism, we budgeted to make £65 million in the coming twelve months, a decent increase on the £50.1 million we made in the previous year (and £37 million the year before that), which I thought was a stretch but achievable. To give ourselves a little head-room, we guided the analysts towards £60 million, hoping to surprise them on the upside.

In May 1987, four months into our financial year, we were still on track and I reported strong trading to the market, adding: 'The group can look forward to another successful year.' Turnover was up 19 per cent, we had plenty of cash and on the surface everything seemed to be going well. But, as the weeks ticked on, I began to realise that things were not at all well. The sales figures were recording a worrying weakness and other retailers were telling me the same thing. More importantly, I was also becoming aware that I had made some unfortunate errors on the management front. Under pressure from the City institutions, as well as the GUS directors and some of my other non-executives, I had been persuaded to restructure my management along more formal reporting lines and bring in some new blood. Some of my board never liked my old East End crowd and told me that they may have been fine for a smaller, family-run carpet retailer but they were not right for a big, modern company with outside shareholders. To my eternal regret, after months of argument, I agreed to remove myself from the day-to-day running of the business, and head-hunted two new managing directors who would run the company day-to-day, ostensibly reporting to me. Peter Carr from Debenhams came in to take over the furniture operation, and Martin Watts arrived from Sears, where he had run Olympus Sports, to take responsibility for carpets, Poundstretcher, Hamleys and the Home Charm business we had acquired a year earlier as part of the GUS package. We also hired Peter Ellis from Dixons to become managing director of Queensway and Roger Pedder, a member of the Clarks Shoes family, to take over electricals.

It didn't take long for me to realise what a mistake it all was. Several of the newcomers were good people, and Roger Pedder in particular was a brilliant retailer, but they were in the wrong jobs. They came in over the heads of my long-serving and most loyal executives, including Tony Behar and Kingsley Elton, who were deeply upset by the changes. David Stockwell, my most trusted lieutenant, had to step down from his managerial role but stayed on as a non-executive director. Others were taken out of their jobs, where they were doing really well, and found themselves propelled into the centre where they were like ducks out of water.

Hugh Sykes was still there but he had moved up north where he was busy running his own affairs in Sheffield. I had isolated myself from my core team, and felt increasingly alone at the top of what was now a troubled empire.

I disagreed increasingly with some of the decisions the new management was taking. Peter Carr decided to upgrade the furnishing ranges and introduced china, glass, pictures, mirrors and household textiles into the Queensway stores, which I thought was a mistake: the bottom to mid-market was our core area and we neglected it at our peril. However, I had agreed to his appointment and had to give him his head, biting my tongue as the year wore on while profits slipped and troubles mounted.

There was barely a week when we made budget and trading profits were running behind the previous year, something which had never happened to me before. By June, sales were slowing alarmingly, and by August things were so bad that I had to warn the City that profits might only be £30 million, half their expectations at the start of the year. The shares dropped like a stone, falling 31p in a day to 165p, half their price of a year before. My reputation dived with them.

On a road show with my finance director, Peter Davis.

One evening, David Reed drove down from the City to my home in Kent and told me that he had just had lunch with the two managing directors, Peter Carr and Martin Watts, as well as Peter Davis, the deputy chairman, and they had a lot to say about my management style. 'Phil, the structure is all wrong,' he said earnestly, 'and you can't go on like this. The company is out of control.'

In David's view, I should either appoint another chairman and take full executive control again, or become a genuinely non-executive chairman, removing myself completely from the day-to-day running of the business – no more visiting stores on Saturday mornings without warning, no more negotiating prices with the suppliers, no more going over people's heads to shop managers I had known for forty years.

David had another suggestion: why didn't we find a buyer for the business before its value slipped any further? Woolworth, now called Kingfisher, might still be interested and there were several other potential buyers. I didn't like the sound of that – I was convinced I could sort out my own business better than anyone.

I now experienced what many wiser heads had warned me about: in my heyday, which was not all that many years before, I virtually walked on water in the City and among the financial journalists, who praised me to the skies. But, as the share price fell and analysts revised down their profit forecasts, I was referred to as a 'faded star', heading up a 'troubled' or 'beleaguered' company. There were even rumours that I was about to resign, or be taken over, which really shook me. I was described as the man whose 'management style was best suited to a family-owned business' but who didn't know how to run a big, diverse group, and so on. I had never known adversity before and I can't say I liked it. But I knuckled down, worked out my plan for recovery and set about trying to make it happen. I had let go of the executive reins, my biggest mistake, and now I took them back, determined I would turn the business around and get back onto the growth track. And I could see exactly how to do it, although it would take time – maybe two years.

One of my immediate problems was the quality of our financial controls, but that improved after the existing finance director resigned in June and I appointed Tony Shanagher, the most professional finance director I had ever had. 'My job is to ensure it doesn't happen again,' Shanagher told the City analysts when they quizzed him about our poor forecasting record. In August, I asked Peter Carr to go and Peter Davis left a few months later. In all, I lost four directors in this period, including Tony Behar, the only one I didn't want to go – he had been with me since the Keith Royle takeover and now told me he wanted to start his own business. All I could do was wish him well. Stephen Fearnley sold most of his remaining shareholding in Poundstretcher to us and took a back seat. GUS's two directors on the board were a steadying force, but they made no secret of their concern for the value of GUS's shareholding, which they were there to protect and which had halved in less than a year. Nor did Leonard Wolfson when I saw him at GUS board meetings, where I was no longer talked about as his successor.

In December 1987, I offloaded the Ultimate electrical chain without even waiting for the Christmas period. The buyer, ironically, was Woolworth, who paid us a nominal £8 million for a business that I had ploughed millions into but had never made a profit. I also sold the Home Charm chain to AG Stanley for £7.5 million. And I put Hamleys up for sale.

I had never been able to make a go of Hamleys, which too late I realised couldn't easily be replicated outside Regent Street. In Luton, where we opened a branch, it was just another outlet and damaged the brand. My son Martin managed the shop in Croydon and realised, sooner than I did, the structural difficulties of turning it into a chain. Belatedly I asked Stephen Fearnley to look after it on the basis that he was the only person in the group who knew anything about toys – he sold some through Poundstretcher. It was Stephen and Martin who persuaded me we should offload it. Finding a buyer, however, would take time.

My biggest problem was furniture. The acquisition of 600 Times Furnishing outlets from GUS had doubled the size of our operation and I couldn't stock them, at least with the merchandise I wanted to sell. There simply weren't enough British manufacturers to make the quantities of beds and suites of furniture we needed, and China – or the Belgians – were no help either. Unlike carpets, furniture manufacturing was a cottage industry, small factories turning out items which were almost hand-crafted. They kept no stocks, and their lead time could be months. That caught us on the hop more than once.

Let me relate two episodes that stick in my mind from these times. We introduced an Airsprung bed into Harris Furnishing and put it on sale at £99.99. It was a nice bed, the first to have drawers underneath, and we promoted it heavily. The factory was making them at a rate of 400–500 a week, which they thought was a pretty big number, but we sold out a year's production in ten days. No one else could make those beds and it took months to fulfil our orders to increasingly irate customers.

Then there was the Colonial three-piece suit, an attractive print with wood around the edges which I liked when I saw it being made in a factory in Wales. They were turning out fifty to sixty a week, which I thought was fine, so we ordered all they had and put them in the shops. Within days we had sold out and couldn't get any more.

Finding a solution could only be done over the longer term. When I told Harry Solomons, head of the Hillsdown conglomerate which owned the Christie-Tyler furniture-maker, of my supply problems, he offered to build a new factory in Scunthorpe where there was high unemployment and grants available. He was as good as his word and a year later I got my friend (Lord) David Young, then the Trade and Industry Secretary, to open the new facility, which could make 500 three-piece suites a week. It was developments like that that could have changed the business for us.

The one bright spot was carpets, which continued to deliver record profits. I often wished I'd stuck with carpets and I solemnly promised myself that, if ever I had a second life, I would foreswear all diversification and stay with what I knew best. The Swanley carpet-cutting centre had delivered us huge savings since it opened in 1985, and the level of service and speed of delivery we offered was unrivalled across the industry. I wanted to move more of our business out of town, which now accounted for 60 per cent of carpet sales, and I signed a five-year agreement with MFI which gave us sole rights to sell carpets and other floor coverings in seventy-eight of their outlets. MFI, by then part of Asda, had tried to do it themselves and when they failed they asked me to take it over. We already had 115 edge-of-town Carpetland stores and concessions in twenty WH Smith Do-It-All outlets and four Homebase stores owned by Sainsbury's. And we were still trading in forty-six Debenhams stores. So, I was doing something right.

I was firing again on all cylinders, relishing the challenge, and I could feel the business beginning to respond. I know in my heart I could have turned it around, but I needed time, maybe two years, to get the furniture side into shape – and I didn't get it.

*   *   *

Early in May 1988, David Reed called me from County with some startling news. I was on our boat off the Italian coast and there was no decent communications system aboard, so we hastily sailed into Portofino where I walked up the hill to the Hotel Splendido to use the phone. David told me he had received a visit from Michael Gatenby, a senior banker at Charterhouse, who told him that the bank had a 'credible' client, a well-known entrepreneur and businessman, who was interested in making a bid for Harris Queensway. Gatenby would not disclose his name, but he said he was serious, Charterhouse would be financing him, and they wanted to reach agreement with me before announcing it. They had apparently already talked informally to GUS, hoping to persuade it to pledge its 23 per cent holding (I still owned 16.3 per cent) in support, and had been encouraged by the response.

'Who do you think it is?' I queried. We ran through the various suspects, Kingfisher (Woolworth) which Charterhouse financed, being the most likely, followed by Asda-MFI and Hanson.

'I don't think it's any of those,' said David. 'It's clearly someone who they have picked to head a highly leveraged consortium bid. But I'll try to find out.'

In the meantime, he went on, we would have to put out a Stock Exchange announcement that we had received an approach from an outside party. We were due to disclose our figures for the year ended January 1988, which were going to be dreadful, but now, David said, we should bring them forward and announce them at the same time as the news of the bidder – which would at least cushion the blow. I flew back to London and on Thursday 5 May, we revealed that we had received a takeover approach from an unknown party. I also announced the worst set of figures I was ever to produce in all my years running public companies.

I had promised the City and my shareholders another record year but, instead of the £60 million the analysts had projected at the start of the year, and the £30 million I was forecasting at the halfway stage, we made £17 million. The only good news I could offer was that we were maintaining the dividend, although it was not covered by earnings (in previous years it had been covered three times). We were now, I told the City analysts and financial press, taking strenuous measures to turn things around, but they were no longer listening. The results were variously described by the next day's papers as 'disastrous', 'abysmal', 'even worse than feared', 'beyond belief' or 'shocking' – and they were.

Fortunately, the market was more interested in the price the bidder might pay, and our shares rocketed by 51p to 170p, still way off the level of 350p we reached at the peak, but also well up from the 100p they had fallen to at the end of 1987 (I had bought nearly 3 million shares at prices ranging from 100p to 115p, reckoning they were absurdly undervalued).

* * *

When we finally worked out who our adversary was, I could not have been more flabbergasted. It was James – or Jimmy as he was better known – Gulliver, the same man who had lost the battle for Distillers to Ernest Saunders. I can't say I knew him well, but we had met several times, always socially, and I rather liked him. He had a house outside Cannes and, a few years earlier when we were nearby, I had invited him to join us for a game of tennis and a day on the boat. He had turned up with a magnificent, fiery red-haired lady called Marjorie, whom he later married. The story put about, no doubt apocryphal, was that he had arranged to marry two different girls on the same day, and both turned up. Pauline couldn't resist having some fun at his expense. He was a small, stocky, straw-haired Scot, not much above five feet, and when Marjorie mentioned he'd had a 'short' commission in the navy, she quipped: 'Was that because of his size?'

He, like me, had once been the darling of the City, a management star who made his name in the food business, starting his high-charged career at the supermarket company Fine Fare. He was a millionaire by the time he was thirty, and was generally credited with bringing the modern supermarket to Britain at a time when Tesco was still in its 'pile-it-high-and-sell-it-cheap' mode. Several successful executives had learned their trade working for him, including Sir Martin Sorrell. Besides Ernest Saunders's 'dirty tricks' campaign, one of the reasons he lost Distillers to Guinness was the revelation, just a few days from the end of the battle, that he had falsified his *Who's Who* entry. He was not, as the entry stated, a graduate of Harvard Business School, but of Georgia Tech, which was not quite as prestigious. It sounds trivial, but the disclosure that he had lied about his academic record mattered to the City, the press and, particularly, his own senior colleagues who never forgave him.

Now, still smarting from that blow, he was back and, supported by Charterhouse, was planning to bid for us.

We found out a lot more than that. Gulliver (or Charterhouse, we were never sure which of them) had indeed been to see GUS to pose the question: if they were to receive an offer of around 170p, how would they feel about it? Leonard Wolfson was too wily to commit openly to Gulliver – that was not the way GUS did business. He may even have gently forced up the price, letting Gulliver know that he required a handsome premium before he was even tempted to sell. My suspicion to this day is that he gave him just enough encouragement for Gulliver to go ahead. GUS was reported to have told one of the analysts: 'We will back Sir Philip to the hilt,' but I was no longer convinced. Leonard was an honest man, who I was fond of – and I think it was reciprocated, in his own, odd, shy way – but when the crunch came I felt let down by him.

After that there was a deathly hush. Despite intense speculation in the press, Gulliver's name had still not surfaced and we pretended not to know who it was. To my surprise, Gulliver never came to see me, which I thought he should have done, given our past contact. I was still on the board of GUS but no one ever mentioned his approach to me, which again I thought was odd. As the weeks dragged on and there was no movement, the market began to become restive and County Bank wondered if Charterhouse were not getting cold feet.

In the meantime, I was encouraged at the way the business was responding and I was hoping Gulliver would go away, but David Reed didn't see it like that. He had been sounding out other potential bidders to see if he could get a counter-offer to push up the price but, he told me, there had been no interest. We should try to force Charterhouse's hand, he urged. 'Look, Phil, things are not going so well down the pipe and we must get this business bought. And with your approval – you're the client – I'm going to leak Gulliver to the press, and once that appears, he won't be able to resist going ahead.'

His point was a good one, which I couldn't really argue with. An offer of 170p, which is what we were talking about, was thirty-five times our last earnings per share, more than twice the average for the sector. GUS would undoubtedly insist that, in the interests of its share-holders, it would be forced to consider an offer seriously if it meant receiving over £100 million for its investment, half of which would be profit. One of the analysts at County NatWest, our in-house broker, sent out a circular saying that 'in the absence of an offer the right price is around 100p' and Leonard would certainly remind me of that. And the other shareholders, including staff, friends and family, would not easily forgive me.

I also knew there was at least one more year of pain before I could convince the markets the company had truly turned the corner, and I couldn't afford to disappoint them again – I had done it twice in the past year and I was sure if it was three strikes I'd be out. I would be in no position to resist a takeover bid, probably at a much lower price.

But there was something else I could do. I could buy the business myself, take it private, complete the restructuring out of the public limelight, and maybe float it again later. If Gulliver could raise the money for a bid, then so could I. So, working with Warburg's, one of the most respected merchant banks in the City, we came up with a scheme and once again I toured the City presenting to potential investors, stressing the recovery prospects. The response was positive enough to convince Warburg's we could mount a credible counter-bid when the bidder made his move.

In the meantime, I reluctantly agreed to David's plan and the next day he called his friend John Jay, the City editor of the *Sunday Times*, and told him he had a story for him which would have to be unattrib-utable and he should specifically mention that both Phil Harris and County were unavailable for comment (a harmless ploy which would fool nobody but would satisfy the Takeover Panel, and Charterhouse could not object).

The following Sunday, 12 June 1988, Jay duly disclosed Gulliver's name for the first time, and the rest of the press followed up eagerly.

The comment was just as David Reed had predicted: Gulliver was presented as a retailing genius, the miracle man who would sort out Harris Queensway's problems in no time.

David was delighted. 'He won't be able to resist that,' he told me with a chuckle, and he was right. Within days of being 'outed', Gulliver broke cover and began briefing people on what he planned to do with Harris Queensway: he would reduce the number of brands under which we operated, consolidate the 'fragmented' carpet market (where we were already the dominant player by a wide margin), operate a single chain of furniture shops under the Queensway brand and sell both Hamleys (which was already on the market) and Poundstretcher.

In the meantime, Warburg's had got the backing it needed for my own offer and I was ready when the serious bidding began. Gulliver, as expected, opened with 170p, and Victor Blank, the chairman of Charterhouse and a good friend of mine, called to ask me if we could do a deal at that price. I said no, and would be bidding myself – starting at 175p a share. They raised that to 180p and I again countered with 185p and they went to 190p, all in a matter of a few weeks.

News of my attempted buy-out leaked to the press.

By then I was beginning to flag. That price valued Harris Queensway at £450 million and my own stake at £73 million and I really didn't see how I could justify paying more. I needed some sane, sensible and independent advice on what to do next and, not for the first – or last – time, I called my old friend Harry Djanogly and drove down to his house in Marlow. Pauline went off somewhere with Harry's wife Carol, and we went into his study, where Harry studied my figures. Finally, he looked hard at me under those great bushy eyebrows of his.

'Phil, if you don't do this deal I will take you to the nearest psychiatric hospital, have you locked up and throw the key away,' he said. 'You've got to do it!'

I knew he was right, but in my heart, I didn't agree. This was my business, it had been started by my father and I had gambled everything and worked hard all my adult life to build it into what it was. Harry could see I was in love with it, but I knew he too had reluctantly sold his business, Nottingham Manufacturing, which had been in the family for three generations. Time and the collapse of the textile industry, however, had shown it had been the correct decision.

'You've got everything at stake here,' he went on. 'These things go up and down, they rely on hire purchase, government interest rates, they are very sensitive to markets … You've got an offer on the table, and the right thing to do is accept it.'

So, with a very heavy heart, I gave in. It was later widely reported that I wept when I called David Reed to give him my decision. I don't think I did, but I had certainly been close to tears at various stages through this emotionally exhausting battle. I told David to accept the offer subject to two conditions: that Gulliver would sell me Harveys, the home furnishing chain, which I thought had great potential – and there would be no 'non-compete' clause. Secretly, I was already planning to start again, determined to show Jimmy Gulliver who was the carpet king. I would steer well clear of furniture and electricals in the future.

On 23 June 1988, I chaired my last annual general meeting of Harris Queensway in Orpington, where I think I genuinely was in tears as I said goodbye to my shareholders, some of whom had been with me from the beginning. The company was valued at £30 million when it floated in 1978 and twenty years later I was selling it for £450 million. I calculated that, adjusting the price for splits and rights issues, £1,000 invested in the shares over that period would be worth around £13,000. That was not too bad a note to exit on. It was also the last AGM for my deputy chairman Hugh Sykes, who later commented: 'I respected Phil Harris enormously, and found working for him tremendous fun, and tremendously stimulating.'

That morning, Gulliver announced that he had hired a 'managing director designate', Eddie Dayan from Dixons, and made some other statements that got up my nose. 'The company seems to have lost its way,' he said. 'It was all right while Sir Phil was able to run it hands-on but once it started making acquisitions the management did not seem to get behind the marketing and selling properly. It started to drift down-market when it should have been going more upmarket. Now we have to try to reposition it.'

It was utter, uninformed rubbish, but I was too tired and fed up to argue. In fact, we had always made acquisitions, and, with a few exceptions, they had been good ones. I also believed he was heading for disaster if he attempted to go upmarket too fast, a lesson he would learn even sooner than I expected.

There remained a few odds and ends to tidy up. We agreed the terms for the buy-out of the 75 per cent of Hardys – about £20 million. Gulliver and Eddie Dayan, however, proved sticky about my non-compete clause, which would have stopped me setting up carpets or furniture shops for at least five years. I said there was no deal without it – and I meant it, although I could not realistically have enforced it. Once again it was the resourceful David Reed who resolved the problem. He took Dayan out to dinner, they both got a bit sloshed and then David told him that Gulliver didn't need a non-compete. 'You'll kill him in the marketplace if he does start again,' he said.

'Yes, we'll kill him in the marketplace!' Dayan agreed triumphantly.

By the time I signed the deal in the first week of August 1988, I was already planning my new carpet business. I went off to the Olympics in Seoul with Pauline, watched David Broome finish just outside the medals riding Countryman, came back refreshed and we opened our first new carpet shop, under the name Carpetwise, in early November. From then on, we opened a new shop every ten days for the next ten years – many of them managed by my old Harris Queensway staff, who couldn't wait to join me.

CHAPTER 22

'ALL CAN ACHIEVE'

Fortunately, there has always been more to life for me than business, and all those years I was running Harris Queensway, I was busy running hospitals and raising money for Westminster Abbey and the Conservative Party – and with creating Britain's biggest schools' federation, which is probably all I will be remembered for by future generations.

My involvement with schools came about like this. Through most of Mrs Thatcher's time in No. 10, I served on an informal advisory committee that advised her on business matters. It was an august group of businessmen (we were all men), chaired by (Lord) James Hanson, and included (Lord) Jeffrey Sterling, chairman of P&O, (Lord) John King, who had turned around British Airways and privatised it, (Sir) Hector Laing of United Biscuits, (Sir) Stanley Kalms of Dixons and various others, all successful business people in their own right, all keen to help in whatever way we could.

We met, usually in Downing Street, about once every three months for a lively discussion on all sorts of matters, from privatisation of state industries such as BT and British Gas, to taxes, the City, competition, trade union legislation and industrial policy. We were able to raise the issues that affected us as businessmen and the Prime Minister would always listen and take note: Mrs Thatcher, despite her reputation for dominating conversations, was actually a very good listener and quite a few useful initiatives came from these meetings. She usually had a couple of ministers with her, sometimes the Chancellor Sir Geoffrey

Howe and, later, Nigel Lawson, or the trade minister, whoever that happened to be at the time (there were ten in her eleven years in power).

One of the topics that kept coming up was youth unemployment and what to do about it. As British industry was restructured in the 1980s – some of it, it should be said, by the people in the room, particularly James Hanson – unemployment rose, particularly among younger people. By 1986, a million people between the ages of eighteen and twenty-four were out of work, and it was getting worse. Mrs Thatcher had been severely shaken by the rioting that had erupted in Brixton in the early 1980s when, for three days, mobs – predominantly young, black, unemployed men – fought police, attacked buildings and set fire to vehicles.

At one of our meetings in 1986, with rumblings of further riots and unrest across the country, the Prime Minister went around the table and asked each of us in turn: 'Why don't you employ more young people?'

The response was pretty much the same: Britain's state comprehensive schools were not teaching the right skills and many kids emerging from school were barely literate. The level of innumeracy was horrifying and our schools were producing kids who weren't qualified to do anything.

Her next question was typical of her: 'Well, what are you going to do about it?'

A few months later I got an invitation to attend an all-day conference in the House of Lords, chaired by (Lord) David Young, the Trade Secretary and a good friend of mine, on the subject of youth unemployment. Mrs Thatcher was there and, to my surprise, given all the other things on her mind, she stayed all day. Ken Baker, the Secretary of State for Education, was much in evidence, but the man who had most to say was his special adviser, Cyril Taylor, a brilliant but eccentric right-wing academic (although he later worked under both Tony Blair and Gordon Brown) who had been campaigning for business to get involved directly in education for some time. He had written several papers on the subject for the Centre for Policy Studies, the think tank that had been founded by Mrs Thatcher's mentor Sir Keith Joseph in 1974. She had clearly read Taylor's papers and understood the problem – and now, in her typically direct fashion, she wanted to find solutions.

Taylor, who had organised the conference, had assembled an impressive group of people that included some of our advisory committee, and I remember Heather Brigstocke, the formidable head of St Paul's School for Girls, also having a lot to say.

The message I took away from a long day of presentations and discussion was one of a state education system that was failing far too many children and which desperately needed reform. Everyone else seemed to be doing so much better than we were: France, Germany, even Italy, were producing much better-educated kids than us, and Singapore, Taiwan and Japan were in a different stratosphere. What were we doing wrong?

There were enough successes in the system to show what might be done, with the right leadership. The failing schools were almost all managed by local authorities, whereas some of the more successful schools – a small minority – were grant maintained, independent schools, run by the Church of England or by charities such as the King Edward VI Foundation in Birmingham, which ran seven excellent schools. That, we all agreed, might offer a way forward.

What emerged from the conference was a recommendation to set up a new kind of school, independent of the local authorities and sponsored by the private sector, which would focus on subjects that would be useful to employers. They would be called City Technology Colleges (CTCs), and would provide free education, paid for by the state, but would be managed by private sector 'sponsors' who would be responsible for forming new boards of governors that would appoint the headmaster. We would each be asked to sponsor at least one school, at a cost of £2 million, and we were urged to get them up and running as quickly as possible. If they worked, then more failing schools could be converted to CTCs. A figure of 100 CTCs was set as an initial target.

I was still thinking of how I might get involved when Mrs Thatcher decided it for me.

'Philip, I want you to run a school,' she told me in a manner which brooked no argument.

When I protested that I knew nothing about schools, she just waved that away dismissively.

'But you know about business,' she persisted. 'And schools should be run much more on business lines.'

You could never argue with Mrs Thatcher in full flow – or at least I couldn't. Weakly, I agreed I would do my best, but secretly I couldn't see what I could contribute other than money.

A few months later, in October 1986, I was at the Conservative Party conference in Bournemouth when Ken Baker announced the CTC programme as part of his wide-reaching education reform proposals. Ken today doesn't get enough credit in my view as a reformer but it was he who introduced the national school curriculum, as well as grant-maintained schools which could 'opt out' of local authority controls after parental ballots. He was also the minister behind the City Technology Colleges initiative, the forerunner of the academy school which has widely replaced the comprehensive today. Baker built on the reforms first introduced by his predecessor Sir Keith Joseph, who was a 'Thatcherite' before Thatcher, including the introduction of GCSEs to replace O Levels. Andrew Adonis, Tony Blair's education guru and the real architect of the academies programme, later wrote that 'it was the Baker reforms to the structure of the state school system which were to have a fundamental impact on my thinking'.

A few days later, I found myself travelling down to Croydon with Cyril Taylor, whom Ken Baker had put in charge of the CTC project, to visit the school I had been allotted. He was in ebullient mood, telling me that when he arrived in his new office in the Department of

Education, donations for the CTC programme were already coming in, including one from me. The civil servants carefully put them in a box, which they solemnly brought in and laid on his desk. 'They didn't know what to do with them, you see,' he said, roaring with laughter.

He was a fascinating man whom I was to see a lot of over the next few years (and still stay in touch with). He had a reputation for being arrogant and self-opinionated, which was not unfounded, but without him I don't think the CTC programme would ever have got off the ground. He brought an extraordinary missionary zeal to the job which was quite infectious, and I learned later that both his parents were indeed missionaries in the Congo. Baker and Taylor were really the two men who paved the way for the biggest transformation in the recent history of Britain's comprehensive education system, providing the base on which Andrew Adonis and later Michael Gove were able to build.

The Sylvan High School in Crystal Palace, my allotted school, was a mixed comprehensive with 400 pupils that wasn't there when I was growing up in the area: it had only opened in 1974, and was already showing signs of wear and tear. We had been told that the teachers and the local authority, worked up by the unions and left-wing lobby groups, were fiercely opposed to the CTC concept and we could expect a rough welcome if we were recognised. We arrived incognito, pretending to be quantity surveyors, and wandered around, talking to people where we could, including the dinner ladies, and inspecting the premises.

It was a really depressing and spiritless place. The 1970s buildings, all concrete and glass, were ugly and shabby, the classrooms and cor-ridors were dirty and neglected, and I could glimpse untidy children and teachers who clearly couldn't keep order. The academic records painted an even grimmer picture: the pass rate was 9 per cent, teachers on average lasted six months, and headmasters not much longer. It was scarcely surprising that attendance was low and teachers were all too ready to expel the kids – who were already at the bottom of the system and had nowhere else to go.

But everything I had seen made me more determined to take it on, and I had begun to formulate a plan. From the start, I decided to treat it as I would a new and troublesome acquisition and apply the same mix of disciplines and incentives. A good paint-job and a few superficial repairs would make a big improvement to the existing buildings and I would lean on Ken Baker to provide funds for new classrooms and facilities. I would recruit the best headmaster available, even if I had to pay him more, and set him the task of assessing the staff, keep the ones we wanted and replacing the others. Many of the teachers had been working too long in a failed school to be redeemable – they were institutionalised. But there would be others who, under the right leadership, I knew would blossom – which is what happened. My experience was that, as in Keith Royle, there was always unrecognised talent in an acquisition if only you looked for it.

First of all, however, we had to get hold of the school, and that proved a long and frustrating exercise. As soon as my involvement was announced, there were fierce demonstrations both inside and outside the school, and the teachers did everything they could to stop us. I attended three rowdy public meetings with parents and teachers which were terrible. But I insisted on staying to the end, standing there for hours while I was abused, trying to make myself heard and convince the parents that my only interest was to give their kids a better education and a decent chance in life. I was not in it for the money, I told them – quite the contrary. I was investing my own money.

Every kind of accusation was thrown at me, and I was taunted with being 'an asset stripper' who just wanted to close down the school and put up a Queensway store. There were professional lobby groups who had nothing to do with the school but came along to stir up trouble and denounce me as 'a rich capitalist bastard and Thatcherite', only in it for personal greed. But the most bizarre moment was when a woman, clearly not well-off, stood up and shouted: 'I don't want my child turned into a yuppie!' I thought to myself: 'Well, it's better than being unemployed,' but I held my tongue.

As we were coming away from one particularly noisy meeting, Cyril Taylor turned to me and said: 'I expect you'll give up on this one, Phil?' But I never had any intention of giving up. 'No,' I replied. 'I'm more motivated than ever. I'm going to give those children a good education, whatever it takes.' I know that sounds a bit pious now, but I really meant it.

Bit by bit, I won the parents over, or enough of them to matter, but the bigger problem turned out to be the hostility of the local authority which tried everything in its power to stop us getting control of the school. Baker pushed through legislation giving CTCs the legal right to take over failing schools, but the local authority owned the premises and held us to ransom by insisting we buy them. Eventually we did, for £4.75 million, of which I put in £1.75 million and the government stumped up the rest. I paid for the whole school to be redecorated and spruced up, which made a huge difference to morale.

All this took time and it was 1990, three years after that House of Lords conference, before we finally reopened as the Harris CTC Crystal Palace, by which stage several others were already up and running. Harry Djanogly opened a CTC in Nottingham in 1989 and Hanson teamed up with Lucas Aerospace to establish one in Birmingham, and another dozen (there were fifteen in the first wave) were on the way. I put over £1 million of my own money into Bacon CTC in Southwark, which the Church of England ran (not very well).

Our first headmaster at Crystal Palace, Lyndon Jones, proved a joy to deal with, and from the start made a huge difference. I found him at Norwood Technical College where, if my father had lived, I would have continued my education past the age of fifteen. The first thing he did was to assess the forty teachers and get rid of all the ones who weren't good enough. He kept just fifteen (nine of them are still with us, three of them principals in our schools), and hired bright, young teachers with a passion for working with children to replace the others. We offered our teachers a small bonus on top of their state salary, and we were flooded with applications from really good candidates.

Lyndon and I spent long hours discussing the changes we both wanted to make. He had the idea, which I thought was an excellent one, of changing titles and descriptions to reflect our academic status: 'school' would become 'college', 'head teacher' became 'principal', 'pupils' became 'students' and 'school leavers' became 'graduates'. Similarly, we had Arts, Communications, Science & Maths and Technology 'faculties' rather than 'departments'.

From the start, he imposed a rigid policy of zero tolerance and set strict standards on attendance. For the first week, Lyndon stood at the gate every morning, greeting the children but also recording who came in and at what time. If a pupil was consistently late or hadn't appeared after two days, he called the parents and, if they didn't have phones, someone went to their home – if they had one. The effect on attendance was astonishing.

Lyndon believed that 30 per cent of effective teaching time is lost because of poor behaviour in schools – and that equals at least five lost terms, which a pupil can never make up. It's amazing what a difference simple things like classroom discipline and attendance can make.

I appointed a new independent board of governors, run more like a board of directors but with parents and teachers on it – and no one got paid. Pauline served as a governor and so did David Stockwell, and they took it seriously, putting a great deal of effort into it.

At my insistence, the teachers were required to wear smart clothes: suits and ties for the men and no jeans for the women. I personally gave the parents the money to buy smart new school uniforms, which the children would have to wear from the time they left home to the moment they arrived back again in the afternoon. The effect of this was out of all proportion to the costs: the kids loved their new blazers and took real pride in them.

I shall never forget Monday 10 September 1990, the day we opened our first college. I stood at the gates with Lyndon to greet 180 excited eleven-year-olds in their new bright green jumpers sporting the college logo, *All Can Achieve*. Part of the deal was that we took on the existing Sylvan pupils, but we were allowed to choose the new intake and these were the lucky ones, chosen from 580 applicants. Later in the week they would be joined by students from other years, whose parents seemed to have forgotten their original reservations and were now eagerly on board.

It was a week of new beginnings for all of us, which came to a celebratory conclusion on Friday 15 September 1991, when I addressed the first whole college assembly, unveiled a plaque and gave out prizes, including a trophy to Sabrina Droom, the twelve-year-old who had designed the new school uniform, who was a real star. I was taken by surprise when a candle-lit cake was carried on and everyone sang Happy Birthday. I was forty-nine that day.

Three conversations stick in my mind from this time: a girl who told me that people kept stopping her in the street to ask what the college was like and she replied that it was 'great'; a boy who said: 'Sir, can I thank you for making the school safe?', and a dyslexic child who asked: 'Please can you make me read?'

I was interviewed by some of the students for the first edition of the new school magazine, *Harris Chat*, and here are some of the more moving bits:

Sir Philip was very honoured when he became a Knight but when he was asked why he was knighted he replied, 'I do not know why I got it really.' Sir Philip said that if he could have anything it would be happiness. It is more important than anything else in the world.

Sir Philip's worst fear is to make a lot of mistakes at home and at the college. Sir Philip, being dyslexic, has a problem with words and also reading. He classed this as his worst pastime. The thing that annoys Sir

Philip is people saying that they can't do something when they don't even try at all.

At the first whole college assembly, when the commemorative plaque was unveiled, Sir Philip received his giant birthday card and cake. It was a very emotional time for him and his family. He said that Lady Harris even had tears of happiness rolling down her cheeks.

There were a lot of kids at that school who thought they were backward – but they weren't, they were just dyslexic or had another form of learning disability. Even in 1991 there were many teachers and academics who were still highly sceptical about 'dyslexia', but I knew from personal experience what it felt like, and I was determined to make the college a centre of excellence for dyslexia and related special educational needs teaching. I invited Sue Fallon, who was married to Ivan and had been very involved in a successful British Dyslexia Association 'awareness campaign', to join the board. She brought very valuable expertise at a time when there wasn't much dyslexia expertise available, and made a great difference to our early success. Sue had a dyslexic son and had taken a specialist teaching diploma. She also ran computer workshops and conferences for teachers and was in touch with the new approaches and technologies that were emerging to help dyslexic children of secondary school age. The Department of Education, which was just discovering dyslexia in a big way, agreed to fund a research project based at Harris CTC, tracking the progress of about twenty of our dyslexic students, and its findings were later used as part of a nationwide initiative to improve the quality of dyslexia teaching across the country.

Pauline, as always, backed me to the hilt in the schools' venture. She not only attended all the governors' meetings, but was on the dyslexia sub-committee, and went along to many of the school functions, such as carol services and prizegivings, when I couldn't make it. Our son Peter also became a governor and there was a total family commitment to make this first Harris college a success.

The school soon became almost unrecognisable from what it was when I first saw it. The government was prepared to support the new CTCs with hard cash and we spent £7 million improving the buildings and putting up new ones. The school was in a built-up area and we had to take away some of the old playground to build new classrooms, but I got David Lewis, a highly successful property developer, to sponsor a new sports facility, and we also found decent sports fields about a mile away. Like all building projects, it took some time to complete and for a time some of the kids had to attend classes in Nissen huts. But nothing dampened their spirits and it was a joy to see them respond to what had basically become an entirely new school in just a few years.

Soon after he became Prime Minister, I brought John Major and his wife Norma down to see the school, which I think he was getting bored of hearing me talk about. They were greeted with a fanfare of trumpets from our music students and I took them around, stopping at the dyslexia unit where the kids were happily working with computers. Whatever their expectations were, they were exceeded many times over, as I knew they would be. Everyone I have ever brought to the schools has had the same reaction. I challenge anyone not to be uplifted by a visit to Crystal Palace – or any of our other schools – as they witness the enthusiasm of the children, the dedication of the teachers, and the modern classrooms and sports facilities. The Majors went away to another fanfare of trumpets and John wrote to me afterwards to say what an encouraging day he'd had – and how he wished he'd had the opportunity to go there when he lived nearby. He might even have gone to university – and never become Prime Minister.

The academic results, I must say, were marvellous – and went on getting better. We went from a 9 per cent pass rate in 1990 to 54 per cent in 1996, when we were awarded 'most improved school in the country' status, an honour we won twice – I doubt if any school will ever do that again. Then Lyndon got ill and we replaced him with a new headmis-tress, Carol Bates, and she took the pass rate into the eighties.

The kids have really thrived in the new sports facilities, and I live in hope we will produce a gold medal winner one day. Today we even have a rugby club, and a football enhancement programme for 16–18-year-olds. In 1989, the kids at that school didn't even play organised sports.

The intake has altered dramatically over the years: from being predominantly disadvantaged when we started, today the school is much more mixed, reflecting the communities in the surrounding areas which have become much more gentrified as property prices in central London have forced young couples further out. But we still have lots of pupils who qualify for school meals, some of whom have been among our biggest achievers.

We increased the number of teachers to about sixty, and today we teach a rich and varied curriculum, including many subjects that were just not available in the pre-CTC days. We also take the children on special visits to broaden their education – kids always love trips and some of them even get to visit NASA's Johnson Space Center in Texas every year.

When I took on the Crystal Palace school, very few from that institution had ever gone on to university. Today, the majority do – and, I hope, to much better lives beyond that.

*   *   *

In 1991, we had two Harris schools, Crystal Palace and Bacons (really a half), up and running – and there we stalled. Only fifteen CTCs had been opened across the country but no new ones were planned and the programme ran out of steam. Ken Baker had moved on in July 1989, before we had even opened, and was replaced by John McGregor, who never had much interest in CTCs. Economic times were not good in the early 1990s, and became even worse in September 1992 with the so-called Black Wednesday crisis, when sterling left the European Exchange Rate Mechanism, so there was no money for CTCs, which were expensive. Ken Clarke was moved to the Treasury, replacing Norman Lamont, and John Patten took over at education followed by Gillian Shepherd in 1994 – making five education Secretaries of State in those last seven years of Tory government.

For the rest of the nineties, the fifteen CTCs remained lonely pariahs, and we had to take our football teams by coach all the way to Nottingham or Birmingham if we wanted to play other CTCs. Cyril Taylor and I still took a lot of flak when we appeared at meetings, but the academic results kept improving and I made sure they were well publicised. In the end, I knew that would be the deciding factor in the success or failure, not just of the school, but of the whole CTC initiative.

But, as the years progressed with no new schools opening, I thought the CTC experiment would end there, an interesting exercise in state education that had helped a few hundred students mostly from disadvantaged backgrounds, but no more than that. The programme seemed to have fizzled out. It would take a Labour government to get it going again.

CHAPTER 23

SECOND COMING

One of the first steps that Jimmy Gulliver took after acquiring Harris Queensway was to drop the 'Harris' which had been part of the name for forty years. It became, for the brief time it survived, Lowndes Queensway, but I had no time to mourn it. After the initial shock of the takeover, I had a wonderful feeling of exhilaration as I started anew, building a new company with no baggage but all the resources I needed to take advantage of a market I knew probably better than anyone in the land. In November 1988, four months after I left my old company, I opened my first new Carpetwise shop, in Canning Town, and was already lining up new sites for what I intended to be a rapid advance. Initially at least, I was careful not to tread on Gulliver's toes. 'We are not out to smash Lowndes Queensway,' I told Fiona Walsh of the *Sunday Times*. 'The carpets market in this country is worth £1.5 billion a year. They've got 15 per cent and we'll be going after the other 85 per cent.'

But the truth was that far from 'killing' me in the market, as Gulliver confidently expected when he agreed to drop my non-compete clause, it was me who was killing him. I had everything going for me. For my 'second coming', I planned a new style of shop, more modern and bigger than the old Harris Carpet shops, which would be on the edge of town, mostly in the new shopping parks that were shooting up all over the place. Harvey Spack moved with me and together we carefully chose the sites we knew from experience would work best.

I was also able to cherry-pick my managers and staff, and took only the best ones, who I had hired and trained in the first place. Some of my old stalwarts had gone: Tony Behar, as I have related, wanted to start on his own and I backed him in a furniture venture, while David Stockwell sold his shares and retired to Spain. But some of the old team stayed with me including Ted Wright, who had first come to work for me as a boy twenty-six years earlier. My loyal secretary, Maritsa Blackman, also stayed on and John Kitching, who would play a leading part in the development of the new company, agreed to take charge of sales. I took David James across to open the new stores I planned.

I did a tour of the suppliers, insisting I got prices even keener than my old company, despite the huge difference in volume in the early stages. I was pretty tough on them – anyone who didn't want to deal with me on that basis, I warned them, would not get my business in the future when I would again be the biggest carpet company in the country. After that they treated me as if I were.

I arranged a meeting with Derek Hunt, CEO of MFI, to ask him if he had any outlets in his stores we could take over. I came away with a lot more than that. For years, Harris Queensway had run MFI's in-store carpet shops, and Derek was keen to renew that arrangement with me. To help me get going, he also offered to handle the accounting and admin side, which relieved me of that burden. And finally, he said, he'd like to invest alongside me in the new venture. So, MFI put in £1 million, matching the £1 million I had already invested and he joined the board.

I didn't need any more finance but when it was offered I didn't refuse. One evening towards the end of 1988, I was in the West End for a function with Pauline and afterwards we went into a wine bar for a late supper. To my surprise, I spotted Stephen Fearnley, who was in the process of buying out Poundstretcher (he paid £50 million for it), dining with a couple of City types whom he introduced as Frank Neale and Ron Hobbs of Phildrew, a private equity company special-ising in management buy-outs and start-ups.

Prompted by Stephen, I began telling them about my plans for my new company. It didn't take long for the Phildrew guys to become interested, and they invested £2 million in return for an 11 per cent stake. NatWest Ventures matched them and I invested another £1 million. The total investment came to £9 million.

Initially I decided to take a less hands-on role at the new company, at least officially, and made Ted Wright managing director. Ted set a frantic pace, opening fifty-one stores in one crazy year, or nearly one a week, and in our first full year we lost £1.5 million, which was more than I had budgeted for. Initially I encouraged him but gradually realised that Ted had a different vision for the company than I did, and our relationship was becoming tense. I confess I was also upset at some of the interviews he gave where he talked about 'my' company – I regarded it as *our* company, certainly not his.

I offered David Reed a shareholding and a directorship after he lost his job at County in July 1989. He, along with half a dozen other executives, had to leave County after a Department of Trade inquiry criticised the bank for its role in the 1987 rights issue of the employment agency Blue Arrow. It was a big scandal at the time, not quite as big as Guinness but getting on that way, and it destroyed several promising banking careers, David's included.

One of David's first contributions as a non-executive director was to advise me that, in his view, Ted Wright was not the right man for the job and if I was to float the company on the stock market, which was what I intended, I must take over the executive reins. That's what the markets would want to see, and it was also right for the company. Others had been telling me the same thing, and regrettably I parted company with a man who had worked with me, man and boy, since we were both teenagers.

I took over as managing director, made Derek Hunt chairman, and slowed the pace of store opening right down. I changed the name from Carpetwise, which I had never liked, to Carpetright, with a schoolmasterish tick to emphasise the 'right', and established our headquarters in Rainham, Essex, where we began building a new warehouse.

Over the first couple of years, I completed the team that I wanted to take the company to the next stage, mostly with old Harris Queensway hands. Someone later calculated that the nine area managers, although their average age was only thirty-three, had been with me for a total of 100 years, or more than eleven years each, and 70 per cent of our personnel had come from the old company. In head office, Shirley Hazell, in charge of the purchase ledger, had been with me for twenty-two years and Carol Sawyer, head of personnel, and Alice Cook, responsible for the computer systems, were also veterans. At the more senior level, I brought in my old stalwart of many years, Ian Horwood, as finance director, and we took back the financial functions from MFI. I was particularly pleased when Paul Lorimer, probably the best buyer I ever worked with, also joined the team.

Two years after we started, we were profitable. In 1990/91, we made £351,000, and I was projecting nearly £3 million for the next year, with more to come. My aim was to list on the London Stock Exchange by 1993 with profits in the £7–8 million range – which was what we did. Well before that, however, things had come badly unstuck at my old company.

*   *   *

Jimmy Gulliver's swoop on Harris Queensway might have caught me at my lowest point, but, as events turned out, his timing could not have been worse – for him. He had borrowed £450 million to buy the company, believing that the 'Lawson boom', which had driven strong economic growth for three years and cut unemployment in half, would keep on going. But it didn't, and as inflation shot up from about 4 per cent to 7.5 per cent by 1989, Lawson, after a ferocious row with Mrs Thatcher, resigned, and the new Chancellor, John Major, slammed on the brakes. In May 1988, when Gulliver began his stalking, interest rates were around 8 per cent; a year later they were 15 per cent, and economic growth basically came to a standstill. By 1990, Britain was in recession, the bottom dropped out of the housing market, and consumer spending dried up. People didn't have the money even to buy carpets, which they had always done in previous recessions.

I was no longer involved in the company's affairs, but I kept an eye on what was happening and often bumped into former colleagues who still worked there. It was clear to me that the new management did not understand the carpet business and probably knew even less about furniture retailing. They did all the wrong things, pushing up prices and moving upmarket when they should have been doing the opposite, getting into all sorts of problems with their suppliers and running out of money to invest in the shops. Gulliver raised over £100 million by selling Hamleys, Poundstretcher and Harveys, but it barely made a dent in his borrowings. He changed the name to Carpetland, abandoning our old brand names that had been established over years and which had been created for a reason. He lost key managers who had been with me from the beginning and knew what they were doing – some came to my new business – and the company suffered a real lack of leadership at the top as a result.

In 1987, we had made a profit of over £50 million, which, because of all the problems I have already talked about, had dropped to £17 million in 1988. In one year, under Gulliver's management, that turned into a loss of £80 million – the first loss in the company's history. When I left in August 1988, it was still profitable, cash flow was good, it had £25 million in the bank and there was no reason why it shouldn't weather the recession, as it had always done, ready for the time when the cycle turned up again.

But it didn't work out that way. In January 1990, after failing to refinance the business, Gulliver resigned, his reputation destroyed, leaving the company in dire straits. On 13 August 1990 I was on our boat in the south of France with Pauline and friends when news came through that the shares had been suspended and the company was in receivership. It was almost exactly two years since Gulliver had taken it over, and I still puzzle to this day over how it could have gone down so fast.

I still don't know why Gulliver took it on in the first place, why he showed so little interest in it afterwards, and how he could have let his reputation, built up over more than thirty years of shrewd deals and turning companies around, be destroyed without lifting a finger to help himself. I had sold the business for £450 million, so my shareholders had done well. I had also received nearly £80 million for my own stake. But I felt sad for the company, upset for the staff and angry it had come to this.

I flew back to London first thing the next morning and met several of the old staff who related how they had arrived for work to find the lights out and the doors locked, with a sign on the windows reading: 'stock-take in progress'. Journalists trying to track down Gulliver were told he was 'on the grouse moor in another country' (I presume they meant Scotland).

The *Sunday Times* did eventually get hold of him and he insisted the fault for the collapse should not be laid at his door. 'When we started negotiations to buy the business, interest rates were virtually half what they are now and the Chancellor was promising steady economic growth of 3 to 4 per cent,' he said. 'We looked at all the worst-case scenarios but we could not have foreseen what would happen. We could have coped with a 10 per cent fall in sales. We were prudent.' Some of my old staff told me they had never even seen Gulliver, that he didn't go near the shops and was seldom in the office. He paid himself £257,000 a year, compared to my £100,000 salary, and Eddie Dayan got a similar sum, but I'm not sure what the company got back for it.

None of it gave me the slightest feeling of satisfaction – quite the opposite. I was very, very upset when I lost Harris Queensway, and I still grieve for it. If I could go back today and have the choice between taking the money and keeping the business, I'd have kept the business – I've no doubt about that.

* * *

In April 1992, I was invited to address the annual convention of the Institute of Directors in the Albert Hall, an event attended by 400 captains of industry and widely covered by the press. David Young, then Trade Secretary, was the main speaker, followed by four others: the heads of McDonald's, Campbell Soups, Unilever – and me. I was the final speaker and as I stepped up to the podium I was more nervous than I had ever been in my life. Because of my dyslexia there was no point in having a prepared speech, so I had about four notes which had to keep me going for forty-five minutes. I took the audience through the history of my life, from the time I ran just three shops to my first encounters with the City, the history of Harris Queensway and then starting all over again and doing it for a second time. I also told them about my schools and my work with the NHS, of which more in the next chapter, and about my underlying philosophy, which was a very simple one: 'it's all about people'. I had little time for management consultants, Harvard Business School theses or formal management structures, I said. 'Running hospitals, schools and even government successfully is all about having the right people and getting them to work together. That's really what matters.'

I then took questions and got a standing ovation at the end which went on for what seemed to me a very long time. Many years later, in February 2017, I bumped into David Young in the House of Lords and he reminded me of that day. 'That was one of the best speeches I ever heard,' he said. I can't tell you how chuffed I was by that.

CHAPTER 24

GUY'S HOSPITAL

In the autumn of 1990, just as Carpetright was getting into its stride, I got a call from 10 Downing Street, asking me to come in and see the Prime Minister. Ken Clarke, the Health Secretary, was with her when I arrived, so I immediately assumed this had something to do with the NHS, with which I had been involved over the past few years.

Mrs Thatcher, as ever, got straight to the point. The Health Service, she said, needed urgent and radical reform and she had been 'impressed with the suggestion that we should make NHS hospitals self-governing and independent', basically competing with each other to provide services as cheaply as possible. 'Hospitals treating more patients,' she went on, 'will generate a higher income and improve their services rather than having to cut back.'

I was familiar with the theme – it had been much discussed in our regular meetings in recent months and in Tory Party circles. It was pretty much the same principle of self-government that was behind the CTC programme, which was yet to get off the ground.

Mrs Thatcher said that she and Clarke had decided to set up several independent 'trust' hospitals, which would have their own boards and would take responsibility for their own budgets, effectively operating along business lines. Guy's Hospital, with its reputation as a world-class teaching hospital, had been chosen as the flagship.

'We'd like you to be chairman,' she said.

I thus found myself at the leading edge of Thatcher's plans to revolutionise both the education system and the Health Service – probably the two most enduring legacies of her ten years in government. I am very proud to have been associated with both.

*   *   *

My history with Guy's, as Mrs Thatcher was aware, went back a long way. It was much more than just another hospital to me – it was really *my* hospital. It is based at London Bridge, in the borough of South-wark, where both my parents were born, and I was often taken there to visit sick relatives when I was a young boy. My daughter Susan was born there.

I also had other, more recent, connections: for the past eight years, I had served as a governor of the joint Guy's and Thomas' medical school, or UMDS, which met quarterly in either Guy's or Thomas', and I was also on various other boards and committees.

I was first introduced to Guy's by Donald Bompas, the secretary of the medical school, whom I must have met at some event or other in the early 1980s. He approached me and asked me to sponsor a new lecture theatre for the medical school which was in desperate need of new facilities. The cost was £1.5 million, but if I were to contribute £500,000 it would have my name on it.

'I don't want a lecture theatre named after me,' I replied. I was happy to be involved in something to do with cancer or childbirth, I said, but I had no real interest in a lecture theatre.

'Well, before you decide that,' said Donald in his precise, clipped, manner, 'come and talk to Lord Robens.' As I was to discover, Donald had a wonderful way of cajoling you along until he got his way – which is what made him one of the best fundraisers I ever met. He was also a thoroughly decent and nice man, whom I still miss (he managed my family trusts for years before he died in 2013, aged ninety-two).

I had never met (Lord) Alf Robens, but I had seen him often enough on television and heard him on the radio, where he liked to present himself as 'the voice of industrial common sense' on talk shows. One of his obituarists later described him better than I ever could: 'Alf Robens was one of those remarkable products from the legendary generation of Labour and trade union talent, largely untutored, who scaled the heights, loved the glamour and successes, yet did not forget their roots.' He was a former Labour MP and government minister who had run the National Coal Board, which then employed over half a million miners, under three Prime Ministers, including Harold Macmillan and Harold Wilson. At one stage, he was even talked about as a future Prime Minister himself, and when that didn't work out, he opted for a string of directorships as long as your arm: he was chairman of Vickers and Johnson Matthey and on the board of the Bank of England, Times Newspapers and Trusthouse Forte.

From the moment Donald introduced me, I was captivated by him, awed by his towering presence and wooed by his irresistible charm. He was a big, bluff man, then well into his seventies, who with his cigars and his handmade suits looked more like the rich industrialist he had become than the trade union official he had once been. By the time I left the room I had agreed to donate half a million to the new Philip Harris Lecture Theatre that is still used today.

When Robens, at Donald's suggestion, asked me to join the board of the medical school, I was happy to do so, little knowing where this would eventually lead me. At my first meeting in the boardroom at Guy's, I remember staring at the large portrait of Thomas Guy, who had founded the hospital in 1721 after making a fortune in the South Sea Bubble, presumably one of the few people who did. After that, someone told me, he went back to his old profession: selling bibles to the good people of Southwark. I never worked out what lesson to draw from that.

After initially floundering in this very different world of academics and medical specialists, I soon came to enjoy the UMDS board meetings. I couldn't contribute much on the medical front but, like every institution of its kind, the medical school was always short of funds and I was good at raising money. I made many friends there, including some of the finest medical brains in the country, acknowledged world specialists in their respective fields. Whatever your ailment, Guy's had the man – or woman – for you, and they were the best.

Then, in the early 1980s, I was introduced by my friend Ivan Fallon to two of the most brilliant geneticists of their day, Paul Polani and Martin Bobrow, both research professors at Guy's, who were working on areas of research not dissimilar to Birthright. Polani, the more famous of the two, was the first to develop a method of identifying the genetic basis of a number of congenital problems, including spina bifida, which changed a lot of people's lives. They were originally supported by an endowment from the Spastics Society (now called Scope) but that had stopped, and they needed £600,000 to keep their Generation Trust going – which they hoped I might help them with.

I will never forget the look on their faces as I told them they were never going to get that kind of money. I paused for a moment, and then went on: '… unless you find someone to get you off to a good start.' So, I said, I would come in for a third, get Gerald Ronson or someone else to match it, and we could then easily raise the rest. In the event, we raised £2 million and I served as chairman of the Generation Trust for ten years. We had some wonderful board members, including Professor Ellen Solomon, one of the world's leading cancer geneticists, and Kay Glendinning, a member of the Dunhill family, who made a very generous contribution to our funds. We also recruited the late Nils Taube, the Rothschild fund manager whose clients included George Soros. Some great, pioneering work has come out of that unit since my first meeting there over thirty years ago.

Long before that meeting in Downing Street with the Prime Minister in 1990, I found myself drawn into the debates, often heated, about the growing crisis in the NHS, which Guy's and Thomas' were at the forefront of, because of their prominence and Central London positions. Often I had to push my way through demonstrators or marches protesting against 'the Thatcher cuts', which were blamed for everything. The newspapers, just as they are today, were full of horror stories of overcrowded hospitals, long waiting lists and underpaid and overworked nurses and doctors. In her speeches up and down the country, Mrs Thatcher tried to point out that spending on the NHS, in real terms, had in fact risen every year she was in power (it rose by 40 per cent in real terms in her ten years in office), and that there were more beds, doctors, nurses and dentists than there had ever been. But she never got the message across, and many people still believe to this day that the NHS was cut to the bone under her leadership, which was never true.

I was at the Conservative Party conference in 1983 when she uttered her famous phrase, 'the National Health Service is safe in our hands', but in private when I saw her she described the NHS as 'like a bottomless pit' that simply had to be reformed. She complained that lots of hospitals deliberately spent their entire annual budgets in eleven months and then, very publicly, closed whole wards, blaming it on her.

In 1987, three years before our Downing Street meeting, I invited Mrs Thatcher to visit Guy's to open the new MRI scanner, the first one in Britain, which I had donated after being given a demonstration of its extraordinary powers. It was a futuristic machine, opening up all sorts of possible treatments, and she was keen to see it. Professor Cyril Chantler, the newly appointed general manager of the hospital, and Peter Griffiths, the general manager of the regional health authority, had another objective in mind that day, which I had been roped in on. After the war, the Guy's governors bought up most of the land and bomb sites around the hospital, and began building on it in the 1960s. The result was a chaotic jumble of patched-up Victorian buildings and a brutal thirty-storey 1970s tower that briefly held the dubious honour of housing the highest hospital ward in the world.

For years, the governors' ambition was to finish the job by building what was simply called 'Phase III', an eight-storey complex first planned in the 1970s that was designed to bring all Guy's clinical services under one roof and make sense of its ramshackle structure. It was an ambitious project, but when I was shown the model I could see it made a great deal of sense, and would complete the transformation of the hospital from the Dickensian buildings I had known in my youth to one of Britain's best-equipped medical establishments. But it was also expensive: the original budget sent to the Treasury in 1984 was for £35.5 million – which had still not been signed off. Cyril hoped he might get the opportunity to persuade Mrs Thatcher to approve it on her forthcoming visit.

On the day she was due, there was a mass demonstration outside Rupert Murdoch's print plant across the river in Wapping and the hospital was on red alert with police snipers on the roof and high security everywhere. But she did her tour in her usual brisk fashion, admired the MRI scanner which she duly declared open for business, and finally, as we had arranged, came to the model of the new medical wing. Cyril had just launched into his well-rehearsed pitch, basically asking her to force the Treasury's hand, when she cut him off.

'I know what you are going to say, doctor, and we cannot say yes today.' Then, seeing his downcast look, she went on: 'But don't look so disappointed, doctor – we can't say yes today, but we are hoping to say yes in two weeks' time.'

She was as good as her word. A fortnight later the Treasury approved the plan and the project began to chug forward again. Only afterwards, when it became my problem, did I realise how unrealistic the original budget was, and later a parliamentary committee accused the hospital of deliberately putting in an estimate which was 'disgracefully low' in order to get to the front of the queue. Knowing the individuals, I don't think that was true. But doctors and clinicians, brilliant though they are at their own jobs, don't necessarily make good property managers.

My involvement with Guy's in these years was largely as a member of the UMDS board, and chairman of the Generation Trust, but I formed a growing friendship with both Peter Griffiths and Cyril Chantler, very different men. Cyril was a paediatrician who, unusually then, passionately believed that doctors should become much more involved in managing resources in the Health Service. 'It comes down to either you manage or you're managed,' he told his fellow clinicians. 'There is just no alternative.' In 1985, although he remained a practising consultant and clinical academic, he became general manager of Guy's, where he did an excellent job. Peter was a born manager of people, one of the best I've come across, who could have run the biggest company in the land but chose instead to devote his considerable talents to the Health Service.

After she won the 1987 election with a majority of 102, Margaret Thatcher finally turned to reforming the NHS, proposing what one medical journal summed up as 'a series of changes that are more drastic and far-reaching than anything that has occurred since socialised medicine was introduced by the Labour government forty years ago'. She obviously felt that poor John Moore, the Health Secretary and at one time her chosen successor, was not up to the monumental task and in July 1988 she replaced him with Ken Clarke.

I liked Ken. Like me, he was a strong supporter of the founding principle of the NHS, which was basically to provide medical treatment for every citizen, paid for out of taxation. 'I have never had private insurance myself and regard it as something of a rip-off,' he liked to say. But he was also a firm advocate of competition and choice, which he was determined to introduce into the NHS. Over the next couple of years, as he tackled the unions and opposition head-on, Ken became probably the most unpopular man in the country, accused of mistreating nurses and young doctors by refusing to pay them a living wage, and of 'privatising' – or 'pillaging' – the precious NHS. He had to contend with mass demonstrations and strike after strike, including a year-long dispute with ambulance drivers which endangered many lives. It got so bad that he and his family had to have special police protection around the clock.

Ken's main proposal for reform, slightly less ambitious than Thatcher's, was that each hospital's management would have the choice to move to the status of a 'self-governing' body, outside the control of the local health authority. They would be free to settle the pay and conditions of their staff and able to sell their services to the public and private sectors at the most competitive price. Hospitals, he argued in that wonderfully eloquent way he had, would be 'freed from bureaucracy' and run by the equivalent of commercial boards, made up of a mixture of non-executive and executive directors.

For this new type of hospital, he invented the title 'NHS Trusts', which he admitted 'was rather meaningless as there were to be no trustees of these bodies, nor any trust deeds'. But, he added, it was a 'reassuring-sounding brand name'. Guy's was to be the first 'trust' hospital off the ground, the prototype of what both Thatcher and Clarke saw as the model for the reforms and management changes they wanted to introduce.

So, when the call to Downing Street came, I was ready for the challenge. Before I accepted, however, I insisted on putting together the strongest team available. Peter Griffiths, who had been co-opted by Clarke to oversee the plan of establishing trust hospitals across the country, was to come back to Guy's as chief executive, and Cyril Chantler, who had been put on the NHS policy board, would also be there to help me as clinical dean of the medical school. I could not have asked for two better men.

We were appointed in late 1990, ready to start when the legislation was in place on 1 April 1991. But well before we got there the political world was turned upside down. In November 1990, the Foreign Secretary, Sir Geoffrey Howe, after being humiliated once too often by Mrs Thatcher in front of the whole Cabinet, resigned and launched a savage attack on her in the House of Commons. Within hours,

Michael Heseltine announced he would stand against her for the leadership of the party and, after weeks of infighting and turmoil in the party, she failed to get the majority she needed on the first ballot. On 22 November, Mrs Thatcher, faced with a revolt from some of her own ministers, resigned. A few weeks later, John Major, the Chancellor, was elected Prime Minister, Ken Clarke was moved to education and William Waldegrave became the new Secretary of State for Health.

So, as I arrived to take up my new job as chairman of the Guy's and Lewisham NHS Trust (Lewisham hospital was almost as big as Guy's) in April 1991, I had both a new Prime Minister and Secretary of State to those who had appointed me only a few months before.

* * *

From the start, I could see there was a lot wrong with the way the two hospitals were run. There was no meaningful information, which meant the budgets we inherited – and for which we were now responsible – were meaningless. Despite the management improvements introduced by Cyril Chantler, there was still an awful lot of waste, duplication and inefficiencies. And money was desperately tight. The Guy's budget had been reduced by more than £8 million (out of over £50 million) between 1985 and 1987. Cyril, with the support of the clinicians, had done a brilliant job in clearing the deficit, reducing the staff by 17 per cent, mostly through natural attrition, with no apparent effect on the service provided, but there was a lot more to be done.

Within days of arriving, through no fault of my own, I found myself in hot water with both the Prime Minister and Ken Clarke. The government had approved all the first-wave trusts on the basis that they were 'financially viable and sound', and our first forecast as a self-governing trust, which we issued in April 1991, showed a profit of £1.5 million for the following year. But, a few days later, Peter Griffiths came in to tell me he had taken a serious look at the accounts and had some bad news. There was, he said, 'a black hole' in the finances and, far from making a profit, we were heading for a loss of £6.8 million – a cash swing of £8.3 million.

I remember a meeting with Peter Griffiths, Cyril Chantler and Professor Maurice Lessof, my deputy chairman, in which we wondered whether we could somehow avoid announcing it. However, sense prevailed and we did – with explosive results. We were in all the newspapers the next day and I was told that John Major was less than pleased with me. Our embarrassment was compounded when Peter, rather naïvely, alluded to the 'black hole' in a chat he had with a room full of journalists. When he was asked: 'Well what kind of scale of problem is this?', he replied, rather casually: 'Oh, it would be something in the region of the equivalent of 600 redundancies.'

Any bad news from Guy's was a national event and that put us on the front pages and the TV news all over again. It couldn't have come at a worse time for John Major, just four months into the job and running well behind in the polls. In the May local elections, the Tories lost 890 seats and were defeated in a parliamentary by-election in Monmouth. The party's exit polls showed that the bad publicity surrounding Guy's was one of the main reasons for people not voting Conservative. In my first couple of weeks in the job I had gone from being flavour of the month to an embarrassment and my relationship with John Major cooled for a while. However, as I later pointed out to him, maybe I did him a favour. The Monmouth loss and the disastrous local election results persuaded him to call off the snap election he intended for June 1991, which he probably would have lost, and made him hold out until April 1992 – when he won.

After the 'black hole' debacle, we changed the finance director and brought in some top people from the City to help. This caused a fresh furore when the unions leaked the salaries we were paying, particularly to Peter Griffiths, who was earning over £100,000 a year when other hospital managers were on half that. I justified it by pointing out that he could get much more in the private sector but it wasn't a popular message, particularly in Whitehall where the government was trying to impose a wage freeze.

In those early months, there was scarcely a day when we weren't in the news. Peter landed himself in hot water again when he told a parliamentary committee that while some of the hospital's 250 consultants worked 'way above' contracted hours, 'there are others who spend too much time in Harley Street and not enough in our facilities'. We had some consultants, he added, 'whose clinical practice is not up to the standards we would wish for'.

That didn't endear him to his professorial colleagues back at Guy's.

I was working seven-day weeks now, raising money for the restoration of Westminster Abbey (of which more later), spending time on my schools, fundraising for the Conservative Party and trying to stay on top of events at Carpetright, which was still progressing in the teeth of an economic recession. I tried to spend as much time as possible at Guy's, though, touring the wards at weekends and talking to the nurses and doctors who worked under terrific pressure. I particularly liked to go to the children's wards, and I had great fun dressing up as Santa at Christmas, carrying as many teddy bears and toys as I could bear. Sometimes I wished I'd managed to hang on to Hamley's, loss-maker as it was.

I also went around the new GP fund-holders, set up as part of the reforms, to try to persuade them to send more patients to Guy's and Lewisham, where we could treat them better at a lower cost – which is what they were now required to do. This was what Thatcher meant by introducing competition into the system. It was the equivalent of drumming up new business, something I was good at.

I have always been humbled by the commitment of doctors and nurses in the NHS to their patients, and their determination to get on with the job no matter what. I was told sternly by one of our oncology professors that the nurses on the wards were 'at their wits' end' because of 'the cuts', drips weren't being watched properly, there was no time for proper coffee breaks and they just couldn't cope. But when I went to see for myself, they told me they were stretched but were managing and they were indignant when I mentioned the unwatched drips. The nurses were always pushed to the forefront by the unions.

Some of the loftier professors clearly resented the prominence of Guy's role in the revolution, which they suspected – rightly – would lead to further cuts in their budgets. But I found most of the physicians supportive of the management changes and the majority were realistic enough to accept the need for what we were trying to do. There were plenty of savings we could make without damaging the actual delivery of services.

The pressure, however, was showing on our top management team, and I was concerned about keeping morale up in the face of the constant criticism and hostility we all had to put up with on a daily basis. I told Cyril Chantler that I'd like to give him a present for all his hard work, and asked him what he'd like. 'I'd like my ward to be redecorated,' he replied. When I asked how much that would cost, he replied: 'I've been told about £250,000.'

That seemed excessive, so I went in and looked at his ward. It needed nothing more than a paint-job and on the NHS, which had its own contractors and way of doing things, that could cost many times what you'd pay in the private sector. So, I got some of our shop-fitters in and over a weekend they painted the ward and the corridor outside for just a few thousand. Cyril couldn't believe it when he came in on Monday morning.

Pauline also played her part when she noticed that visitors to the hospital and outpatients, who often had to hang around for hours, couldn't get any fresh fruit to eat. So, she organised for a little market stall to be set up in the main foyer, which is still there.

The main task, though, was to get costs down, and that could only be done meaningfully by tackling the staff issue, difficult at the best of times but potentially explosive then. In my first year at the hospital, we reduced the numbers by 800 (out of 8,000), mostly through a freeze on hiring, and made other savings and improvements across the hospital. Peter Griffiths discovered that £4.5 million a year was spent on employing agency staff at substantially higher rates than we paid our own people: £250 a week, while Guy's employees were paid only £186. We quickly came up with a plan to phase out our agency staff and we gave our own employees a pay rise.

The problems of completing the Phase III building, which was now called Philip Harris House, ran right through my three years as chairman and often dominated everything else. The design was still altering as new demands were made by the clinicians, and the project managers seemed to come and go at disturbing speed. So did the 'project sponsor', the person in the hospital given responsibility for it, who, when I arrived, was a psycho-geriatrician with no experience whatsoever of managing capital projects. Several contractors had gone bust, bills were not being paid and there were several legal actions outstanding.

By 1990, the costs of the building had risen to £83 million and two years later they were £118 million, three times the original estimate. By that stage I was committed to personally contributing £6 million, and we had total promises of over £35 million, a huge amount to raise from the private sector. A lot of that had to do with the tireless efforts made by Donald Bompas, but I had personally persuaded friends and other business people to contribute.

Philip Harris House was still far from finished when, in July 1991, I got John Major to top it out. As with Mrs Thatcher's visit five years before, we had security all over the place and there were the usual demonstrations outside, but the visit went well and the Prime Minister duly thanked us all for our pioneering efforts, saying that 107 hospitals now wanted to follow Guy's down the trust path. 'You opened the doors,' he said. It made me even more aware how much depended on our success at Guy's and how exposed we all were – including John Major.

The general election was now approaching, and we knew that Guy's would be one of the issues Labour would campaign on. The shadow Health Secretary, Robin Cook, had made no secret of his antipathy to hospital trusts, and particularly to the two people most publicly associated with them: Sir Philip Harris and Peter Griffiths. 'We might as well pack our bags now,' Peter said gloomily after a particularly bad poll put the Conservatives eight points behind. When Major called the election for 9 April 1992, no one thought he would win, except for Peter Griffiths, who bet me £5 on it. I took the bet and was never happier in my life to pay up when the Tories won with a majority of twenty-one. Peter made me sign his £5 note, which he had framed. He told me recently he's still got it.

In my first two years at Guy's and Lewisham, Peter and I, working closely together, saved £20 million a year on a total budget by then of £150 million, which included mental health clinics, for which I was also responsible, and we treated 60,000 more patients. We got all the costs down, right across the board, but we went on improving the service. When we were accused of neglecting our older patients, we could show conclusively that we were treating more people, at a lower cost and with a shorter waiting list. I felt I was proving that a private sector style of management could work in the NHS, and it *was* possible to run a hospital more efficiently, save costs and offer more services. That's what Mrs Thatcher and Ken Clarke had asked me to do, and I was justifying their faith in me and Peter Griffiths, who did most of the hard work.

The criticism however never seemed to abate and I was accused of all sorts of misdemeanours, including allegations about our overspending and extravagance. One of the trade unions even accused me of planning to privatise the hospital and sell off the land for my own private gain; when I threatened to sue, it retracted. That was typical of the vitriol that was thrown about, which upset my team rather more than it did me.

There were about thirty people at the hospital who really put their hearts and souls into the reforms and one evening, as a way of saying thank you, I invited them all – at my expense – to a Chinese restaurant in Greenwich. We took over the whole place and it was a great, fun party – all these professors in paper hats having a great time – and then someone at the hospital, who hadn't been invited, ratted on us and reported it to the press. A few days later, there was my face on television where I was accused of wasting NHS money on extravagant dinners when nurses weren't paid enough to make ends meet.

Shortly afterwards I received a call from Downing Street summoning me to meet the Prime Minister, who I was told was furious with me. I was actually on my way when a message came through cancelling the meeting: Downing Street had been attacked by the IRA, which had fired two homemade mortar shells into the garden, narrowly missing the room at the back where the full Cabinet was in session. Later, John Major took me out into the garden to see the damage, which was extensive. Poor Norman Lamont, the Chancellor, had all his windows blown in at No. 11. By some miracle, no one was hurt.

I still got into trouble though – I had to go to a press conference with Peter Griffiths and Donald Bompas and explain away my Chinese dinner. When someone asked me what I was going to do for a party next year, I said defiantly: 'Exactly the same!'

All of this brought us closer together as a management unit in Guy's and I was particularly moved one day when I was ushered into the boardroom where the portrait of Thomas Guy, which I had gazed at in such awe at my first UMDS board meeting, was taken down and mine was put in its place. That still ranks as one of the proudest moments of my life.

* * *

Behind the scenes, however, events were in motion that would eventually undo a lot of the good work we had done. In October 1992, a report into the London health services by Sir Bernard Tomlinson, a 72-year-old professor of pathology in Newcastle, recommended the closure of ten hospitals, including Bart's, one of the oldest and most distinguished medical establishments in the world. More importantly for me, Tomlinson also recommended that Guy's should merge with St Thomas', on a single site under a joint management trust board.

I was actually in favour of merging Guy's with Thomas' and at one point I proposed a plan to Virginia Bottomley, who replaced William Waldegrave as Health Secretary in 1992 (she was our third Health Secretary in two years), that we should do exactly that, possibly incorporating King's and St Mary's too. Lewisham Hospital, for which I was also responsible, and King's would remain as two ordinary hospitals, and all the specialist stuff could be concentrated into Guy's and Thomas', one for oncology and one for cardiology. The joint Guy's and St Thomas' medical and dental school (UMDS), of which Cyril Chantler was the principal, was in the process of merging with King's College London and should be based in the new Philip Harris building, while A&E and acute would go to Thomas'. Cyril Chantler and I had been through the figures several times, and had satisfied ourselves it would work, and the savings and efficiencies would be considerable.

Mrs Bottomley, however, saw it more as a Guy's takeover than a merger and was not impressed. 'You'll be too powerful if we do that,' she told me.

'How could we be too powerful?' I replied. 'You control the money that would go into it.' But she wouldn't agree and so we left it.

But if Guy's and Thomas' were to merge, I was particularly keen that Peter Griffiths should get the job of manager while I would step down to make way for a new chairman. I also strongly believed that the site for a single, merged hospital should be Guy's, where the facilities, once Philip Harris House opened, would be more modern. Guy's had a much better track record and in a straight fight I had no doubt we would win. It wasn't to be a straight fight, however.

What I had totally underestimated was the physical position of Thomas', which is right opposite the Houses of Parliament, and the emotion that was attached to it. An MP or peer taken ill could be driven straight across the river in minutes, and it was the nearest major hospital to Buckingham Palace, Westminster Abbey, Downing Street and the whole Whitehall establishment. 'The last hospital to close in this country will be St Thomas',' Cyril Chantler told me gloomily. 'You just have to look at where it is – right opposite the Houses of Parliament.'

The normal rule in any commercial merger is that one side appoints the chairman and the other the CEO, and I had every reason to assume that would be the case this time round. I duly told Mrs Bottomley that I would step down at Guy's but stay on as chairman of Lewisham, on the clear understanding that Peter Griffiths should be chief executive of the joint Guy's and Thomas' hospital. She accepted my resignation, and a few weeks later appointed (Lord) Barney Hayhoe, a rather ineffectual former minister of health, as chairman-designate of the new 'shadow' joint trust board, which would have an annual budget of £240 million.

But, in March 1993, I was stunned to learn that Tim Matthews, the chief executive of Thomas', had been appointed CEO and had already been tasked with submitting plans to Mrs Bottomley for merging the two hospitals – with Thomas' in prime position. Peter tried to put a brave face on it, but I could see he was badly hurt, and I really felt for him. I bumped into Mrs Bottomley a few days later at a cocktail party and she said: 'The job you have done at Guy's and Lewisham was fantastic.' I was in no mood to be flattered and retorted, probably rudely: 'You did the wrong thing in not appointing Peter Griffiths.'

'But you let him have two cars,' she replied. There had been a lot of criticism of Peter's package, which had been made public, and clearly it rankled with her. But she had got this one wrong.

'I don't know where you got that from,' I said angrily. 'He never had

two cars – every senior manager gets a car and he only ever had one.'
Peter resigned and left soon afterwards.

In February 1994, Bottomley rejected the one-site solution and
opted for two sites, but with Guy's reduced to a very junior partner.
All the acute and specialist services would go to Thomas', and Guy's
would be left with research and outpatient facilities, basically a shell of
a hospital and a shadow of its great self. Bottomley told the House of
Commons that the decision had been finely balanced but Thomas' had
won out because of its 'strategic position and accessibility'.

But what would happen to the still-unopened Philip Harris House?
one MP asked her. She was forced to admit it would not be used for the
purpose for which it was built and that donors might 'have grounds for
asking for their money back'. The consultants were equally angry and
puzzled. 'This is the most prestigious building in the NHS,' one told
the *Telegraph*. 'Our fear is that it will now become the most prestigious
white elephant.'

The next day's *Independent* read like the death knell for my troubled
building:

> Philip Harris House at Guy's Hospital in south London stood opulent,
> empty and silent. It was nonetheless the most articulate tribute to the
> disbelief in the NHS's flagship trust yesterday. The £140 million build-
> ing was to be Britain's most sophisticated hospital wing. Instead, along
> with what little else will remain of the 273-year-old hospital, it is set to
> become a health centre and medical school.

The decision to downgrade Guy's created a storm of protest. People
who had contributed to the new building complained we'd accepted
their money under false pretences. They were not only angry at the
government but angry at me, too, for getting them involved in the
first place, and I spent days apologising, as did Donald Bombas, who
took the brunt of it. I suspended all further payments and wrote to the

new trust requesting them to repay the money I had already contributed. The Imperial Cancer Research Fund did the same, as did Kay Glendinning, who had promised £7 million for the building. Research charities threatened legal action, and a Save Guy's campaign got under way, with growing numbers signing up to it.

I asked for my name to be taken off and for a time it reverted to 'Phase III'. It stayed closed for three years while they considered what to do with it, and when it did finally open, its costs had gone up by another £20 million.

After I stepped down from Guy's in 1993, I stayed on as chairman of Lewisham Hospital for a few years, and Maurice Lessof, my deputy at Guy's, came with me. There were lots of things to be done there and we made some significant improvements. We managed to buy the local library and set up a post-graduate department, turning Lewisham into a university hospital. I raised the money to install a new entrance, and with the proceeds from the sale of land at the back to Tesco, we built a children's unit, which Pauline is still patron of. It's a very decent, modern hospital now.

In the end, Guy's didn't fare as badly as I feared and has kept its place as one of the world's great hospitals. Within a few years of the merger, the management at St Thomas' came to appreciate the importance of the work done at Guy's, and the two hospitals now operate as a genuine partnership. The merger of the UMDS with King's College medical school, housed on the Guy's campus, has produced a great medical school capable of taking on the big US institutions that had begun to dominate the world of medicine. After its many vicissitudes, the new wing is used pretty much for what it was intended for, significantly improving the efficiency of the whole hospital.

Cyril Chantler retired in 2000 to become chairman of Great Ormond Street, where between us Martin and I gave him over £5 million.

My biggest regret is that the trust hospital initiative fizzled out without being properly tested. Virginia Bottomley was not a natural reformer and John Major had too many other problems to get involved. We were well down the road to proving that even the most complex of hospitals – and there are not many more complex than Guy's – could be made to work efficiently once it was freed from the dead hand of the local district council and given responsibility for its own budgets and management.

Ironically, the concept of the trust hospital was picked up a decade later in Tony Blair's second term with the creation of NHS foundation trusts, which are a similar but less ambitious form of what we set out to create. At one point, he asked me whether I would come back and help put together King's College with Guy's and Thomas', as I originally proposed to Mrs Bottomley. But I had lost my team by then and it didn't tempt me.

Despite all the battles, politics and money issues, I look back on my three years at Guy's as among the most important of my life. But I cannot help feeling that so much more could have been done if the government had held its nerve even for another year. The whole NHS could have learned valuable lessons from our experiment and maybe be more manageable today.

CHAPTER 25

PARTY POLITICS

In April 1992, John Major astonished everyone but himself by winning the general election, the fourth Conservative Party victory in succession and their last outright victory until 2015, twenty-three years later. I was delighted for him. In my view, he was one of the best Prime Ministers this country has had since the war, and certainly since Margaret Thatcher. He is also a thoroughly decent man and I am honoured to claim him as a friend.

I originally met him at one of Mrs Thatcher's Boxing Day lunches in Chequers. Pauline and I were usually invited and we always enjoyed the occasions, chatting to old friends and meeting new ones. It was soon after the 1987 election, in which I had been heavily involved working with the party chairman, Norman Tebbit, to raise money. Tebbit, who had fallen out with the Prime Minister during a bad-tempered and tense campaign, had startled everyone by resigning a few days after the election, despite another sweeping victory that he had done much to bring about. In the Cabinet reshuffle that followed, Nigel Lawson was promoted to Chancellor and John Major became the Chief Secretary to the Treasury, the most junior job in the Cabinet but also one of the most powerful. It is the Chief Secretary who has a very big influence on who gets what when it comes to the public purse.

At Chequers that day, Pauline sat beside John Major on one table and I sat beside Norma on another and all four of us got on well. We discovered we had a lot in common: John and I were almost the same age (he is six months younger than me), came from modest family backgrounds, grew up in the same part of London, both left school at a young age (me on my 15th birthday, he on his 16th), and we – and our parents – shared very similar political views. His childhood, however, was a lot more colourful than mine – his parents were music-hall performers, much more exotic than running lino shops – and he only discovered he had a half-sister after the 1997 election, when he left Downing Street for the backbenches. One thing we could never agree on, however, was football: he was a life-long supporter of Chelsea and I found it hard to forgive him for that – particularly if they were winning.

Norma was an almost exact contemporary of Pauline's, went to school in Dulwich and then Peckham School for Girls where she was head girl. Like Pauline's mother, she was a skilled dressmaker, although her real profession was teaching. I am still surprised none of us had met before that day.

After the Chequers lunch, we saw a lot of each other, and when Michael Heseltine challenged Mrs Thatcher for the party leadership in November 1990, I backed John, who was the Chancellor by then, for the leadership with both money and all the support I could muster. His opponents were Heseltine and Douglas Hurd but, as Thatcher's favoured candidate, he had the inside track and won easily, moving across from 11 Downing Street to No. 10 right in the middle of the First Gulf War – which he handled with great skill and decisiveness. We were at his Boxing Day lunch in 1990, just days before he flew off to the Gulf to meet the British troops, when he looked remarkably relaxed. Three weeks later the invasion began. In the middle of all that, on 7 February 1991, the IRA mortar-bombed Downing Street, as I have already related, saving me from the embarrassment of a severe dressing-down for entertaining my friends in a Chinese restaurant.

The manner in which he handled the war helped both his self-confidence and his standing in the party, but he was still not given much hope of winning when he called the election for April 1992. Once again, I was heavily involved in the campaign, helping Chris Patten, the party chairman, to raise funds, which were much needed. The financial position was dire, and the party was running on an overdraft with little chance of paying it off. Maurice Saatchi complained to me that Saatchi & Saatchi were not being paid for their ads, and still had unpaid bills left over from the 1987 election. Alistair McAlpine had done a great job in his fifteen years as the party treasurer but he retired when his great friend and heroine, Mrs Thatcher, resigned in 1990, and his replacement, Max Aitken, the 3rd Baron Beaverbrook, was hopeless. Just two weeks before the 1992 election, Beaverbrook told me the party was short of £900,000 and asked me to lend it to them for a couple of weeks – which I duly did. Afterwards, of course, I couldn't get it back, even with Chris Patten's help. Beaverbrook also told me the economic recession had hit him so hard personally that he urgently needed £500,000 to pay off the bank. Foolishly I agreed to guarantee a loan and a few months later the Royal Bank of Scotland issued a writ against me demanding the money. It all became embarrassingly public, more for Beaverbrook than for me, and I was forced to sue him in an attempt to get my money back. But I was just one among many others – a few months later his lawyers announced he couldn't pay his creditors, many of whom had lent him money against the security of his collection of Ferraris which were said to be worth millions.

After the election, I urged John to bring in a heavyweight treasurer if he was to have any chance of winning again (which, in reality, seemed unlikely). Chris Patten, whom John had earmarked as his Chancellor, unexpectedly lost his seat in the 1992 election, but was compensated by being sent to Hong Kong as the last governor before the colony went back to the Chinese. I visited him there several times, where he lived in great splendour and pomp, and did a very good job. Norman Fowler took over as chairman, and Tim Smith briefly became the treasurer until he became involved in a 'cash for questions' scandal and stood down, leaving the finances in an even bigger mess than Beaverbrook had.

In August 1993, John Major, out of the blue, asked me to take on the treasurer's job. I was just finishing up at Guy's and had already told Virginia Bottomley I would step down as chairman, but hadn't intended to take on something as time-consuming as this, particularly after two such undistinguished predecessors. Conservative Party treasurers are appointed by the party leader only, not by the chairman or any of the various committees, but John's style was to be as inclusive as possible. Norman Fowler, it turned out, had already tapped Sir Charles Hambro, the leading City banker, for the job and Sir David Sieff, of the Marks & Spencer family, was also in the running.

In the end, Major asked Charles and me to share the job, and I was happy with that. We worked really well together, splitting the work between us. I would host dinners at our house in Cadogan Square for potential donors and he would follow up with one-on-one meetings, which proved very effective at extracting funds. But it was an uphill task. In our first few weeks in the job, we discovered something no one seemed to have noticed up to that point: that the party owed £19 million to the Royal Bank of Scotland, which was charging interest of 10 per cent, and another £600,000 to Saatchi. At Christmas time 1993, four months after we started, Central Office couldn't pay the wages and about six of us had to put the money in from our own pockets.

In desperation, I went to see John Major in Downing Street and told him we needed his presence at our dinners with donors if we were going to get them to make the donations we needed. 'We're never going to get rid of this overdraft otherwise,' I said. He reluctantly agreed and we had some good fundraising dinners. When he couldn't be there, I sometimes asked Ken Clarke or one of the others, but people naturally preferred to meet the Prime Minister. The existence of these dinners, when they were discovered, caused some controversy in the press, but they were entirely above board and we made no attempt to keep them secret – I paid for them, they were not held on government property and we offered no knighthoods or peerages in return for cash.

By 1994, a year after we took over, we had repaid the bank over-draft and were back in credit. Some of our big donors are well known, and their names are in the public domain, but others contributed on a strictly confidential basis and I promised never to disclose their names – a promise I will keep, even though some of them are dead now. Alistair McAlpine famously used to keep his list of donors so private that he refused to share it even with the Prime Minister, arguing that a citizen is entitled to privacy in the polling booth, 'so why should they declare which political party they support financially?' The Labour government, jealous of the way we raised our money (as opposed to their dependence on the unions), changed the rules in 2000 and now parties must disclose large donations.

Let me just say that my great friend (Lord) Graham Kirkham (DFS) was a big donor, as were (Lord) Irvine Laidlaw (conferences), Martyn Arbib (fund management) and Eddie Healey, who built the Meadow Hall shopping centre in Sheffield. In the four years we worked together, Charles Hambro and I raised £118 million, enough to fund the deficit, buy and refurbish Central Office, pay off Saatchi and finance the 1997 election.

* * *

During this time, I saw a lot of John Major. Norma and Pauline put on a series of opera evenings at Chequers at which they raised over £7 million, half of which went to Norma's favourite charity, Mencap, and the rest was split between different charities. John and Norma were always there, greeting the guests, posing with each couple for photographs at the door, and generally making themselves as hospitable as possible. No Prime Minister had ever done anything like that before at Chequers, which was normally used only at weekends.

John went through a terrible time during those years, undermined by the Eurosceptics in his own party (and even members of his own

Cabinet) who were virulently opposed to his decision to sign the Maastricht Agreement, which paved the way for the euro. With great foresight, for which he is never given proper credit, he negotiated an opt out from the euro, an enormously important action as time would prove, as well as other concessions. Without that, I'm certain Britain would be in the euro today, making Brexit a lot more difficult even than it is – and probably impossible. And we would not have had the strong economic growth of the past ten years when the Eurozone was in a mess.

I often popped in to see him at No. 10 or saw him at weekends in Chequers to talk about party business and offer him my sympathy and support. And my goodness he needed it. At one stage, exhausted after months of negotiations with his fellow European leaders, John, not realising he was still being recorded after a TV interview, referred to his most vociferous Cabinet opponents – Michael Portillo, Peter Lilley and John Redwood – as 'bastards', an untypical lapse that did him great damage with the right wing of the party.

He not only had to endure the unrelenting bitterness of the Eurosceptics, or 'Maastricht rebels' as they were known, but a series of tawdry episodes of 'sleaze' that damaged the whole party. He lost minister after minister, some of them good friends, who were forced to resign after the press revealed details of their extra-marital sex lives or something equally salacious. His biggest blow was the loss of David Mellor, his so-called Minister of Fun (he was actually in charge of arts and culture, about which he knew a lot), who had been his sponsor in the leadership campaign in 1992 and they remained close. Mellor was revealed by the tabloid press to have been of conducting a relationship with an actress, a revelation which, as John remarked, wouldn't have raised an eyebrow in France. Mellor's forced departure from government was followed by a long line of others who found their sexual escapades brutally exposed.

But it was the unrelenting hostility of the Maastricht rebels which did the most damage, to the party as much as to John, and the after effects haunt it to this day. Support for the party in the summer of 1993 sank to a low of 23 per cent and in July a Conservative majority of 23,000 was turned into a Liberal Democrat majority of 16,000 in the Christchurch by-election. John came within a hair's breadth of losing the Maastricht vote – he suffered one defeat in the House of Commons, when the Eurosceptics voted with Labour and a Tory rebel was smuggled in on a stretcher to vote – but eventually he won through with the help of the Speaker's deciding vote.

In June 1995, I called Howell James, one of his closest advisers, and arranged to meet John in Downing Street late one evening. He looked terrible: he had been working eighteen-hour days and he was just preparing for a G7 meeting in Halifax on top of all his other issues. He was suffering severe pain in his back and shoulder, a problem which he said had been recurring for years but was getting worse, and he wasn't sleeping, 'not because of the political situation,' he said with a half-smile, 'but because of the pain'.

He wanted to talk and ranged over all the people lining up against him and their various motives. I told him he had to take them on or they would have him out. He said Willie Whitelaw and his friends Richard Ryder and Robert Cranborne had told him the same thing.

He left the room for a bit and Howell, who had been observing all this, said quietly, 'Be careful with him – or he'll go.'

I replied that I didn't think he should go, but he needed to hit back. At that moment, John came back into the room and said, 'I've got to leave for Nova Scotia early tomorrow – what are you doing for supper?'

I replied that I was going home and would probably have some beans on toast, which was about the extent of my culinary skills. I thought for a moment he was going to ask if he could join me, but instead he announced that he was going upstairs and wished me goodnight.

'Thank god you didn't invite him to dinner,' said Howell. 'Because he's starting so early, all his security people have left – there would have been a real flap.'

Matters came to a head a few days after he came from the G7 and announced he was resigning, triggering a leadership contest – for which he would stand again with the aim of winning an overwhelming majority, sidelining his enemies.

Three days after his resignation statement, John and Norma drove down to our home near Edenbridge in Kent, for Sunday lunch. He appeared remarkably relaxed for a man facing the biggest crisis of his career, and after lunch, to which we had invited a group of friends and neighbours, he and I strolled in the garden to discuss how it was all going. It was a beautiful, sunny June day and the Kent country-side was looking its best. John told me that he had heard that John Redwood was already preparing to run against him, 'sniffing around' among other potential runners to find out what they were up to. He expected him to announce his candidacy by the end of the week. He thought Michael Heseltine would keep his promise, which John had extracted from him a few days before, not to run on the first ballot, but he had heard that Michael Portillo was gearing up for a challenge.

Underneath his relaxed air, I could see John was desperately tense, which wasn't surprising given what he had been through, totally un-fairly, and I tried to reassure him. 'Win or lose,' I told him, 'there's a lot of life left. There's much more to it than politics.'

'Those are my sentiments exactly,' he said with a laugh, and we went back into the house. On the way back to London, he wrote later, 'I was feeling positive' and up for the fight.

A few days later, Redwood, as expected, launched his campaign for the party leadership but he was the only other candidate and, after some nervous times, John Major won by 218 votes to 89 on the second ballot (there were eight abstentions and twelve spoiled votes). His supporters were jubilant but he told me later he was disappointed – he had hoped to win by more, to silence the Eurosceptics once and for all. For the rest of his time in Downing Street, he presided over an openly divided party that would go on to lose three elections in a row and be out of power for thirteen years.

The 1996 New Year's Honours list brought some momentous news for me: I was awarded a peerage and took the title Baron Harris of Peckham, in the London Borough of Southwark, the greatest honour I will ever enjoy. I think I am the first peer to use Peckham in his title – and quite possibly the last. I was proud to do so.

* * *

After the 1997 election, I retired from the treasurer's position but only on the condition that I was replaced by Graham Kirkham. We lost so many good people in that election that for years the party wandered in the political wilderness. Michael Heseltine might have rescued it but he had a heart attack and never fully recovered. Chris Patten had lost his seat in 1992 and Michael Portillo in 1997, both potential leaders. We then got three new leaders in quick succession, of which my favourite was William Hague, who I felt would have been a great Prime Minister with just another five years' experience. After him, Michael Howard, an underestimated politician, steadied the ship. I was initially very impressed with David Cameron and backed him for the leadership, which he won after beating Ken Clarke, who ran three times. Later however I was disappointed in Cameron and don't think he was a patch on John Major.

I backed the Brexit campaign in 2016, but with no great passion either way, and was surprised that Mrs May got the job when David Cameron resigned. I guess I'm just getting old, but politics doesn't seem to be as much fun as it once was.

CHAPTER 26

CARPETRIGHT

On 17 September 1992, we opened our 100th Carpetright store in a modern retail park on the edge of Sheffield, the type of site I now preferred. Seventy of our shops were stand-alone, purpose-built premises all personally chosen by Harvey Spack and me, and thirty were shared sites with MFI. The warehouse at Rainham, a mini-Swanley, was working flat-out and I could see we were going to have to move to bigger premises if we went on expanding like this.

Even when I was chairman of Guy's, I still did most of the carpet buying with Paul Lorimer, dealing with a dwindling number of UK suppliers. We still bought 70 per cent of our carpets from domestic manufacturers but during the recession they were closing at an alarming rate. I struck such keen deals that they never made much money from me, but we kept the mills running and the workers in jobs. Today the industry is recovering again but employs only 6,500 people, a fraction of its peak.

After Derek Hunt left, I took over as executive chairman and recruited the best board of non-execs I've ever worked with: Gerald Dennis, former deputy chairman of BAT, Lionel Ross, ex-finance director of Whitbread, and my friend Harry Djanogly, who, as he always did, put his money where his mouth was and invested over £1 million in our shares. (Baroness) Judith Wilcox joined a little later. It was comforting having Harry there, knowing nothing would get past him – Harry never let anyone get away with anything he disapproved of. After his City travails, David Reed had to step down from the board but he kept his shares and later did very well out of them.

By early 1993 I was getting ready to go back to the City and float the new company and when I tested the waters, I found it was ready for me too. In a curious way, my reputation had been enhanced by the timing of the sale of Harris Queensway, where I had fortuitously got out at the top, after which the company had lasted only two years without me. I hadn't intended it to be that way of course – I had just been lucky, even if I still felt aggrieved.

As the date for the float approached, there was a flurry of publicity and whole-page profiles devoted to me in *The Times*, *Sunday Times*, *Sunday Telegraph*, *Independent*, *Retail Week* and various others. Once again it was 'King of Carpets', 'Making a Pile', 'Magic Carpet', 'City to roll out carpet for Sir Phil' and so on.

And then it was roadshow time. I recently found my schedule for these busy days and I can't believe what energy I still had then, starting with breakfast meetings, then a presentation every hour on the hour to institutions and journalists, breaking off to go to the lawyers, the bankers, the brokers, the PR people, holding board meetings to bring the directors up to speed, lunch with a group of analysts, then more of the same running into the evening, starting again the next day. When I had exhausted the London institutions, I went up to Scotland for more presentations in Glasgow and Edinburgh. I developed a little trick of taking a sample of one of our new and revolutionary carpets, the Stainprooof, putting it on the floor and asking my audience to spill coffee, tea, bleach or whatever they wanted onto it. Then I wiped it clean. That, I said triumphantly, was what technology was doing for carpets, and we were leading the way.

I demonstrated this to Judi Bevan, one of my favourite financial journalists (she is married to John Jay), who wrote a funny little sketch on this:

> Sir Philip Harris bustles into the room, a sheaf of carpet samples under
> his arm. Before I can stop him, he whips out a rectangle of burgundy

twist, scrubs a felt-tip pen onto it, pours on hot coffee and then calls for the bleach. 'No, no,' I beg. 'Not that!'

She need not have worried: I cleaned it off in seconds.

It must have worked, because we sent out an initial 28,000 prospectuses and had to print more. On 16 June 1993, we learned that the issue was oversubscribed 2.6 times.

In the build-up to the flotation, County NatWest (now, alas, without David Reed or Charles Villiers, who had retired from the bank) and our brokers, Warburg's, tentatively put a value on the company of £70 million, which, as I whipped up interest in the issue, they raised to £90 million and then went even higher. In the event, we got the shares away at 148p a share, valuing the company at £114 million. I retained a 29 per cent stake, worth £34 million, and took out £7 million in cash, which I used for my various charities. I had originally invested £3 million. MFI's investment of £1 million was worth £20 million and the other backers, Phildrew and County, also made a hefty profit. Overall, the £9 million of capital I had invested myself or raised from MFI, Phildrew and County had multiplied 12.6 times.

Senior executives, including John Kitching, did very well out of it, well merited after the support they had given me. And I received a nice letter from David Reed thanking me for letting him keep his shares, which he said had helped him get his life back on track.

A few weeks later, on 7 July 1993, I gave a party in the ballroom of Claridge's to celebrate the success of the issue. Everybody came – friends, family, suppliers, staff, advisers, politicians, the press – and I really enjoyed myself. One report afterwards said that someone asked one of our Belgian suppliers about his experiences of selling to me. 'He cuts your throat,' he replied. 'But still you love him.' He at least loved my champagne, which flowed freely that evening.

CHAPTER 27

AN OXFORD COLLEGE

I have been privileged in my life to have been involved in some of the great British institutions: the House of Lords, Guy's Hospital, Westminster Abbey – and the University of Oxford. I have loved them all, in their very different ways, and each of them has given me back as much as I have given them.

My relationship with Oxford started, as many of my connections have, through fundraising. In February 1990 John Patten, who was then a minister at the Home Office (he would succeed Ken Clarke as Education Secretary after the 1992 election), invited me to dinner in Oxford, where he was the local MP. I was fond of Patten, a gentle, Jesuit-educated, donnish man, who was more of an academic than a political heavyweight like his namesake Chris Patten.

Patten wanted me to meet Dr Ralph Waller, principal of Manchester College, which, he said, was 'one of the best-kept secrets in higher education'. It was the only college in Oxford exclusively catering for mature students and the only mixed mature college in the country for both graduates and undergraduates.

Its problem was that, although it had recently become a residential hall of the university, it did not have full collegiate status and was in danger of closing without an endowment to enable it to get its royal charter. I confess, as I drove up to Oxford, that I was not terribly interested in supporting a struggling college, even if it came with naming rights. I felt I was doing my bit for education already by investing in two City Technology Colleges, Crystal Palace and Bacon, and I was getting a bit stretched with Guy's, the Conservative Party and Westminster Abbey, all of which required both time and money.

I changed my mind, however, when I met Ralph Waller and his wife Carol. Ralph was a charming man, a Methodist minister and theologian as well as an academic, who had been struggling to turn the college's fortune around since his appointment in 1988. He took me around the college, which, although it wasn't as ancient as some of the more famous colleges (University College, Balliol and Merton are all about 800 years old), had a wonderfully peaceful, scholarly air about it. It was ideally situated in the City, just a short walk from the Bodleian Library, the Sheldonian Theatre and the Randolph Hotel where I was staying. Most of it had been built in late Victorian times, including the beautiful chapel where I admired the stained-glass windows which were the work of the Victorian artists Edward Burne-Jones and William Morris, their last stained-glass scheme in Oxford.

I was particularly interested in its 'mature students only' policy. I had known so many bright people who had missed out on a proper education for all sorts of reasons – poverty, broken homes, immaturity, poor teachers or whatever – and I loved the idea of them getting a second chance. I would have loved one myself.

I had come to Oxford out of a sense of obligation to John Patten, but now I found myself falling under its spell. I liked the college building and I liked Ralph, and, despite my initial reservations, I began to think seriously about the proposal he put to me. He had no money to do anything, he said, but he had lots of plans. Everything hinged around getting full 'chartered collegiate status', as he called it, but the university authorities had told him he would have to prove that Manchester College was financially viable before he could even apply – and that meant proving he had an endowment of at least £4 million in place. That's where he hoped I might come in.

In return for a commitment to a donation of that order, he was prepared to change the name to Harris College Oxford, if that was what I wanted. The Manchester title was no longer that relevant – the college had actually been founded in Warrington in 1758 as a 'dissenting academy', moved to Manchester in 1786, where it stayed for only seventeen years, before moving to York, back to Manchester, then to London and finally to Oxford in 1889. The intention was to get full collegiate status then, but it was still waiting over 100 years later.

My thought was to name it, not after me, but after my father, and I asked Ralph, if I were to go ahead, could I have the right to erect a statue of him in his army uniform in the main quadrangle? That was one of the few conditions I asked for and he readily agreed.

The process of getting college status, Ralph thought, could take up to ten years, and in the meantime he needed funds to build up the college again. It had a splendid baronial-style dining hall, named after a Victorian family called Arlosh who had presumably paid for it, which was unused for the very good reason that it had no kitchens, and staff and students had to make do with a much smaller space. The building cost of a new kitchen and other facilities was over £1 million, which I helped with. There was also a lovely library that Ralph was keen to enlarge with state-of-the-art electronics and more room for books. I agreed to give him a contribution towards that if he would name it after my mother's brother, Frederick Ward, my beloved uncle Fred, who came up to open it. Uncle Fred was tickled pink: for a retired rag-and-bone man from Peckham, and prospective batman to my father, having an Oxford library named after him was quite something.

It was through Ralph that I met his great friend Sir Roger Bannister, the master of Pembroke College next door. Bannister was one of my all-time sporting heroes and I remember as a twelve-year-old listening with my father to that legendary race in 1954 (which was in Oxford) when he ran a mile in under four minutes for the first time in recorded human history, with Chris Chataway and Chris Brasher pacing him all the way. He retired soon afterwards to become an eminent neurologist, almost embarrassed by his sporting fame. When someone asked him whether the sub-four-minute mile was his greatest achievement, he said he was much prouder of his medical research into the nervous system.

He was often at dinner or events in Manchester college, which he told me he considered the most beautiful in all of Oxford – 'after Pembroke of course'. He retired as Master in 1993 but remained a mentor to Ralph through his most difficult times – of which there were many.

A couple of the tutors, who were on the college council, opposed Ralph's reforms every step of the way and he found himself accused of all sorts of malpractices and high-handedness, which for such a decent, transparently honest man was bizarre. Fortunately, he had the majority of the council and his fellow college heads on his side and he held out. But it was an unpleasant time for him.

Early in 1994, I committed the Harris family to a £3 million endowment, spread over six years, with the promise to consider extending it at the end of that period. I had already given them the best part of £1 million, which had helped attract a few other donors including Robert Wills and the Rank Organisation, but much more was needed. Other than the two dissenting tutors, the council was happy with that and the application for full collegiate status was finally submitted. Ralph had been steadily building up the student numbers and every time I visited him I could sense this beautiful college becoming more and more vibrant. I loved it and I loved Ralph and his enthusiasm and his ability to make things happen.

All was going well until June 1994, when suddenly I found myself back in the headlines all over again, just as I had at Guy's and the Tory Party. Oxford dons can be a tricky lot, and out of the blue poor Ralph found himself in the centre of a rebellion over his decision to give me naming rights. Several former governors wrote furiously that they didn't mind a quadrangle being named after my father but to rename the whole college 'in return for charitable monies is quite breathtaking in its audacity'. Some of the graduates announced publicly that they would oppose the name change at the next governors' meeting.

Magnate threatens to cancel £3.6m donation to Oxford

By Ben Preston, Education Correspondent

A CARPET magnate yesterday threatened to withdraw a gift of a £3.6 million donation to an Oxford college if opposition mounted to plans to rename it after his father.

Sir Philip Harris, a leading Conservative Party fundraiser, said he did not want any 'aggro' over his proposed gift, which would help Manchester College to raise the £4 million needed to become a full member of the university.

Some academics and graduates oppose the move to rename the 200-year-old college, which caters for mature students. They will seek to have the proposal rejected at a meeting of 450 governors next week.

Sir Philip said: "I am just a retailer trying to help schools and colleges. If they do not want that help, the money can go elsewhere. I do not want to be involved in rows ... I do not like people knowing where I give my money."

Sir Philip, who left school at 15, said: "I am a great believer in mature students. I have been involved with Manchester for five years. It is a great college, very well run. It deserves to get full college status."

Sir Philip has a long record of making charitable donations, including support for two city technology colleges. One in south London bears his name.

He said the idea to rename the college was Manchester's and that he had simply agreed to the proposition. He added that it would be a great source

Charles Harris, who died of cancer aged 38 in 1957, founded the carpet business that Sir Philip used as a springboard for his business success. As an army captain in the Second World War, Charles, aged 23, was awarded the MC for bravery in action.

John Patten, the Education Secretary, is understood to be the broker who introduced Sir Philip to the college. Mr Patten, a former Oxford don, has close links with the university.

Dr Ralph Walker, Principal of Manchester, said he was confident the name change

> **(I am just a retailer trying to help. If they do not want that help, the money can go elsewhere)**

would be approved. Both students and fellows supported the plan, which had already been unanimously endorsed by the college council.

He believed the controversy was being stirred by a small minority seeking to embarrass Sir Philip into withdrawing his offer.

He said: "Sir Philip and Lady Harris have been very generous and supportive of the college aim to provide the best education for mature students. Sir Philip has been enormously encouraging.

leges, for example Wadham and Wolfson colleges."

Brian Andrews, 57, formerly the chief auditor of Unilever and a theology undergraduate at Manchester, said students were "very relaxed" about the proposals. He said the attitude was generally positive.

Gillian Carey, senior tutor and longest-serving staff member after 27 years, said: "The ethos of the college and its continued effectiveness is more important than the name. Those of us who have been here a long time are 100 per cent behind the move."

Opposition to the name-change has come largely from within the Unitarian Church, which founded the college in 1786. Graduates will propose at next week's meeting that only part of the college carries the Harris name.

The change of status would give Manchester representation on all Oxford University committees and finance for certain lectureships. The proposed charter would hand control of the college to its fellows, removing the direct influence of the 5,000-strong Unitarian Church.

Manchester is one of the best-kept secrets in higher education. The country's only mixed college for mature students has established a formidable academic reputation. Its 120 students range in age from 25 to 62. They come from a variety of backgrounds, many having left school at 16.

The college, one of the last in a long line of Nonconformist academies founded in the

The Times *headline in June 1994.*

When *The Times* education correspondent Ben Preston called me for a comment, I wearily responded: 'Look, I am just a retailer trying to help schools and colleges. If they don't want that help, the money can go elsewhere. I don't want to get involved in any more rows.' That remark, which I meant every word of, caused quite a furore when it was reported.

The opposition died after that and when the compromise name of Harris Manchester College was proposed, I accepted. And that's what it's called today. And, to tell the truth – I prefer it. If I do anything more in Oxford, which I plan to, I will do it under that name.

In 1996, much sooner than we expected, we became a full Oxford college, the 39th and last (there are now thirty-eight after a couple of colleges merged). It was a big turning point, making it possible for Ralph to attract serious donations for the first time. Two very generous Thai ladies, Maevadi Navapan and Karnitha Karnchanachari, gave us $3 million to build the beautiful Siew-Sngiem Clock Tower, which looks as if it has been there for centuries, and the Sukum Navapan Gate onto Mansfield Road. Rooms in the college have been renovated and look to my eye more like five-star hotel rooms than student accommodation – no dusty old students' garrets without toilets in our college. The whole college looks a different place to what it was on my first visit nearly thirty years ago.

The main addition for me is my father's bronze, life-size statue in the main quadrangle. I used as a model the picture of him in officer's uniform receiving his Military Cross from Field Marshal Montgomery in 1945, and I commissioned the sculptor Etienne Millner, who had made statues of several leading military figures, including General Allenby and General Auchinleck, to carry it out. He did such a good a job that I also got him to do one of me and I shall stand opposite Dad, looking across the quadrangle at him, I hope for ever – or a few centuries at least, certainly a lot longer than I knew him in real life. I sometimes wonder what he'd make of it, but I think he'd be proud. One thing is for sure: he is the first, and will probably be the last, person from Peckham to have an Oxford college named after them.

Ralph has always been very generous with his acknowledgement of my role, stating that without me he wouldn't have got full college status which has changed his life, and I'm pleased for him. Our schools have benefited too. There is now a powerful link between the Harris Federation academies and the Oxford college, which I never anticipated when we started. Even in 1996, when Manchester became a proper college, I still only had two CTCs, not the forty-four academies I have now.

Today, our English and maths teachers come to Harris Manchester two or three times a year, thirty or so at a time, for intensive weekend courses. They stay in the college and we show them Oxford in all its glory, hoping to inspire them to point their students in this direction. Every year I give a dinner for all our school principals, and Dan Moynihan gives them a full analysis of their performance in the past year, praising the ones who have done best, encouraging those (very few) who have had a disappointing – by his exacting standards – year.

Of course, none of our academy students has been to Harris Manchester yet – you have to be at least twenty-one (we have some students who are more than fifty). I'd like to do something about that, and would dearly love to find a building, preferably connected to Harris Manchester College, where we could take some eighteen-year-old students straight from school. Some might even be graduates of Harris academies, which I'd dearly love to see. Ralph, who is as keen as mustard to expand, is on the lookout for the right premises.

CHAPTER 28

THE QUEEN AND
THE ABBEY

I watched the Queen's coronation in 1953 as an eleven-year-old with my parents on a black-and-white television, one of the few in our neighbourhood (we lived in Millfield Road, Thornton Heath). We all had the day off school, and there were street parties and parades across the country, although it rained solidly. It was the first time the BBC had been allowed to film a royal event inside Westminster Abbey and my mother, my nan and their friends were in a frenzy of excitement. The cameras were positioned high up over the nave, presenting a wonderful view of the main body of the church, and even on our flickering fourteen-inch screen, it looked magnificent.

I think the first time I ever went inside the abbey was on a school trip, and I learned, like every British school kid, that every monarch since William the Conqueror to Her Majesty Queen Elizabeth II was crowned there (I later discovered this is not entirely true: Edward V died at the age of twelve in 1483 and Edward VIII was never crowned). That's a fantastic history, unequalled anywhere else in the world.

Yet for much of my life it looked like a big, black old church, which I scarcely gave a second glance to. It was under scaffolding for years and it was only when that began coming down that I was aware of the startling white stonework that had been hidden from view for more than two centuries. I went to a few events there over the years but it had barely touched my life until one day in about 1991, Lord (Alf) Robens, my chairman on the Guy's and St Thomas' medical school, proposed that I head up the appeals committee of the Westminster Abbey Restoration Fund, started by the Duke of Edinburgh nearly twenty years before. I was incredibly busy at the time and I told Alf, who had obviously volunteered me for the job, that I didn't think I could do it.

'When the Duke of Edinburgh writes to you, you can't turn him down,' he replied.

I was still thinking about that when, a few days later, I duly received a letter on Buckingham Palace notepaper, signed simply 'Philip' in the grand way that royals have. And, of course, Alf was right – I couldn't resist. The abbey, said the Duke, was 'a place of unique religious, historical and architectural interest', which had been saved through conservation, rebuilding, restoration and repair 'ever since the first building on the site was dedicated by Edward the Confessor, its founder, on 28 December 1065'.

But over the centuries, London smog, German bombs and a lack of proper maintenance caused by two world wars interspersed with the Great Depression, had left their mark. 'The most extensive restoration carried out since at least the time of Sir Christopher Wren,' Philip wrote, had begun under his chairmanship in 1973, but £10 million and eighteen years later it had still not been completed.

As a first step in my new job, I was invited to meet Michael Mayne, who was the dean and 'surveyor of the fabric'. Mayne explained that the Duke's restoration programme was the second since the war. The first, in 1953, had been more modest, raising just £1 million to clean up the inside, which was 'quite literally black' with the dirt of London and had not been seen, let alone properly appreciated, since the seventeenth century. The task of restoring the main fabric of the building had proved many times more difficult and expensive than anyone expected and still required another £10 million, which they were hoping I would raise.

Buttress then took me on a tour of the abbey, a fascinating experience. He was a scholarly, bearded north countryman who seemed to know the history of every stone and carved decoration, and enjoyed nothing more than talking about them, particularly to potential donors like me.

High on the roof of the building, Buttress gave me a short history of this great building, explaining that the abbey was indeed a thousand years old but very little of the Confessor's original Romanesque structure still existed. The abbey we are familiar with today is largely the thirteenth-century church built during the reign of Henry III from 1269 onwards, greatly enhanced by Wren and Hawksmoor who added the twin towers 500 years later. All of it had been hidden for years under a thick coating of London soot, and on my first visit I couldn't even see the front of the abbey, where the towers and main entrance are (I learned to call this the 'west front'), which was cloaked by a latticework of scaffolding.

I thought old buildings like this were merely cleaned with a good scrub with a wire brush and a pressure hose, but nothing could have been less true. 'Some of the pollution we're taking off is two to three inches thick,' Buttress told me, illustrating his point by chipping off a chunk of it, exposing the corroded stone which came off with it.

Sulphur in the air and moisture in the atmosphere had eaten away at the softer stone like a cancer, and in the 1930s iron and bronze straps, used to stabilise the building, had rusted and swelled, splitting the stones. Cupolas built from inferior stone used by the Victorians were crumbling and he showed me carvings of fantastical greyhounds, lions and grotesque beasts that had been worn down by the weather and looked like lepers, their noses and half their faces long gone.

Every hundred years or so the building required major restoration, and different surveyors used different stone, with the result that where it had already been cleaned the abbey looked like a chequerboard. Christopher Wren rebuilt and refaced much of it in a creamy-brown Burford stone, and his Victorian successors used a softer stone from Chilmark, near Salisbury, which Buttress called 'an explosive disaster'.

He showed me parts of one of the towers where two successive layers of stone had been added, the first in the fifteenth century, the second by Hawksmoor 200 years later, underneath which was some of the original Norman stone from Caen. Now it had to be repaired again.

As we finished our tour, I began to realise the scale – and importance – of the job I had taken on.

* * *

I attended my first meeting of the Westminster Abbey Trust, presided over by Prince Philip at Buckingham Palace, shortly afterwards. I knew most of the other trustees: Lord Catto, the City merchant banker; Lord Robens; Sir John Quinton, chairman of Barclays Bank (and, along with Rupert Murdoch, founder of the Premier League); Sir Peter Walters (chairman of BP); Sir John Templeton, the hugely successful fund manager; and Garry Weston, the Canadian-born billionaire. The Duke of Westminster was also a trustee but he didn't often attend. At my request, Hugh Sykes also joined – I reckoned I was going to need his support. The Duke proved an excellent chairman: precise, knowledgeable and often witty. One of his favourite greetings was to ask: 'Who got you into this then?' In my case, I was able to reply: 'You did, Sir.'

As chairman of the restoration fund, I was set the task of raising £10 million, a hefty sum for a charity that had long ago exhausted its traditional donors. I formed a little committee, which included Ivan Fallon, and started by calling Garry Weston who was a big supporter of the abbey. He invited me to his London office for a meeting at 7.30 in the morning and, after listening to me for a few minutes, he suddenly excused himself, left the room and came back with a cheque for £5 million.

I added £1 million to that, and once again Harry Djanogly was typically generous, as was the former US ambassador to Britain, Walter

Annenberg, and Captain John Latsis, the Greek billionaire. Most of the members of the trust were also major donors, including John Templeton (who matched my million), and Hugh Sykes.

I reached the target of £10 million in my first year and by March 1992 work on the main building was basically complete. Prince Philip commemorated it by unveiling an inscription cut into the lowest part of the north-west tower and the scaffolding began coming down at last. By the summer, the façade was revealed in all its glory, with every detail of the towers standing out in gleaming ochre and white sandstone. It is one of the great sights of London and to this day I stop to admire it every time I pass.

I thought I was off the fundraising hook at that point, but the Duke had other ideas. The job, he said, was not quite done, and the finest part of the abbey, which needed attention badly, had not yet been touched. The Henry VII Chapel, the ornate (Gothic) chapel that juts out directly opposite the peers' entrance to the Houses of Parliament, was built in the early 1500s by the father of Henry VIII and most famously houses the tombs of Queen Elizabeth I and her cousin Mary Queen of Scots. The current dean, Dr John Hall, describes it as 'one of the most stunning ecclesiastical spaces in the world', which is no exaggeration.

It was in a worse state even than the nave and the two transepts, pockmarked and blackened from the smogs, and had been damaged by a German bomb that blew a hole in the wall (it's still there, preserved for posterity) and destroyed its fine stained-glass windows. Prince Philip and the surveyors originally intended to make the chapel part of the bigger restoration project but abandoned it because they didn't have the funds. Now I was asked to raise another £5 million to finish it.

Over the next three years, the chapel's twelve great cupola tops, each weighing ten tonnes, were reconstructed, flying buttress arms made sound, badly eroded carved beasts replaced and parapets, pinnacles and buttress tops rebuilt in Portland stone. All the external ornaments were replaced: over 300 pieces of stone carving, including Tudor badges, lions, dragons and talbots, a truly prodigious job of work done by seven carvers over a period of three years – probably the most extensive programme of architectural stone carving in the past century. By the time they finished, the stone masons were as skilled as anyone in the Middle Ages.

The work was finally finished in 1997, at a total cost, over twenty-four years, of £37 million, of which my committee was responsible for raising £24 million. The major donors, including me, were honoured with heraldic glass windows in the church bearing their coats of arms – mine is the one that features rolls of carpet, end-on.

I had still not yet done with the abbey, however. I had grown to love this building, with its immense sense of history, and I hated leaving things unfinished. The windows of the Henry VII Chapel had been repaired after the war with plain glass, and I proposed that we should replace the large central east window with a modern stained-glass one – which I would pay for. After holding a competition, we chose Alan Younger, one of the most important British stained-glass artists of the post-war era, to design and build it. The central figure in the window is the Virgin Mary, surrounded by angels, but in the bottom right-hand corner are two small, penitent figures, on their knees and praying to heaven. Look closely and you might recognise them – they are Pauline and me, immortalised in stained glass in one of the greatest buildings of the world.

The Queen formally unveiled it a few years later, suitably acknowledging my role.

One of the rewards for my contribution to the restoration of the beautiful King Henry VII Chapel was that I could use it for very special occasions. Outside the royal family, very few people have been married there, but the dean very generously allowed the use of it for the wedding of my son Martin to Julie in 1993.

CHAPTER 29

LAST OF THE
GOOD TIMES

All this time, while I was busy at Guys, expanding my schools federation and raising money for the abbey, Carpetright continued
to motor strongly. By June 1994, when we announced our first set of
figures as a public company, the shares were 255p, buoyed up by pre-
tax profits which were up 79 per cent to £14 million on turnover that
topped £100 million. That was more than we ever made from carpets
at Harris Queensway – in 1988, my last year, the carpet division made
an operating profit of £12.8 million on sales of £127 million. At that
moment, I could truthfully say I had done it – I had got back to where
I was, and more if I hadn't diversified into furniture and electricals.

We now had 116 stores and 9 per cent of the carpet market. A year
later, that was nearly 150 stores and profits of £19.7 million and our
market share was 12 per cent. And so it went on, year after year, the formula working perfectly as the economy, first under John Major, later
Tony Blair, went on booming. In 1996, the shares climbed above 600p,
dropped back in 1998, and then set out on an almost vertical climb to
cross the £13 level. The market value at that point was just over £900
million, twice what we sold Harris Queensway for.

At the time of the share listing, I had publicly set myself a target
of 260 stores, but by 1998 we had 307 outlets and made profits of £30
million; by 2004 we had expanded into Europe, with 77 stores in the
Netherlands, 28 in Belgium, 11 in Poland, 26 in Ireland and 533 in the
UK. When someone asked me if, as a boy in Peckham, I thought I'd

ever be selling carpets in Poland, I replied, only half-jokingly: 'I didn't even know where Poland was.'

I was now able to boast that we were the biggest retailer of carpets in the world.

That year we made £65 million, more than all sectors of Harris Queensway made at its very peak. And we paid out £35 million in dividends, of which I received £7 million, most of which went straight into my charities.

I also tidied up some of my other interests, including the sale of Harveys the Homemaker, which I had bought out of Harris Queensway when I left in 1988. I had put Rob Templeman, who had joined Queensway straight out of school, in as managing director and asked Harry Solomons to be chairman, and by the mid-1990s it was doing so well we floated it on the Stock Exchange. But a few years later, by which stage Rob had moved on to Homebase and later to Debenhams as chief executive, I received a good offer for it and I accepted. I was sorry to see it go but I did well out of it, more than trebling my money.

I was now sixty-four years old and had been in the business for the best part of fifty years and, although I wasn't even thinking of retirement, I was increasingly asked about succession. I replied, truthfully, that I'd like to keep the company in the family. Charles, after trying the carpet business, left to do his own thing, and Peter wasn't terribly interested. Martin however was passionate about the business and joined the main board as commercial director in 2002, with responsibility for the marketing operations. I thought he was more than capable of eventually running the whole company when I retired – which I didn't intend to for a few years yet.

'Of course, as a father I'd like to see my son take over,' I told Harry Wallop of the *Daily Telegraph* in 2006. 'I think Martin now has the capability of doing it but if there is someone better the board will make that decision, not me.' And if Martin didn't make the grade, I added, there was my eleven-year-old grandson Charlie. 'If he takes up retail, he'll be really good. He's got the gift of the gab, he's good with people.'

* * *

In February 2007, the shares hit 1335p, which meant that anyone who had invested £1,000 when we went public in 1993 would now be sitting on over £9,000. My own shares were worth over £200 million, a huge increase on my original investment of £3 million, and Martin owned shares worth nearly £12 million in his own right. Little did I suspect it at the time, but that was to prove the all-time peak for Carpetright. Although we would have another go at scaling the heights, the good times were coming to an end.

The first hint of trouble came in early 2007, when I began to notice something strange about the weekly figures. Suddenly, for no reason that I could put my finger on, sales were running behind budget and even further behind my expectations, which admittedly were always on the bullish side. It was an uncanny replay of my Harris Queensway experience and I was immediately on the alert. Our financial year ended on 28 April 2007 and I had confidently forecast profits of £65 million, fully expecting to make £100 million the next year if I could get all my plans into line. Now we were running well off that. Ian Kenyon, the young finance director, remarked that sales had been going fine up to Christmas and had then stopped. 'The only thing I can think of is interest rates,' said Ian. But that seemed unlikely: interest rates had indeed gone up, but only by half a point to 5.25 per cent in the early months of 2007 and that wasn't a show-stopper. Other retailers, however, were reporting similar slow-downs and all retail shares had begun to slip.

In April, Carpetright shares dropped below the £10 level as the market sensed something was wrong – which there was. Trading was definitely slowing down, well behind budget and, even worse, below the previous year. We had always been a bellwether for the rest of the economy, the first into a recession and the first out, but at that moment there was nothing to indicate that the economic boom had come to an end. True, the US housing market boom had cracked in the summer of 2006 and there was much talk in the press and the City of a 'sub-prime banking crisis', but all the experts said it was an American phenomenon – nothing to do with Britain, where the economy under Gordon Brown seemed to be going nicely.

But I knew it wasn't. I had been through too many recessions not to recognise the signs of an approaching one, even if the Treasury and the Bank of England hadn't seen it yet. And I didn't like the feel of this one. Recessions in Britain usually lasted two years, which meant this one would take us to around to the middle of 2009 – and that's what I would plan for, although I felt in my bones there was something worse coming down the road.

On 28 April 2007, I had to put out my first profit warning since those final days of Harris Queensway, nearly twenty years earlier, indicating that profits would only 'marginally' exceed the previous year's income of £57.2 million, well short of what the analysts were expecting – and even that would be flattered by £8.5 million of property profits. But I didn't want to slow the momentum, and we went on opening stores, seventy in the UK and Ireland that year and another eleven in Poland and the Netherlands.

Rather than wait for the recession to bite, I decided to anticipate it and brought forward plans I had been working on for some time. In the spring of 2007, I was approached by Lazards, the City bank, proposing a merger with Allied Carpets, my old competitor and still the second biggest floor covering retailer in the country. In 1999, Allied had been bought by a French company, Tapis Saint-Maclou, controlled by the Mulliez family, who had put it up for sale.

It was still a big business in the UK, with 1,600 staff and 220 stores, but it was a business in its death throes and I wasn't really interested.

However my interest was piqued by the wonderful freehold properties owned by its parent company across France, and I suggested to the Mulliez brothers that we should merge our two companies, lock, stock and barrel, creating the biggest carpet chain in Europe.

But, when I bounced the idea off my non-executive directors, I hit a blank wall. There was no appetite, with profits turning down and the share price well off the peak, to take on Allied and venture further into an uncertain European market. Someone tartly suggested we focus on our own problems and leave others to sort out theirs.

I had been expecting that, and it suited me just fine. For some time I had been working on a plan to bid for Carpetright, take it private, merge it with the French company and radically revamp it away from the public eye. We could take rafts of costs out of the enlarged group and negotiate much lower prices with the big Belgian manufacturers who dominated the European industry. We might float the company again on the other side of the recession, when our new £25 million IT system and a giant new warehouse at Purfleet would be fully in stream, but that could wait.

At the next board meeting in June 2008, I dropped my bombshell. I wanted to make an offer in my private capacity for the whole company, I announced. Would they give me the go-ahead to explore that possibility? There were some surprised faces in the room, but there was nothing they could do to stop me. They formed a committee of independent directors, chaired by the senior non-exec, Baroness (Sheila) Noakes, to handle the matter.

The baroness was a formidable lady with an impressive record who behaved impeccably, if a little formally, in the boardroom. She was a brilliant chartered accountant who was the first woman president of the Institute of Chartered Accountants. She had also done a successful stint as a manager in the NHS, and had served on the court of the Bank of England and the London Business School. I often met her in the House of Lords, where she was a shadow Treasury minister.

She was a stickler for corporate governance, which I'm the first to admit was one of my weaknesses, and she sometimes chaffed at my impatience and what she probably saw as a rather casual approach to what for her was a serious matter. She was right of course, but I hated the long committee meetings, preferring to discuss sales figures or expansion rather than remuneration policy or audit procedures. I suppose I was never really cut out to run a large, public company with all the regulations and red tape involved that, to my mind, got in the way of managing a business. I was always more at home visiting suppliers, renting properties, opening shops, talking to staff and customers and getting the feel for what was selling and what wasn't. But I accepted it had to be done and Baroness Noakes and the other non-execs kept us on the straight and narrow.

It was corporate governance, rigidly interpreted, that had caused me to lose two of my favourite and most supportive non-execs who I badly needed most at this moment. Baroness Judith Wilcox, who had a brilliant career in the food industry behind her, was forced to leave the board after a nine-year stint, the maximum recommended under the corporate governance code. Harry Djanogly had to go too for the same reason, depriving me of my two major supporters. If Judith and Harry had still been on the board in the summer of 2007, when I announced my intention to bid for the company, I think the others would have taken a more pragmatic and flexible approach and things might have worked out differently.

I worked very hard on putting that bid together. I started off with the advantage of owning 24 per cent of the company and, together with Martin's shares (873,000 of them), other family trusts and Harry's shareholding, I could muster nearly 30 per cent. There were two other major shareholders whose support I also sought: the Olayan Group, a Saudi pipeline company seeking to diversify its investments, owned 14 per cent, and Harris Associates, an American fund with no connection to me, had an 8 per cent holding.

The shares were just over £10 on 16 June 2007 when I announced my intention to make a bid and they immediately rocketed 314p to close that day at £13.40, a figure that lodged itself in the minds of the independent directors and became their target price. Looking over the edge at the recession I was now convinced was on the way (the official figures gave no hint of it yet, and the Brown government took no defensive action), I thought a more realistic price was about £10, but was prepared to go to £11.50, even if that was stretching it a bit. It put a value on the company of £780 million, which meant I would have to raise £550 million – which I was convinced I could find.

My timing, however, wasn't good. The storm clouds were now gathering across the Atlantic, where a full-scale banking crisis was about to break, eventually threatening the whole global financial system. Most of the big European banks had stopped lending with the exception of the two Scottish banks, RBS and HBOS, who were still competing with each other to provide loans for buy-outs or takeovers at a time when they should have been running for cover. County NatWest was part of RBS, which, under Fred 'the Shred' Goodwin, was in full flight in its quest to become the biggest bank in the world – which it achieved, briefly, in balance sheet terms at least, a year later. So, I started my journey there.

We had an overdraft facility with NatWest of £50 million, and RBS agreed to add a loan of £200 million to that and get HBOS to match it – which is when I met Peter Cummings, the head of corporate finance at Bank of Scotland, now part of HBOS. He had backed some of the most successful entrepreneurial deals of the day, including Philip Green's acquisition of BHS which made him a billionaire. Cummings would later achieve notoriety for the huge bets he took at the top of the cycle (which led to the bank losing over £40 billion), and at this stage was lending merrily away as if the boom would never end. After not much more than a cursory glance through my figures, he agreed to a loan of £250 million.

Carpetright shares had slipped back to £10.29 by the time I got my finances together early in September 2007 – just in time for the biggest financial crisis for eighty years to hit us. The storm broke on Friday 14 September 2007, the day before my 65th birthday, when Britain witnessed its first run on a bank in 140 years. At 7 o'clock that morning, queues began building outside the branches of Northern Rock and by nine they were stretching around the block. The news channels and newspapers picked it up and soon it was running on live TV around the world, fanning the flames. I was just putting the finishing touches to my deal and in the City that morning I could sense panic spreading through the financial community. Bank runs are scary things and even Gordon Brown later said it was the lowest moment of his entire time in No. 10. 'It was like a scene in a film or a text book, but not something I had ever expected to see in my lifetime or under our watch,' he said. To stem the panic and bring some stability back to the system which was close to a financial melt-down, the government stepped in to bail out Northern Rock and take it under state control, the first time that had happened since the Bank of England was nationalised in 1946.

The banking world was a different place after Northern Rock. The sub-prime crisis had arrived with a vengeance and most of the banks simply stopped lending altogether, even to each other. Liquidity completely dried up and HBOS began to lose some of the huge deposit base of the old Halifax building society. I fully expected Cummings to get cold feet and pull out, but he held his nerve and, after a wobble, carried on as if nothing had happened.

I presented my buy-out proposal to the Noakes sub-committee of the Carpetright board in late September 2007. I told them that the market was expecting us to make profits of between £62 and £65 million for the year to April 2008, which we were unlikely to hit in current trading conditions, and in the absence of a bid, the shares would probably be trading around 700–800p. But I was prepared to offer £11.50, a handsome premium on that.

That went down like a lead balloon. Baroness Noakes gave me a steely look and said the committee could not possibly recommend anything less than £13.40 to outside shareholders – and she refused to budge, even when I nudged my offer up to £12, which was the maximum I thought I could afford. I went back to the drawing board, did yet another roadshow with Martin and Ian Kenyon, determined to have one last try. But I could feel the financial atmosphere changing by the day and the rates and the conditions the banks were demanding were getting increasingly onerous. I didn't want to find myself in a Gulliver-like situation, owning a business with huge amounts of debt heading into a recession, and I was getting dangerously close to it. Alan Dickenson, our man from NatWest, certainly began to show some nervousness and I had great difficulty getting him to agree to remain in the deal.

By November 2007, I was all set to offer the baroness £12.50 a share when Alan Dickenson called me from Scotland to say that RBS was unhappy with its level of commitment to the deal and wanted to reduce it by £50 million to £200 million. I called Peter Cummings, who said he would not only fill the gap, he would cover the whole thing, cutting RBS out altogether.

But there were conditions. We would have to move our account from NatWest, where we had our overdraft facilities, to HBOS, and that could not be done overnight, and the interest rate would be higher. I still tried very hard to do it and almost brought it off, but when Cumming's superiors at HBOS eventually decided it was too big a loan to do in a recession, the deal was dead.

By that stage I was glad it was. If the Carpetright board committee had been more reasonable back in June 2007, I could have raised and paid £12 a share. But raising money in the post-Northern Rock world was almost impossible. Only banks as mad and crazily run as RBS and HBOS were prepared to do highly leveraged deals. And maybe only people as optimistic – or mad – as me were prepared to borrow.

As it turned out, RBS and HBOS both effectively went bust in September 2008, following the crash of Lehman Brothers. I survived and the biggest losers were Carpetright shareholders. By February 2008, the shares were 700p and by December, in the post-Lehman world, they were 311p. In September 2017 they were 190p and the market value had shrunk to £144 million.

*　　*　　*

The British economy was now deep into a recession which was much, much worse than anything I had known in my fifty years in business. Asked by an analyst to describe trading conditions in early 2008, I responded that they were 'bloody awful' – and they got worse. This recession, I told everyone, was going to be longer and deeper than anything since the 1930s, but I was confident we would get through it and emerge in better shape. And, my goodness, we worked hard at it. We were still cash generative and we went on investing in our stores, mopping up small chains that went bust, rationalising the property portfolio and expanding on the Continent, where the market was better.

We moved all our carpet cutting, distribution and our head office to Purfleet and closed four warehouses with substantial savings. The new £25 million warehouse facility, within sight of the QE2 Bridge on the M25, was even more efficient than Swanley and Rainham and chopped two days off our average delivery time. Against board opposition, I also made two acquisitions that year, Storey Carpets, with thirty stores in the north-east of England, and Carpetworld Manchester, which cost £33 million between them. Yet our net borrowings still came down from over £100 million to £57 million at the year end, mostly through the sale of excess properties and positive cash flow.

Somehow or other, we ended the 2007/8 financial year still in reasonable health, with profits, helped by property sales, marginally up at £62 million. But, against my better judgement, the board insisted on increasing the dividend by 2p to 52p. I thought that was a bad idea, but once again I was overruled. Some of the independent directors had come under attack from shareholders for rejecting my bid and felt the least they could do was give something back. It was not the right time to do it.

There were some lighter and more cheerful moments in this gloomy time. The first came in May 2008, when Bill Gates suddenly popped up to take a 4 per cent stake in Carpetright, through his Cascade Investment company. I never met him but his fund managers came and grilled me, clearly liked what they saw, and the next thing I knew they had invested nearly £16 million in the company. That, of course, was a mere fleabite compared to his fortune of $58 billion, or £29 billion at the going exchange rate, but it received a lot of publicity.

BILL GATES TAKES STAKE IN UK'S CARPETRIGHT

Daily Telegraph, *16 May 2008.*

One of the more pleasant events at this time was when I was chosen to represent Britain in the Ernst & Young World Entrepreneur of the Year Award. I have won a lot of awards in my life and I have a cupboard full of trophies, but this was special. I really didn't know anything about it until I was invited to Cambridge to compete in what was a sort of heat. I didn't win but I did well enough to get through to the UK finals, which were held in front of 1,100 people at the Grosvenor.

I won that and in June 2008, Pauline, Martin, his wife Zoe and my secretary Judy Willett came with me to Monte Carlo for the world finals, where we were put up in the opulent Hotel Hermitage, and I must say I had one of the most exhilarating weekends of my life. I had to give over forty TV interviews and appeared before a series of panels, and on the night before the finals I was told by Ernst & Young that I was one of the favourites to win.

But the next day I fluffed it. I answered all the questions perfectly until we got to the last one, which was really the easiest: 'If you win, what will you do with the award?' I was asked. I should have answered along the following lines, which would have been true: 'Give inspiration to a lot of young people,' but instead I went into a ramble about the need for more entrepreneurs and my own experiences, and I knew I had lost the interest of the judges. I felt very stupid afterwards, and Pauline and Martin, who were fantastic with me that weekend, had to work hard to pull me out of the doldrums.

*   *   *

Martin celebrated his 40th birthday on January 2008 and we gave him a big party but I was sad for him. The failure to take the company private had scuppered my plans to make him my successor, which had been a key part of my motivation in the last few years. He had worked in the business, with only a brief period off, for more than twenty years, and it was he who handled the move to the new warehouse in Purfleet, which was effectively his baby. In interviews and meetings, I had made no pretence about my preference to make him my successor as CEO, while I would stay on, for a few years at least, as chairman, but there was considerable opposition on the board to that. In an interview with *Retail Week*, I said that there were clear differences between father and son but we also complemented each other: 'We're both thinkers but we're from different generations. I don't use a Blackberry or the internet. But we're good for one another.'

In an attempt to explain to the board what was happening in our industry, Martin presented a paper analysing what he called 'the social change', pointing to the boom in sales of flat screen TVs, iPads and smartphones, which matched the decline in sales of carpets. He also pointed out that a lot of modern homes had been designed to have 'that minimalist look', which didn't necessarily include carpets, and so we should move more into vinyl and wooden floors. He also insisted we invest heavily in the internet, well ahead of the sector. But, despite all his efforts, footfall in our stores went on dropping.

In the outside world, there was now nothing but gloom. The Lehman crash in September 2008, almost exactly a year after the Northern Rock run, caused business to fall off a cliff and house prices to collapse. I later reckoned the carpet market in Britain fell by 25 per cent in a year and the impact on our margins was horrible.

There was no way we could come through that unscathed and I had nothing good to say to the market through most of 2009, the worst of the recession. We were still profitable, but only just – that year our sales fell by 7.4 per cent, dropping back below £500 million, but our profits fell by three-quarters to £17 million. To preserve cash, we cut the dividend to just 8p a share, or by 85 per cent. I rued the day I had been talked into increasing it.

An indication of just how bad things were came in August 2009, when its French owners threw in the towel and put Allied Carpets into liquidation. It had been the giant of the industry when I started, a whale to my minnow, and now it was bust, its stores up for sale. My mood by that stage was such that I didn't even bid for them – my board probably wouldn't have let me anyway. But, again, I fumed over what might have been: if I could have taken Carpetright private and injected Allied into it, I could have made huge savings, grown the business across Europe, and been in much better shape to get through this seemingly never-ending recession.

It was around this time that Baroness Noakes decided to stage a coup. One day she asked to see me and told me that the non-executives had met the previous day and had taken a decision. I could stay on as non-executive chairman but they wanted to replace me with a new CEO and the search was already on. Martin would not even be considered for the job.

To say I was furious would be an understatement and I refused to accept it. I called the four biggest shareholders together, explained the situation, and within a few days the baroness received a phone call to say that if she wanted a showdown, shareholders representing more than 60 per cent of the company would support me, not her.

She backed down, but from then on the Carpetright boardroom was not a happy place.

CHAPTER 30

'EDUCATION, EDUCATION, EDUCATION'

In October 1999, nearly a decade after the Harris CTC Crystal Palace opened, I got a call from Andrew Adonis at 10 Downing Street. I had never met him, but knew of him. He was one of the powers behind the New Labour government and an influential member of Tony Blair's Policy Unit in No. 10, where he had special responsibility for education policy.

Could he come down and see my Crystal Palace school? he asked. He said he had heard lots of very good things about us and would like to see it for himself. I told him I would be very happy to show him around and that he could meet and talk to anyone he wished.

Without exception, each of the fifteen CTCs that had opened by 1991 (none had opened since) were in the top fifty in the country in terms of contextual value added, and were recording an average pass rate of 72.4 per cent, well above the national level. Our Crystal Palace school was recording over 80 per cent and was still climbing, but with the Conservatives now out of power and the CTCs as controversial as ever with the (mostly Labour-controlled) London local authorities and teaching unions, I was not expecting much enthusiasm from a new Labour government. I could not have been more wrong.

In 1996, a year before the election, Tony Blair defined his three priorities as 'education, education, education'. In response, John Major quipped that he had the same priorities – 'but not necessarily in the same order'. After the election, Blair made David Blunkett Education Secretary, an inspired choice in my view, and gave Adonis the task of developing a detailed policy for reforming what was universally acknowledged as Britain's 'failing' comprehensive school system. However, as Blair was forced to tackle more immediately pressing issues and because of the growing rift with his Chancellor Gordon Brown, education slipped down the priority list and it took another two years for Adonis to discover the Harris CTC in Crystal Palace.

I made sure I was there to meet him and show him around. I was very proud of the school, in which by that stage about £10 million had been invested, including a couple of million from me and contributions from David and Hannah Lewis, for new buildings, sports facilities, a language centre, a dyslexia unit and new classrooms. We were also achieving outstanding results, and that year we attracted more applicants for every place than ever before. But, like all the CTCs, we remained an outcast in state school circles.

Adonis was a bit wary of me because of my well-known association with the Conservative Party, but he was clearly impressed by what we had done at the old Sylvan school. He later wrote that when he asked me why I did it, I replied that the school was 'one of the most important things in my life'. He seemed surprised – I guess he didn't expect that of a loyal Thatcherite and businessman.

He was particularly keen to know whether I could take on more failing schools and if the same formula would work across what he called a 'chain' of schools in south London, based on the proven model of Crystal Palace. He told me that Thomas Telford, the Midlands CTC that was sponsored by the Mercers Company (a rich City guild that also sponsored two of London's historic public schools, St Paul's Boys and St Paul's Girls), was keen to roll out its model across the West Midlands. Under its visionary headmaster Sir Kevin Satchwell, Telford was recording a points score of over 90 per cent – the equivalent of nearly twelve A* grade passes – beating many grammar schools, and most of the public schools, in the country. Peter Vardy, the Sunderland-based motor dealer who sponsored Emmanuel College in Gateshead, also wanted to expand in the north-east. We were the top three performing schools of the fifteen CTCs, which is why he came to us first.

Peter Vardy, it turned out, was an old friend of Tony Blair – they had been at the Chorister School Durham together – and Blair knew all about Emmanuel CTC, which was attracting entrants from his neighbouring Sedgefield constituency. Adonis later revealed that Blair called him on his mobile when he was in Gateshead attending 'an inspirational session with a group of sixth-formers telling me about the brilliance of their school and their ambitions to get on'. Adonis told Blair this was the kind of school the Labour government should use as its model and the Prime Minister replied: 'OK, let's work out how to go for it.' I was his next port of call.

Adonis was an impressively bright and energetic young man (he was thirty-six at the time), who I later discovered came from an un-derprivileged Greek Cypriot background. He had been abandoned by his mother as a baby, taken into care when he was two and brought up in various state institutions, where, contrary to what you might expect from all the various horror stories, he had a relatively happy childhood and received a good education. He got a First at Oxford where he was briefly an academic before becoming a journalist on the *Financial Times* and, later, *The Observer*, where he wrote largely about education.

Over a cup of tea after our tour, he told me that from what he had seen of the three CTCs he had visited – and he planned to see the other twelve, which he did – he thought this was 'the model of future schooling'. He was impressed with the commitment of the sponsors who not only offered inspiration but stability. They were not, he said, 'here today, gone tomorrow, like all too many local authority chief ed-ucation officers. I can see you have made a long-term and passionate commitment to this school.'

He reported this back to Blunkett, who was also being advised by my old friend Cyril Taylor who had moved seamlessly from working for the Conservative government (unpaid) to advising Labour (he advised eleven Secretaries of State in total, surviving well into Cameron's time). Adonis's recommendation was a simple but hugely ambitious one: take all of Britain's failing schools out of the control of the local authorities and give them to private sector sponsors to manage, with their own independent boards of governors and the power to appoint their own heads and staff. They would in effect be very similar to CTCs but no Labour government would dare call them that – that was a Tory term, anathema to the trade unions. So, he decided to use the more acceptable and neutral title 'academy'. The big difference in his proposal was that, whereas Ken Baker had conceived CTCs as 'the harbinger of a new form of technical college', with a target of just 100, Adonis's ambitions went much further. He wanted them to replace the standard state secondary schools with academies, providing a general rather than a more technical education – which we were doing anyway – for all.

'If fifteen independent state schools could be so successful in this way,' he proposed to Blair and Blunkett, 'why not, in the right conditions, 150 or 1,500?'

Blunkett embraced the concept enthusiastically and in March 2000 he and Blair announced that, after the next election, which they looked certain to win, a Labour government would introduce City Academies, a 'new type of school designed to improve life standards in deprived areas', directly modelled, as they privately acknowledged, on the City Technology College. Cyril Taylor was working hard behind the scenes and helped do the modelling, remarking in his usual modest way that 'its essence [the school model] remained as I had envisaged it in 1992'. He was right – it was basically his idea, although it had come a long way since then.

*   *   *

I met Tony Blair for the first time in October 2000, when we were both guests at Margaret Thatcher's 75th birthday party. It was a very lavish affair with the Queen and Prince Philip in attendance as well as John Major, former Cabinet ministers and dignitaries from all over the world. As she often did, Mrs Thatcher put me on her table, although poor Pauline had to sit at a table miles away – Mrs T didn't much care for other women. Over dinner, Blair, sitting opposite me, quizzed me about my Crystal Palace school, asking me what in particular made it work so well and whether it could be replicated. He clearly liked the idea of sponsorship from the private sector and the involvement of business, and said he would like to talk to me again about it. His office would be in touch.

A few weeks later, Adonis called to invite me to a meeting in No. 10, the first time I had been there since John Major's time. Blair was very courteous, telling me how much he admired what I had done at my school, which Adonis was full of praise for. He had, he said, a major problem with education in London particularly, which was well behind the national average, and I seemed to have found a way to unlock it.

'Will you open some new schools for me, if we help you?' he asked me.

I answered yes, I would. But when he asked if I would call them academies, I said no, I preferred City Technology Colleges, which is what we were known as. He persevered – and he could be very charming and persuasive – suggesting that I might take on some failing schools in south London and manage them under the new academy formula. I said I would think that over, discuss it with Cyril Taylor and Andrew Adonis and see how it might be made to work. In fact, I had no ideological problem with his concept of 'academies' at all – I just wanted to get my head around it.

As it happened, I had been thinking about expanding on the basis that, if we had more schools, I could set up a central organisation that would share costs, expertise and promote teachers from within. The catalyst for me was the arrival in my life of Dan Moynihan, whom I had lured away from a successful school in the East End of London to take over Harris Crystal Palace when the previous principal retired. It was one of the best decisions I ever made. Dan had already been receiving attention from the media and education officials for the improvements he had made at his old school, which Tony Blair had personally visited. When I interviewed him and asked him to tell me about himself, he told me he was from a 'disadvantaged Irish immigrant background' and went to school in Kilburn, one of the poorest areas of north London in those days where the Irish 'navvies' mostly lived. Its intake was a mixture of Irish immigrant and African and Caribbean families and the teaching, he said, 'was rubbish and the discipline was rubbish too.'

He became head boy, where his main job was to patrol the door to the staffroom so teachers were not disturbed by punch-ups in the playground. 'It was an early lesson in how not to run a school.' From this unlikely background, he got to university, studied economics at UCL and then joined the accountants Price Waterhouse. Accountancy, however, was not for him. 'I wanted to do something for the type of kid I was,' he said. He became a teacher, then a brilliant headmaster – and then I hired him to come to Crystal Palace.

Our school was doing very well already but I told him if he could take it from 'Good' to 'Outstanding' I would find him the resources to take on more schools and he would run them for me – although, for the moment at least, he would still have to double-up as a headmaster. I reasoned that if I could create a successful chain of shops I could also put together a chain of schools, replicating the formula and techniques that had made Crystal Palace such a success, with a strong central management controlling the whole operation. It had never been done before, but I could see no reason why it shouldn't work. I was ready when Tony Blair gave me the resources to do it.

Labour was duly re-elected in 2001 with another landslide (a majority of 166 seats) and this time around, against opposition from Gordon

Brown, Blair immediately put his plans for school reform in motion. My part in it began when Andrew Adonis asked me to take on one of south London's most notorious gangland schools, Warwick Park in Peckham, and turn it into an academy. This was where I was brought up, so I took it on and the Southwark council, instead of opposing me, was delighted to get rid of it. That should have made me suspicious of the school, which was really awful. Even walking across the play-ground made me feel threatened, and its academic record was worse that Sylvan's when I first took it on.

I was already trying to help Peckham in other ways and I contrib-uted to the cost of transforming a run-down youth centre into the Damilola Sports Centre in honour of Damilola Taylor, a ten-year-old boy who was killed on his way to Peckham Library in 2000. It was an event which shocked the nation, and me in particular as Damilola was found bleeding to death in a stairwell in one of the blocks of flats that had been built on the site of my nan's house, attacked by a couple of boys not much older than him. He had been stabbed in the leg with a broken bottle, just months after moving to Britain from Nigeria, and was captured on CCTV staggering towards shelter in the stairwell in the grim block of flats where he bled to death in thirty minutes. It took three trials before the perpetrators, two brothers called Preddie, were convicted of manslaughter. The BBC later made a heart-breaking documentary about it and the anguish of his parents.

I asked Tony Blair to come down and open the centre – which he did, making a fine speech in which he acknowledged my support.

We opened the Harris Academy in Peckham, close to the scene of the crime, in 2003 to a storm of local opposition and protest that almost overwhelmed us. It seemed extraordinary that anyone would want to keep a school that was failing so badly, but even the local newspapers, worked up by the local politicians, were against us. One carried the wonderful headline: 'Campaigners: Hands off our failing school'. No one seemed to notice the irony.

But with Dan Moynihan in overall charge of the central federation, we turned it round in a few short years and got the pass rate up from under 10 per cent to above 50 per cent, with students making great academic progress. Today, the Harris Academy in Peckham is housed in modern, purpose-built premises, has been designated as one of the most successful in the country and is rated by Ofsted as 'Good'; student progress is regularly in the top 10 per cent nationally. That's a huge turnaround, particularly when you consider that over 90 per cent of its pupils come from deprived backgrounds not that different to Damilola's and his killers. A growing proportion now go on to university, unheard of in the previous school where most of the kids left at fifteen for goodness knows what kind of futures.

After Peckham, they kept coming at us. Every time Adonis had a problem school in our area he would call me and say, we have this failing school in South Norwood or Merton or somewhere else, would you be the sponsor? We took all of them on, applied the same formula and every single school responded. Within two years, none of them were failing and many of them were getting into the 'Good' and, later, 'Outstanding' categories.

But it wasn't all easy. Many new schools involved full-on battles with unions, teachers and parents and I seemed to spend many evenings, when I should have been at home with my family, being shouted at and abused at public meetings. There was a group calling itself the Anti-Academies Alliance, which worked up the teachers, some of the left-wing newspapers and the local authorities, accused us of creating 'exam factories' and undermining the whole state education system. Dan always stood beside me and we endured a lot of personal insults together over the years.

When we were given the Merton school, there was a demonstration outside the local Carpetright shop on a busy Saturday, but I got word of it the night before and called the staff to warn them to be ready. By the time Dan and I turned up there were several hundred protesters with banners and placards, accusing me of sacking staff at the store to raise money for the school – or it might have been the other way around, I can't remember now. I'm not sure how much carpet we sold that day, but the staff, all of whom supported the school, were completely unperturbed by it.

Merton's pass rate, before we reopened it as an academy in September 2006, was 20 per cent, which meant that the other 80 per cent were failing to achieve the minimum required to progress on up the ladder or get a job. We took it to 'Outstanding' in record time, with a pass rate that soared into the sixties and then the seventies. We built a new sixth form block and high-quality classrooms and it now offers specialisms in a wide variety of subjects that had never been taught there before, including enterprise for future entrepreneurs. It has extensive playing fields and sports facilities, mostly paid for by the state but with a contribution from me, none of which existed before we became involved. We now have over 1,750 students at the school compared to 750 when we took it over. Most importantly, parents now have faith in us, which took some years to engender – but it's been worth the journey.

Merton took us up to six schools and it was clear that Dan could no longer continue as a head teacher if we were to continue growing. So, I appointed him as the first chief executive of the Harris Federation and encouraged him to build a professional organisation with qualified staff around him, capable of taking on even more schools and improving those we already had. Dan formed a team of specialist teachers (we now have over sixty of them), a sort of task force, to go into our schools, mentor the younger teachers and work with them, often one-on-one, to improve their skills and generally help the principal and staff to raise the whole educational level. We also fast-tracked a pool of potential head teachers ready to take on new schools or replace the older ones, and today more than a third of our principals are home-grown. Dan worked really hard to keep improving results, developing standard systems for discipline, phonics, reading, numeracy and for tracking pupil progress in every school. Crystal Palace remained the template and we applied it to every school we took on, all the time improving and developing it. I think it was Dan who created the phrase 'Harris in a Box' to describe the formula we applied to new schools. It couldn't be too rigidly applied of course, because schools differed from area to area, but the principles – or 'Harris DNA' as Dan calls it – were applied universally.

After Merton, and some of the other early turnarounds, we got a reputation for being a robust sponsor, prepared to tackle failed schools, hostile unions and reluctant local authorities and unafraid of the hard-left lobby groups that turned up at every meeting to heckle and boo. Our reward was to be given the worst schools in London, which probably meant in Britain: political minefields with appalling standards, depressed teachers, entrenched opponents on all sides and not much friendly support. The Labour government kept asking us to do more, and we did: we took on Alwyn Girls School in Bermondsey and two East Dulwich schools, one for boys and one for girls, each with nearly 1,000 pupils, and later moved into Bexley, Bromley, Haringey, Newham, Sutton, Thurrock and Westminster.

In 2008, Adonis was given a peerage and promoted to the Cabinet to take charge of transport, by which stage 133 academies had opened across the country, with another 200 in the pipeline. In his last interview with the *Financial Times*, he was very generous in his comments about me:

'Lord Harris now has an incredibly strong brand in south London, and I now have local authorities coming to me saying that they want a Harris academy. Not saying they want an academy – saying they want a *Harris* academy.'

Several times in that interview he referred to the Crystal Palace school, and one remark he made is worth quoting in full:

Harris has an outstanding academic track record, developing from the City Technology College in Crystal Palace, which is one of the most successful state schools in the country both by results and in terms of

value added in a deprived area. Its record of turning around underper-
forming schools and making them schools of choice in their locality
with dramatically improving results is outstanding.

In Dan Moynihan, Adonis added, we had 'one of the most effective
school leaders in the country'.

Adonis was a brilliant minister to deal with and I was sorry to see
him go. Blunkett had moved on too, succeeded first by Estelle Morris
as Secretary of State, followed by Charles Clarke and, finally, in the
dying days of the Brown government, we got Ed Balls for a brief spell.
None of them showed the same interest in the academy programme
and Gordon Brown saw us as very much a Blairite initiative, to be
viewed with suspicion. As Adonis, who didn't much care for Brown,
later wrote: 'Inadequate leadership, drive and support for academies
within the Whitehall machine dogged the academies programme
throughout its life.' In thirteen years of Labour government there were
six Secretaries of State, three permanent secretaries and four direc-
tors-general in charge of the schools' directorate. And there were ten
education department officials with responsibility for the academies
programme during its first eight years.

In all, I've dealt with fifteen secretaries of state in twenty-seven years
with continually changing shifts in attitudes to academies, and we've
learned to tread warily and plough our own furrow, confident that we
are going in the right direction with a set of principles and a formula
that produces the right results. By contrast, with the fickle nature of
government, we have had the same sponsor – me – from the beginning, one chief executive since 2002, and many of our principals and
senior teachers have been with us for most of their careers. Children
spend up to fifteen years at school and deserve a bit of stability – which
governments don't provide.

CHAPTER 31

TOTTENHAM BURNS

In 2010, Labour finally departed and we got a coalition government under David Cameron, who appointed Michael Gove, a former *Times* journalist, as his Education Secretary. It was another inspired choice. Gove proved to be a genuinely reforming and intelligent minister who embraced the academy principle from the moment he arrived and improved on the work already done by Ken Baker, David Blunkett and Andrew Adonis. I worked with him better than any other minister, with the possible exception of Adonis.

We needed his support badly at that particular moment because we were going through a bit of a revolution ourselves. Up to that point, all our schools were secondaries, and we were becoming seriously concerned by the number of primary school children we were taking on who couldn't read or write. However good our secondary schools were, there was a limit to the extent we could pick up the pieces – as the saying goes, 'kids can't read to learn if they haven't learned to read'.

One day, after a particularly bad intake, I said to Dan Moynihan: 'We're going to have to get to them earlier' – which meant primary level. Gove immediately grasped the importance of what we were proposing and, with his backing, we started taking on primary schools, going right down to the age of three. As with the secondaries, they were mostly in tough, disadvantaged areas of south London, including Peckham, some of the most socially deprived in the country.

Little did I know what I was walking into. If the protests had been rough outside the secondaries, they were mild in comparison to what we faced now. We had demonstration after demonstration, which sometimes became really nasty and went on for years, long after we had turned the schools around. I remember a protest where one of the parents was a senior member of a public sector trade union and they had the kids, in their uniforms, parading outside wearing Michael Gove masks and shouting abuse at us.

We were about a year into our new programme when an event occurred that highlighted for me the importance of what we were trying to do. On the evening of 6 August 2011, I began getting messages that our Carpetright store in Tottenham, which we had only recently renovated and reopened, had been set ablaze by rioters who were rampaging through the streets. I switched on the TV and there it was, our lovely store on the corner of Tottenham High Road and Foster Road, burning like a torch with hundreds of police on the streets fighting mobs that were clearly out of control.

Even as I watched, horrified by what I was seeing, the disorder was spreading across London and into other cities with astonishing speed, and eventually more than 15,000 rioters were rampaging through the streets, 4,000 of whom were arrested. In London alone, 3,800 shops were damaged and five people died.

The original cause of it all was later identified as the police killing of a local man, Mark Duggan, who was shot during an attempt to arrest him. Duggan was black, the Metropolitan Police Force was predominantly white, and racial tensions ran high in Tottenham. In this case, the riots probably started off as a racial protest but within hours an opportunistic thuggish element took advantage of the chaos and went on a looting spree. Many of the rioters didn't even know what they were rioting about and simply joined in the fun, kicking in a Dixons window just for the hell of it and carrying off a flat screen TV.

The electrical stores and clothes shops were the worst hit and there was footage of rioters going home to fetch their cars so they could carry away their booty. There wasn't much to take from our stores, which contained nothing more than samples and hollow cardboard tubes wrapped in carpet, but twenty-two of them were damaged that night.

My immediate concern was for the safety of our staff in Tottenham, but fortunately the riots started in the evening after the shop had closed and the staff had gone home. However, there were people living in the flats above the store who, even if they got out alive, were going to be homeless. I heard one of them on the radio saying they had only the nightclothes they were wearing and I saw children with no homes. It was, in some ways, a smaller version of the Grenfell Tower disaster in June 2017, except this fire was started deliberately.

Although the people living in the flats were not legally my problem, I wanted to help them, and early on Monday I drove up to Tottenham to see what I could do. The store was a disaster, a blackened, burnt-out, twisted shell, still smouldering, everything destroyed. The flats above it were owned by a finance company and let by a housing association, and I extracted a promise from them that no one would be worse off if they had to rent other accommodation. I met some of the occupants – or ex-occupants as they were now – and offered to buy clothes for them and find whatever else they needed to get by. I even offered to carpet their flats if they could be renovated, although goodness knows when that would be (the Carpetright shop reopened in 2014, three years after the riots, but the flats took much longer).

That day I also checked on my schools to see if any our kids had been involved in the riots. Thank goodness, they hadn't been – which bore out another principle of mine. Most of those arrested and charged turned out to be unemployed or underemployed young men with little prospects of improving themselves and nothing better to do than join in the fun. The students in the Harris academies were motivated, responsible and busy and didn't have the time or inclination to riot – and that included our graduates.

I have always believed that people don't riot without a reason and there were plenty of reasons why it should have started in Tottenham.

In 1985, the Broadwater Farm estate was the centre of the most horrifying riots, which seriously rattled Mrs Thatcher and the Conservative
government (and led, as I have described, indirectly to the whole CTC/
academies initiative), and despite large amounts of money spent on
improvements, nothing much had changed. Tottenham had some of
the worst schools and the highest unemployment level in London, and
the Northumberland Park ward, where the rioting began, was among
the bottom 5 per cent of the most deprived areas in the country. Housing was – and still is – overcrowded, with illegal landlords packing
families into tiny homes. Gang conflicts were common and I was told
that young men, who should still have been at school, would not even
turn up for job interviews in territories controlled by their rival gangs.

I found the riots sad and pointless. It had damaged our shops and
other businesses around us but it was even tougher for small local retailers who had done nothing wrong. Riots, like bank runs, shouldn't
happen in a modern economy and I couldn't rightly say whether it was
the police's fault or the rioters' fault that this started, but one thing was
for sure – it wasn't good for any of us.

In September 2011, a month after the riots, Michael Gove gave a
speech in which he referred to the torching of our Tottenham store as
'an act of nihilistic destruction' and contrasted it with what the Harris
Federation was doing for education.

> The buildings which tell the real story of what London's young people
> are like, and are capable of, are the academies Phil runs which turn out
> hundreds of brilliant, talented, wholly admirable young men and women
> every summer … And we have to make sure that the future for our young
> people is shaped by the values which have made the Harris academies
> such a success, not the values which ran riot on our streets this summer.

The riots brought back a memory to me of a troubled Peckham teenager I used to see at one of our schools. I saw him every couple of

weeks and took him to watch Arsenal at Highbury. But that boy went on to commit a grisly murder. He was a different person with me – he wasn't a bad boy and could have come good if he'd had a chance. I thought about that boy when I watched the rioters.

I don't think they were bad either: just bored and frustrated. It made me even more determined to give our kids a better start in life.

* * *

After the Tottenham riots, Gove asked me to take over the infamous Downhills Primary School in Haringey, north London, not far from where the trouble started. This was a seriously failing school, which, following an inspection ordered by Gove, was placed in special measures by Ofsted in February 2012, resulting in the resignation of its head teacher and the sacking of the board of governors. Against fierce opposition from the teachers and some of the parents, Gove appointed a five-member board, which included two Harris appointees, Dan Moynihan and Robin Bosher, and we took over the management of the school, setting off the biggest storm of protest we had yet encountered – or indeed, were ever to encounter. Professional protesters appeared from all over the place, inflaming the already angry teachers, who in turn whipped up the parents.

Opposition to the Harris presence at the Downhills school, or Harris Primary Academy Philip Lane as we renamed it, went on long after the new school opened and even after it was judged, in only its second year, to have improved from 'special measures' to 'Good' by Ofsted. Graffiti was sprayed on the walls and a ceramic plaque, mourning the death of the previous failing school, mysteriously appeared overnight, bolted to the wall. The caretaker had to chisel it off in the morning, but another one replaced it a few nights later. After one particularly vitriolic attack, Dan issued a statement saying that the school was 'finally giving its children the quality of education they had been denied for far too long under the predecessor school'. At the end of the day, that's all that matters.

We eventually won through, and in 2014, two years after we got control, the number of eleven-year-olds in the school reaching the required reading standard rose sharply, as did the maths pass rates. I don't know what happened to those hostile teachers, but to my knowledge none of them has ever acknowledged what has been achieved since they departed in such high dudgeon. Michael Gove, rightly, has still not forgiven them. In a speech in 2014, he asked:

> Have we had a sorry from those who stood in the way of these children being saved? Or even a wry head scratch from the Labour Party as it finds that a millionaire Conservative is more progressive and practical than its own leaders? All one hears is the silence of consciences unexamined.

In Tottenham today we have an 'all-through' 3–18 school (primary-plus-secondary) rated as 'Outstanding' by an Ofsted report in 2017. Given the intake and the opposition we have had to deal with, that is truly remarkable.

In all, we now have eighteen Harris primaries, each teaching about 600 kids. Three of them are in the top 3 per cent in the country and four are rated 'Outstanding'. Before we became involved, some of these were among the worst-performing schools in Britain. We now reckon on average we improve a child's educational levels by one-and-a-half terms' progress compared to other state primary schools.

*   *   *

It's not all hard work – I've had some moments of sheer delight too. I love nothing more than walking into one of the schools unannounced to be greeted by the kids running up to tell me breathlessly about their latest adventures and achievements. There is so much talent, energy and enthusiasm in these young people that it really lifts my spirits and fills me with hope for the future. One day, not very far from now, some of these young kids from Merton or Norwood or even Peckham – particularly Peckham – will be running our biggest institutions and maybe, one day, even the government.

I particularly love it when our schools produce serious achievers, as they have done. One of them is Louisa Johnson, who was a student at our Chafford Hundred school in Thurrock. She was the youngest winner of *X-Factor* in 2015 when she was only seventeen, and Simon Cowell told her: 'Louisa, what is incredible is that you have no idea how talented you are. We have witnessed the birth of a star.' It's a real inspiration for all our kids when someone like that strikes it big, in whatever field.

Our biggest star yet is probably Stormzy, or Michael Omari as I knew him, now a world-famous figure who appears all the time in the media, and in the summer of 2017 commanded an eight-page profile in GQ magazine. I call him a 'rapper', which is a form of music I can just about understand, but I'm told he's not: he's a 'grime MC', which means the master of ceremonies who holds a room together while performing music which is a mixture of raga, hip hop and rap. I've never seen it but apparently it emerged in London in the early 2000s and Stormzy is the leader of the new pack.

He seems to have strong political views too, although they are not mine. He was one of the founder members of a group calling itself 'Grime for Corbyn' and did an interview with *The Guardian* in which he declared the Leader of the Opposition to be 'My man, Jeremy!'. Everyone to their views.

I remember Stormzy very well from school where he stood out from all the others, not least because he was huge even as a teenager. He was a clever boy but naughty, always in trouble with his teachers at Harris Academy South Norwood, 'a little poet and a little terrorist' as he described himself in a recent profile. His English was fantastic and from the age of eleven he was writing in verse, but infuriated the teachers with his non-stop rap singing, and they found him a disruptive influence on the other kids. When the headmaster, who knew I liked him, asked me to have a 'straightening out' talk with him, I took him around the stores once and probably to Arsenal and I told him his school believed he was easily good enough to get into Oxford or Cambridge – which he was. But he told me he 'wasn't feeling this education thing' and eventually the teachers, having tried everything to tame this wild, talented spirit, reluctantly had to suspend him for a period.

He grew into a tall, good-looking boy who took on the name 'Stormzy' because, he said, 'storms are powerful'. But he quit school in the middle of his AS exams and moved up north, where he took some menial jobs while continuing writing his poetry. He clearly retained good memories of the school – or of me – because a few years later he sent me a lovely poem that revealed a remarkably profound and mature mind. It ended with the lines:

I see the joy. The bliss that can only be
conjured by that of the fortitude of
enlightenment.
I feel the spirit which is Harris Academy.

It is signed 'Michael Omari June 2009'.

No one had ever written a poem about a Harris academy before, particularly about South Norwood, which is one of our less romantic establishments. And quite possibly no one ever will again.

I had the poem framed and put on my office wall. The next thing I knew everyone was talking about this new rap star called 'Stormzy', which meant nothing to me until one day I saw giant posters across London advertising what looked like a pop star. I recognised him as the Michael Omari I had known as a schoolboy. He's now huge, rapping

– or 'griming', I'm not sure which – all across the world, mobbed by his millions of fans and earning a fortune. He released an album, *Gang Signs & Prayer*, in February 2017, which became number one on the UK Albums Chart.

**Sensations of success at
Harris South Norwood**

The tattered doors of a previous legacy closed,
only for the firm roots of a new innovation to be
embedded and sown.
The aspiring passion to educate and teach,
the flame which enlightens knowledge-seeking
souls,
the unyielding whisk which reforms rebels and
directs the stray,
the buoyant prospect which is Harris Academy.
I speak the wisdom which I have heard from the
mouths of scholars,
I taste the only flavour that has bared my
tongue: the taste of victory and perseverance,
I hear the echoes of debate and discussion that
bellow through the corridors of this
establishment,
I see the joy. The bliss which can only be
conjured by that of the fortitude of
enlightenment.
I feel the spirit which is Harris Academy.

Michael Omari June 2009

Tribute from the rap star, Stormzy.

He and Louisa are the best known of the many successful youngsters we have produced, often from schools where previously there had been gang violence, murders, rapes and goodness knows what else. By providing great schools we can bring hope and the prospect of transformation to many disadvantaged children. As with Stormzy, we do our best to give all our kids a better chance in life.

Sometimes we can do something really special for the kids. In 2016 my friend Lord Jeffrey Sterling arranged for some of our children, none of whom had ever rowed a boat before, to take part in the Gloriana Achievers Day on the Thames. The two Harris Federation academies with the most improved results over the previous academic year (Chobham Academy and Harris Academy Chafford Hundred) each sent forty students to learn to row and then compete for the ultimate prize of crewing Gloriana the Queen's Bowbarge, a beautiful vessel conceived and commissioned by Jeffrey for the Queen's Diamond Jubilee. Jeffrey later told me that his day was made when he overheard one of our students, a towering lad of over six feet, come ashore and remark in awed tones: 'Just think: I just sat in the same seat as the Queen.'

CHAPTER 32

STRIKING GOLD

For years after the Barcelona Olympics and the shabby treatment of David Broome I was basically out of international showjumping. But I loved the sport and when Pauline and I discovered that our great friends, Graham and Pauline Kirkham, were also keen on it, we decided to get back into it and create a new stable that would be owned jointly by the two Paulines. One of the first horses we acquired had such an ugly and unmemorable name that the grooms started calling him 'Sailor' – from which it was a very short step to 'Hello Sailor'. And so, the Hello Stables came into existence and all our horses had the 'Hello' prefix after that.

Despite my Barcelona experience, I had never given up my ambition to win an Olympic gold medal, and was only interested in horses that had a chance of achieving it. I had travelled to the Olympics in Seoul and Barcelona just to see my horses jump but in 2012 the games were on my doorstep, the East End of London, and work on the new stadium, velodrome and all the other facilities was well advanced. The equestrian events were to be held in Greenwich Park, home territory for me, where a magnificent 25,000-seater stadium was already taking shape. What a place that would be to win an Olympic gold.

Britain had still not won gold in an Olympic showjumping event since Harry Llewellyn on Foxhunter in Helsinki, sixty years earlier, and I was determined to do better than that on our home turf. Hello Sailor, ridden by Tina Fletcher, had made it into the British team in 2010 and I had high hopes she would make it all the way to the

Olympic team, and Hello Ursula was coming along nicely, although not yet ready. Early in 2007, I began thinking about adding another string to our bow.

Graham Kirkham and I were both working members of the House of Lords and often had dinner there when the house was in session, where we discussed everything from party politics to retailing – and horses. He is a Yorkshireman, the adopted son of a miner, and left school at sixteen with no qualifications to work as a croupier and a carpet fitter, not that dissimilar to my background. We shared a wide range of interests: he was a big donor to the Conservative Party and, as I've said, succeeded me as treasurer. He was also one of the most gifted retailers of my lifetime, who found his niche as a furniture salesman. In 1969, he and Pauline set up Northern Upholstery, which became the furniture chain DFS, in a disused Yorkshire billiard hall with £100 capital. He floated it on the stock market in 1993, the same year I listed Carpetright, which was roughly the same size.

In 2004, he did what I wanted to do with Carpetright a few years later and took the company private in a £507 million deal, later selling it on again at a handsome profit. However well-off he became, he never lost either his Yorkshire accent or his values, which he described as 'being down to earth, a very strong work ethic and loyalty, and knowing the value of money'.

He and Pauline are a lovely couple and we often get together as a foursome. One evening, in the autumn of 2011, the four of us had a long discussion about the Olympics and our prospects of winning that elusive gold, which I didn't think we would do with our existing horses, good though they were. David Broome had talked to me about buying a horse for a promising young (he was twenty-six) rider from Scotland, Scott Brash, whom he wanted me to meet and whom I'd watched on TV several times. He was the top-rated showjumper in Scotland, had first represented Great Britain the previous year (2010), and was now ranked number four overall in the country. David reckoned he was better than that: maybe the best rider in Britain after Nick Skelton, who was more than twice his age. At the end of the evening we all agreed that I would call David and see if Brash would ride for us. We still needed the right horse for him, but finding the rider would at least be a start.

We were leaving it desperately late if we were to have any chance of a medal. It was now October and the equestrian transfer deadline, allowing a horse to represent Britain under the international rules, was 31 December 2011, which gave us no time at all. It usually takes several years to train a horse to Olympic standards and you can't just go out and buy one off the shelf. Top riders also need time to bond with their horses and they work to a carefully prepared plan of training and performances over several seasons to peak at the time of the games. We couldn't do that.

The next day I called David and asked him to arrange for me to meet Brash as soon as possible. 'And I want you to find him a horse, which is going to win the gold for us,' I added. David said that was not going to be so easy but he was working on it. He called back to say he had spoken to Brash, who already had a 'trusty old campaigner' called Intertoy Z that he was thinking of entering in the Olympics, but was happy to ride for us. 'It will be a miracle if we find the right horse for him though at this late stage,' David added gloomily.

But miracles do happen. A few days later, David called me in great excitement. There was a showjumper for sale in Germany that had actually been in training for the London Olympics but the owner, a Ukrainian billionaire whose name he couldn't remember (it turned out to be Alexandr Onishenko), had fallen out with his rider, Katharina Offel, and wanted to sell him. He was a ten-year-old bay gelding with a pretty fancy name, Sanctos van het Gravenhof, and an unusual background: Belgian-born and bred, stabled in Germany, owned (and ridden) first by the American gold medallist Peter Wylde, and then by the frustrated Ukrainian oil tycoon. David knew Wylde and the

breeder, Willy Taets, and said the horse had attracted a lot of attention at the big international events in the past few years. His record
was pretty remarkable: he'd had only three fences down in thirty
grands prix.

'We'll have to move very fast – and keep it very quiet. If word gets
around we will lose him for sure,' said David. The price, he warned,
would be a hefty one.

David couriered over some videos and I watched them over and over
again. I liked the look of Sanctos immediately and later learned that
Peter Wylde, who won team gold for the USA in 2004 in Athens as
well as countless other medals, had come out of retirement just to ride
him. 'Sanctos made me realise all the parts I love about showjumping,'
he said a few years later. I didn't know that at the time of course but
was mesmerised as I watched the horse jump clear round after clear
round. Sanctos seemed to work out his own way to tackle each fence,
often clearing them by just an inch, instantly sizing up the next one.

I got the videos on a Tuesday and on Friday I called David and told
him to get across to Germany immediately and try him out. If he liked
him, we should buy him on the spot, whatever it cost. I would love to
have gone myself but I was in the middle of something and couldn't
get away that weekend.

David took Scott Brash with him and they drove to the German
stables where, for forty-five minutes, Scott put Sanctos through his
paces, jumping the course laid out in the paddock. As soon as I could I
called him to ask how it went. It was the first time I had talked to him.

'I think he's a very careful horse,' he replied cautiously. 'Careful' was a
very important quality in jumpers, which riders particularly looked for.

'But do you think he'll be able to jump in the Olympics?' I asked
anxiously.

He took some moments to consider that. 'I'm not sure he can at the
minute, to be honest,' he replied, explaining the horse had been out of
competition for a couple of months. 'He's not ultra-fit, and I just don't

know if he's got that last bit of championship jumper in him – it's very difficult to say right now.'

Probably sensing my disappointment, he added: 'But he's certainly a very good horse and even if he doesn't win the Olympics, he'll win a lot of classes.'

I had only seen him on video but somehow, as I had with Philco, I had a feeling about this horse and I was determined to have him. I got David back on the phone and we discussed what we should offer for him. David had established that the Ukrainian wanted $3 million, which was a pretty fancy figure for a showjumper (although not, as was widely believed, a record), and wasn't prepared to haggle. Neither was I, and without consulting the Kirks I made an instant decision. 'Let's not argue, just buy him,' I told David, who later told me that was the first time in my life I hadn't tried to get the price down. I just thought the guy wasn't going to take anything less. It truly was a miracle.

Scott brought him back to his own stables in Peebles and he was registered just in time to meet the Olympic deadline. None of us could pronounce, let alone remember, his German name, so we renamed him just plain Hello Sanctos. When I called Scott in Peebles to enquire how he was doing, he told me that 'he already thinks he's the king of the stables. When you try to pat him, he's like, "Bugger off, I'm eating – I'm doing what I want."' I could hear in his voice that Sanctos had won his admiration, if not yet his affections, as Scott, always modest and polite, was winning mine. I already liked this boy even though I hadn't even met him yet.

Now the hard work began. We were really running against the clock. The horse was still something of an unknown quantity, was not match-fit and somehow he and Scott had to win enough points on the international circuit by June to be selected for Team GB. 'I'll take him to Florida in January for six weeks,' Scott proposed, 'and ride him in as many events as possible.' I thought that was a brilliant idea.

From January to March every year, Wellington, near Palm Beach, becomes the equestrian centre of the world, attracting the best horses and the best riders, many of whom would compete in the Olympics in London. 'That's the best place to go to get to know a horse in the time we have available,' said Scott.

In March 2012, I flew to Florida to meet Scott and watch Hello Sanctos jump in the ring for the first time – and it was awful. He had four fences down before I could even draw breath, and it didn't get any better. Graham was coming over the next day and I thought: 'What am I going to say to him? I've spent half his money on this horse and he's knocking all these fences over.'

This was also the first time I had met Scott, who tried to reassure me as best he could. 'We're jumping some big courses and we'll have some good rounds and we'll have some bad rounds,' he said philosophically. 'This is the making of us as a partnership and without coming here and working hard, we would have no chance of going to the Olympics. You'll see a different horse tomorrow.'

He was right. The next day, in front of Graham and Pauline, Sanctos jumped a faultless round and won the competition. Sunday, three days later, was to be the big day, when he would be jumping for a $60,000 jackpot in a World Cup qualifying event and, after the experience of the past few days, I was looking forward to it. But, on Friday 14 March 2012, I got the really sad news that Harvey Spack had passed away and I immediately flew back for the funeral. He had been ill for some time but I was devastated and very sad for Jane. I had lost a really great friend who had played a huge part in my life, both professionally and personally, and my children had been brought up to regard him as one of the family. He taught me about property, schooled me in the art of negotiation, and helped me buy whole companies including Queensway and Hardy's. He knew everyone in the property world and in the Jewish community, where he was much loved. He was a generous, kind, funny man – and I still miss him.

My consolation, even though I wasn't there to see it, was that Hello

Sanctos won the jackpot that Sunday and went on winning just about everything from then on. In mid-March, he jumped a double-clear for the British team in the Nations Cup in Rome and was clear again every day in bigger classes in La Baule. He would have won even more except, as the date of the games approached, Scott stopped competing in minor events in order to work flat-out on his fitness. He put Sanctos – and himself – on a seriously tough regime, trying to make up for the late start. Sanctos was ridden hard twice a day and was put through exercises every bit as strenuous as athletes on the track went through – he was, after all, an athlete too. Scott told me later that in those months leading up to the games he never thought about anything other than the Olympic gold. 'It's a massive mind-set,' he said, 'just waking up every morning thinking about that one goal.'

The selection of the Olympic showjumping team takes place much closer to the event than in other sports and Scott and Sanctos still had to earn their places. The last part of the selection process was the grand prix in Rotterdam and Sanctos once again jumped brilliantly. He would have won but for 'an unlucky fence', which should have stayed put but dropped after he just lightly grazed it, but it didn't matter. By that stage the selectors had seen enough: it was obvious to the whole showjumping world that Scott and Sanctos were really growing as a partnership and clicking at the right time. In June, they were selected for the Olympics.

The British equestrian team in 2012 was led by Nick Skelton, one of Britain's best showjumpers of all time and also a thoroughly decent man. He had jumped for me many times after David Broome retired and we had remained good friends. He was now fifty-four and had been winning championships since 1974, well before Scott was born. He had broken every bone in his body, including his neck, but kept on riding in search of that elusive gold. This was his fifth Olympics and everyone, including Nick himself, expected it to be his last. Ben Maher and Peter Charles were the other members of the four-man team, and someone pointed out that their average age, including Scott, was forty. I had hoped that Tina Fletcher would get in but she wasn't chosen, although her horse, Hello Sailor, was picked as a reserve.

No one who saw it will ever forget the opening ceremony of the London Olympics on 27 July 2012, with the Queen apparently parachuting down in front of 62,000 people in the huge stadium. The battle for the equestrian medals started in the second week and Team GB started well when Zara Phillips and the eventing team won a silver. Now it was up to us. On the night before our event, we had a party in Martin's house in Blackheath, right opposite the equestrian stadium, and the whole of the British team came. Expectations, raised by the success of Team GB in the field events, were high and there was a terrific determination among the riders that they were going to end the medal drought and bring home gold this time. It was a memorable evening, made even better by the singing of some of the girls from our local academy schools. This was the heart of Harris Academy territory, south-east London, and I wanted the schools to feel part of the Olympic spirit too.

The next morning the team performed well but in the qualifying round Sanctos brushed one of the fences and it fell. Fortunately, it was only a qualifier and he did enough to get through and things improved after that. The British team jumped brilliantly in the next rounds and as the day wore on country after country was eliminated until, finally, it came down to two: Team GB and the Dutch, who would split gold and silver between them.

It was to be the best of three rounds and Nick Skelton and Scott both jumped clear in the first. Then Ben Maher had one mistake on Triple X and Peter Charles ended on eight faults, so we lost that one. Another clear by Sanctos in the second just kept Britain in contention. The Dutch had a great chance to win if they had jumped clear but Gerco Schröder, their top rider, clipped the second barrier in a row of three and the competition was tied.

We then had a jump-off against the clock, the nearest thing in show-jumping to a penalty shoot-out, some of the most nail-biting moments of my life. The course was reset and both teams went again, with the best three scores from each team counting towards the overall result. Skelton began the jump-off with a clear round in 47.27 seconds, only to be matched by Jur Vrieling, the first Dutch rider. Maher delivered a second clear round – marginally slower than that of Skelton – but when the next Dutch rider had eight faults the crowd scented victory. But then, to my horror, Sanctos clipped a fence, losing four faults, and the pressure was all on Peter Charles, who was the last to go. Time was irrelevant – the gold was Britain's if he could just go clear. An eerie silence descended over the stadium as he jumped faultlessly over the first seven fences, with one to go. As he approached the last, his horse Vindicat soared up and over and into the history books. Britain had won team gold.

The noise coming from our seats could probably have been heard all the way to Peckham, just a couple of miles away. With the cheers ringing in their ears, and the team dancing for joy, the team then did the usual post-match TV interviews. 'Everyone had said to me there'll be so much more pressure at a home Olympic Games,' Skelton, who had jumped clear three times that day, said, 'but it was totally the opposite. The crowd were unbelievable – they got us the gold.' From our position in the stand, we had more than made our contribution to that.

When the sports commentator Clare Balding asked Scott how winning gold would change his life, he replied mischievously: 'Well, I really hope it improves my pulling power with women, to be honest with you.'

A bewildered Balding couldn't believe what she was hearing. 'You were doing it all for that?' she spluttered. 'Yeah, pretty much,' he responded coolly and walked off grinning to himself. Scott never had any problems on that front. That flippant remark received almost as much coverage the next day in the tabloids as did his gold medal.

But we hadn't finished yet. The biggest event of the equestrian games was still to come: the individual gold, the medal most coveted in all showjumping. Both Scott and Nick Skelton were highly fancied and, to be frank, I wouldn't have minded which of them won. I just wanted Team GB to get another gold.

Alas, it was not to be, at least this time around. Scott started with a clear round and was in with a good chance as he came out again, but in the second round he just touched the top of one of the smallest fences. Several horses had rattled that fence quite hard that day and it stayed up, but now I watched it agonisingly teeter and then fall. If he had cleared that one he would have been jumping off for gold or silver. Instead, he was out of the individual medals.

Poor Nick Skelton had a similar experience but he would make up for it four years later in the 2016 Olympics in Rio, when he won the individual gold at the age of fifty-eight, the oldest British competitor ever to win a medal.

I would have liked two golds, but I was more than content with one. After nearly fifty years of trying, I had achieved one of my last outstanding ambitions.

*   *   *

After the games, we were inundated with offers for Sanctos and we could have made our money back many times over. But the two Paulines, who owned him, refused even to consider selling – he was the horse that had made our dreams come true and we wanted to keep him.

The Olympic gold medal was just the start for Scott and Sanctos. In 2013, Scott got a well-deserved MBE and became the world number one showjumper, the youngest rider ever to finish top of the Global Championship Tour, showjumping's richest series, which he won again the following year. His earnings by that stage were spectacular, bigger than anything ever seen in showjumping before: in 2014, he won majors in Monaco, Estoril, London, Cannes and Florida and prize money of $1.8 million. In 2015, he was awarded the Rolex Grand Slam of Showjumping after winning the three biggest majors of the year – Geneva, Aachen and Calgary – a feat no other rider had ever done before (or since). The prize money for those three events alone was $2.2 million.

At the end of that year, Scott sat at No. 1 on the Longines world rider rankings, and in 2016, riding Hello Ursula, he won Spruce Meadows, the most lucrative grand prix, with prize money of $1 million, for the second time. His extraordinary success, remarked one authoritative equestrian commentator, was 'thanks largely to his top horses and the support of their owners, Hello Stables'. The Kirkhams and the Harrises appreciated that, but we didn't want anything back – we had all we needed with the gold.

Hello Ursula, who had played second fiddle to the great Sanctos, astonished us all by overtaking him to become the number one in the world's rankings, even though she had never won a grand prix (she had come second in five, gaining lots of points). So, we found ourselves in the position of owning the world's number one and number two horses, just as we had all those years ago with Philco and Sportsman. That was a pretty amazing feeling, not something that any amount of money could buy.

Scott missed out on the 2016 Olympics in Rio because both our top horses, Sanctos and Ursula, had slight injuries. Sanctos won't make another Olympics, but we have Hello M'Lord and Hello M'Lady coming along nicely, and a whole string behind them.

I can't wait for 2020. We are not done yet.

CHAPTER 33

BOWING OUT

I finally left Carpetright in June 2014, twenty-six years after I founded it, at the age of seventy-two. It had been a rollercoaster ride: more than twenty years of exhilaration, excitement and fulfilment, when the little company I had started, partly as a reaction to losing Harris Queensway, became the biggest carpet retailer in the world with a market value of close on £1 billion. The last few years were disappointing but nothing could take away the sense of achievement I got from creating a great company from scratch. That first store I opened in Canning Town at the end of 1988 had become over 600 outlets and from half a dozen employees we went to over 3,300.

I confess I didn't enjoy the last bit, when we were weighed down by terrible economic times, the collapse of the carpet trade and board meetings which at times bordered on the bad-tempered. It's no doubt a weakness on my part, but I have not had great experiences of non-executive directors, who, when professional management is most needed, seem to want to take over the running of the company. Some poor decisions were taken that I was not in a position to prevent: for instance, Christian Sollesse, a brilliant motivator who somehow seemed to get his people to work twice as hard for him, was taken out of his job as sales director, put on the board as managing director and given too many jobs to do. Sales, predictably, suffered as a result. He resigned on 2 June 2011.

Those last few years were challenging ones but we slowed the decline in profits by cutting our costs, becoming even more competitive on price and service and continued to invest in our stores and our warehouse. But, between 2010 and 2014, despite increasing our market share, our sales fell by 15 per cent to £450 million and we could not stop the erosion of margins. We paid no dividend for three years, which affected me more than anyone else as the biggest shareholder. Our cash flow, which I had concentrated on all my life, held up, however, and right through those recessionary years we kept reducing our debt, from £100 million at the peak to £5 million by the time I left.

We tried everything, including shuffling the management, and in 2012, when I reached my 70th birthday, I agreed to split my role and bring in a chief executive. I let the non-executive directors choose him and they found him already on the board: Darren Shapland, who had served as finance director for three years between 2002 and 2005 and had rejoined the board as a non-exec six months earlier. He agreed to take the job. Darren had originally left us for Sainsbury, where he was tipped to replace the highly regarded Justin King as CEO, but he was overlooked and came back.

He didn't stay long. His return to Carpetright coincided with another downward lurch in the market and, after only eighteen months and yet another profit warning, he decided to go. I was in Spain at a health spa when I got a call from Baroness Noakes to say that Darren had just told her that he was not committed to the company for the five years as he had promised and he was leaving. She asked if I would take over again while the board looked for another CEO. The retail analyst Nick Bubb was later quoted as saying: 'I guess Darren thought he would be able to preside over a great profit recovery before going off to do something else and it dawned on him it would be a long haul.'

I had no desire to step back into the breach but Darren's abrupt departure left me with no choice, so in October 2013 I found myself as chairman and chief executive again, running the company in trading conditions which weren't getting any easier. I had no intention of staying on and instructed the baroness, still on the board after thirteen years, that as soon as she found a new chief executive she should also look for another chairman.

Wilf Walsh, who had run the bookmaker Coral, took over as CEO in July 2014 and Martin stepped down in September, twenty-three years after he first joined. And, in October, the company announced that Bob Ivell, who had thirty years' experience in the brewing industry, would become chairman. I welcomed him to the board, told him he was taking over a great team (which he was) and he in turn complimented me on 'the strong legacy' I left behind. I would have liked it to be even stronger but he inherited a good company, with some excellent properties, a good brand and a depth of decent management.

I was flattered by some of the sentiments that acknowledged my passing. 'Lord Harris's reputation among Britain's pre-eminent entrepreneurs is secure,' wrote *The Times*, and went on to quote some of the analysts: 'He has been Mr Carpets for years,' said one, 'he's killed off the competition.' 'His career stands on its own,' said another. There was a lot more in that vein, qualified by remarks that 'fresh blood' was probably needed to rekindle the salad days when we were growing in double digits.

I'd have liked that fresh blood to have been Martin, but by then he had ambitions of his own and was no longer interested. It was time for another new company, the family's third foray into the carpet market. In January 2016, we launched Tapi Carpets, with Martin as its CEO.

Carpetright shares were just over 600p when I announced my departure but they had dropped to 300p when I sold my shareholding a few months later, basically because the dealers were waiting for it and went short. I should have waited a bit because they went straight back to 600p again once the sale was completed, but then began a long decline all the way back to 149p at the end of 2016 – which was where we started all those years ago. But it's a good company, with lots of excellent people, and will carry on. I wish it well.

CHAPTER 34

WINDOWS AT THE ABBEY

By the Queen's Diamond Jubilee in 2012, Westminster Abbey was probably in better physical shape than it had ever been, the interior restored in all its great beauty and grandeur, the outside made strong, stable and ready to withstand another century at least, and the beautiful towers and walls exposed as Wren and Hawksmoor intended them to be. But I still had a nagging sense of unfinished business. Alan Younger's window in the King Henry VII Chapel had been well received by the critics as well as the public, but to my eye the contrast with the windows on either side, which were still in plain glass, was unsettling. These were big windows, twenty-seven feet high, and replacing them with stained glass would be a major task. But I was up for it and so was John Hall, the dean, when I suggested it to him, so we began working on a plan to have new windows commissioned and installed in time for the 60th anniversary of the Queen's coronation in 2013.

Alan Younger had died in 2004, aged seventy-one, so we had to find another stained-glass artist and eventually decided on Hugh O'Donoghue, whose work John and I both liked. I told him I didn't want anything too challenging that would jar with the ancient chapel or the main window and he came up with a beautiful design of lilies and stars, symbols of the Virgin Mary, which I loved.

Before the Queen could open it, we had a bizarre event in the abbey which I am still trying to get my head around. To mark the occasion of her Diamond Jubilee a year earlier, the Queen had agreed to pose for just one official portrait in her full coronation robes. She actually sat for the artist, the Australian painter Ralph Heimans, in Buckingham Palace, but he placed her standing on the very spot in the abbey where she had been crowned on 2 June 1953. It was a huge canvas – 9ft by 12ft – and was commissioned by Lady Penny Mountbatten, a cousin of Prince Philip, but no one seems to have thought about what would happen to it once the celebrations were over. John Hall saw it at an exhibition in the Lanesborough Hotel and later that day we had a meeting of the abbey's campaign development board, of which I was a member. I happened to arrive early and was chatting to John when he told me about the picture, which he thought was marvellous. 'Don't you think it belongs in the abbey?' I said. 'If I were to buy it for you, would you find a home for it?'

Lady Mountbatten sold it to us for the cost of the commission, which was about £100,000, and in May 2013 it went on public display in the Abbey's Chapter House as part of an anniversary exhibition. A week after it opened, I got a call from an excited BBC reporter telling me that someone had come in at lunchtime and scrawled the word 'help' across it in spray paint. It turned out to be the work of a desperate father belonging to Fathers4Justice, but I didn't see much justice in it. Why take it out on the Queen?

Fortunately, he was grabbed by a security man before he could do too much damage and we had it restored and the artist came back to touch it up. It is now destined to be one of the main exhibits in the new Queen's Diamond Jubilee galleries, the ambitious project that John Hall, by far the most imaginative and energetic Dean of Westminster in my time, has been working on for three years. Since he arrived in 2006, he has already made many improvements, including an education centre aimed at young people who know nothing about their heritage; and a new café/restaurant, which is very popular with the two million visitors the abbey gets every year.

The new galleries, however, are his masterpiece: the transformation of the medieval triforium, a huge hidden gallery space high above the nave, previously only accessible via a narrow wooden spiral staircase. The last time anyone could remember it being used was when Richard Dimbleby sited the BBC cameras to cover the coronation, and it had become a dumping ground for generations of workmen to leave their leftover materials. John's plan involved building an entirely new tower, with a lift and staircase, opening the galleries up to the public for the first time, and Guy Weston, son of Garry, who died in 2002, headed up the appeal, on which I served, to raise £23 million. It is a terrific addition to the abbey, the first significant development other than repair work for nearly 200 years, and will house a fantastic treasure trove of manuscripts, silverware, statues and old artefacts – and the portrait of the Queen, now in pristine shape again, which I have donated.

For what may be my final contribution to the abbey after nearly thirty years, Harry Djanogly and I have commissioned David Hockney to decorate one of the few remaining plain-glass windows (in the north transept) with a stained-glass celebration of the Queen's reign. It's a very tall window, 20ft high and 6ft wide, and Hockney, whose work I love, has never worked in stained glass, but he appears undaunted. Hockney's exhibition at the Tate Britain in 2017 set new attendance records and his window will be a towering tribute to the Queen.

He promises a 'landscape full of blossom that's a celebration every year' – which seems very fitting. It will be a great addition to the abbey, and my swansong. After this, there will be no windows left to restore.

CHAPTER 35

HARRIS WESTMINSTER

I was startled one day to hear that the Westminster public school, next door to the abbey, in an average year sends more pupils to Oxbridge than all the children who qualify for school meals across the country put together. That meant that if you could afford the £36,000-a-year fees your child had a one-in-two chance of getting into Oxford or Cambridge. For students on free school meals, it was one in 1,000.

I found that a seriously sobering statistic and a real criticism of both the state education system and of the big universities. I couldn't accept that Westminster pupils, even if they were carefully selected to admit only the best, were all that much brainier than our kids. They just happened to have gone to the right school, got the right teaching and were guided along a path that maximised their chances. How can we ever have a more equal society if money and privilege, rather than brains and talent, still determine who is accepted by the country's top universities?

Even with our much-improved results, only half a dozen students a year from our Harris academies went on to Oxbridge, and that's better than most state schools. It was not part of their culture, whereas it was bred into the DNA of schools like Westminster. In 2007, the Sutton Trust, the highly respected education charity, found that 43 per cent of state school teachers either 'never or rarely' advised their academically gifted children to apply for Oxbridge. It carried out the same study again in 2016 – with exactly the same result. Britain's rate of social mobility, which lifted previous generations out of poverty and into the professions, is in danger of grinding to a halt.

I decided I would find a way to redress the balance even by a minus-
cule amount and give kids from disadvantaged backgrounds a better
chance of an Oxbridge degree. I first began thinking about it one
day in Westminster Abbey, when my mind must have wandered off
a service, and I found myself, for the thousandth time, contemplating
the majesty of the great church. How marvellous it would be if we
could somehow combine the academic record and reputation of the
1,000-year-old Westminster School with our academies, I thought.

I first raised the possibility with John Hall, dean of the abbey, and
the school's headmaster, Dr Stephen Spurr, in around 2008. They were
sympathetic but they were not sure how it could be done. Other schools
such as Eton and Winchester, partly to protect their charity status and
partly out of conscience, had created partnerships with state schools,
but not many had succeeded, and Westminster was understandably
protective of its reputation.

But I never give up easily and I kept on at it. I got on particularly
well with John Hall, whom I first met when we were both governors of
Bacon's CTC in Bermondsey in the early 1990s. Bacon's was run by the
Church of England – who John represented as a governor for a time –
and, although I gave it well over £1 million, we never got control of it, a
situation I always found unsatisfactory. I lost touch when John moved
to Lancashire to become the director of education for the Church of
England, but he came back into my life again in 2006 when, much to
my delight, he was appointed Dean of Westminster Abbey. That auto-
matically made him chairman of the governors of Westminster School
as well as of the Abbey Choir School, which exists solely to educate
and care for the thirty or so boys who sing as choristers in the abbey
choir. I wanted him to make it a full house by adding a Westminster
state school to his portfolio.

Over the years the Westminster governors had been approached
several times by local authorities about assisting state schools to
become academies and they had thought about it long and hard, but

each time had decided they simply didn't have the necessary expertise and the risk of failure was too great.

I wanted them to see what could be done in the state sector, so I took the dean and the headmaster to visit one of our schools, Harris Falconwood in Bexley, where we had just opened some new school buildings. The principal there was Terrie Askew, one of the original teachers at our first school in Crystal Palace, and I was very proud of her and the school, which was already showing a marked improvement in just a few months. This had been one of our tougher schools in 2007 and the opposition we got from some of the parents when we took over was at times unpleasant. My reply to the more vocal of them was to say: 'Look, if you're happy with a school where the pass rate at GCSE is only 17 per cent, I'm not. If we can't improve on that, we'll give the school back to the local authority.' In just two years we got those results up to 42 per cent (it has since received two 'Outstanding' ratings from Ofsted).

At the end of our tour, I said bluntly to our two visitors: 'What can we do with Westminster in regard to schools?' They had all this expertise, I said, with brilliant teachers and facilities, and an unrivalled success rate for Oxbridge entry. There had to be some way they could share all that with a wider community.

They were both keen to help but they were still wary, and nothing happened for some time. Then one day the dean called me to say that he and Spurr had been talking and had come up with what they both thought was an inspired proposal. Why didn't we set up an entirely new state school for sixteen-year-olds which would be selective but have a clear preference for taking kids from disadvantaged backgrounds? Pupils would be taught by Westminster-mentored teachers on a Westminster timetable right down to lessons on Saturday mornings, and they would receive expert guidance on Oxbridge entry. It would come under the Harris umbrella and of course would be free.

Over the next few months we refined the idea, eventually agreeing that it would be a Harris Federation-run school and all the liabilities and management would rest with us. We agreed to call it the Harris Westminster Sixth Form, and Westminster School's role would be to guide our teachers and provide lessons for our pupils in subjects where numbers of applicants were small, such as history of art, Latin and music (and bridge). We would offer to pay the travel costs of poorer students coming in by bus or tube, which we calculated would cost about £80,000 a year – not much more than the fees for sending two boys to the neighbouring public school.

As always, Michael Gove immediately saw the merits of it and, after checking with David Cameron, said the government would give us its full backing.

The first task was to find the right premises. We all preferred to be within walking distance of Westminster School and, as luck would have it, there was a building that was just becoming available in Tothill Street, almost within sight of the abbey. It was occupied by the Ministry of Justice but they were moving out and we could have it if we wanted it. I went along to see it with Dan Moynihan and thought it was just right, although it would need a lot of work. It was a 1930s building, with a façade featuring stone Greek gods, inside which was the usual warren of civil service offices. The government didn't own it and the costs of buying and refurbishing it would be £45 million, far more than we bargained for. Gove, however, didn't blink and, against the opposition of his officials and some adverse publicity, he went ahead with it.

As our first principal, we hired James Handscombe, an almost scarily bright man. He was a maths prodigy who did brilliantly in his comprehensive in Sheffield, achieved one of the highest Firsts in his year at Oxford, and then went to Harvard where he seemed to be all set for a glittering academic career. But his passion for teaching brought him back to the state system in the UK and when we advertised the job of principal at Harris Westminster in 2013, he applied and got it. We had some good candidates but Dan, the dean and I agreed this was the man for us – and we were so right.

Long before the extensive refitting of Tothill Street was complete, prospective students were turning up for their interviews dressed in everything from torn jeans and leather jackets to smart religious wear including hijabs. Handscombe set pretty formidable targets for them: only children with the ability to make it to the world's top universities would be selected. Successful students, he told them in his opening address, would need to do more than just study – they would be required to prepare themselves for university by taking part in the debates, societies, competitions, clubs, sports and other opportunities in the school. They would also be expected to read widely and complete at least sixteen hours of independent study a week outside their lessons. Vacation time would be spent reading, revising, doing work experience or volunteering – 'as well as for rest and relaxation'. It didn't sound to me as if there would be much of that. 'I want their brains to hurt every day,' Handscombe told me.

Harris Westminster Sixth Form was up and running within a year and we had 340 applicants for 125 places, which we managed to squeeze up to 139. In the second year 1,000 applied for 250 places and in 2017 the figure was 1,600 applicants for 300 places, taking the total number of pupils to 550.

The Westminster School staff and governors met their end of the bargain, providing training and academic guidance, but the finance and leg-work was done by the Harris Federation. More than two-thirds of our teachers are Oxbridge-educated, and have willingly responded to Handscombe's requirement that they teach subjects well beyond the curriculum. One student told me that he could email his teacher at any time and another teacher bought an iPhone so that he could reply to his students' emails anywhere, anytime. Many Harris Westminster students now get taught at least one A Level at Westminster School, where they get the chance to mix with their better-off peers, receiving the same education the public-school kids pay thousands of pounds for. To broaden their education, the London Academy of Music and Drama runs workshops in the school.

James Handscombe encouraged a couple of newspapers to visit the school shortly after it opened and *The Times* education correspondent, Helen Rumbelow, who had been to sixth form in Westminster School (and went on to Cambridge), described a fascinating contrast between the two establishments. 'Up to the age of sixteen,' she wrote, 'I went to a school that rarely sent students to Oxbridge – one girl in our year went. But for sixth form my parents switched me to Westminster, and there it became almost harder *not* to go to Oxbridge. You underwent precise and ultra-staffed preparation like an expensive machine in a grand prix.'

She sat in on one of Handscombe's pep talks to a group of sixteen-year-old applicants, which she was amazed by. 'In this room we have some of the brightest and most interesting people in London,' the principal told them. 'We want to see that type of student aiming at Oxford, Cambridge, Harvard or Princeton.' That didn't happen in any other state school in the country.

It is always fascinating to get an outsider's perspective and I was very taken with hers. 'One of the first girls I speak to is waiting for interview in her hijab,' she wrote, 'her bag dusty and worn but her shoes meticulously shined. If this school represents for her another league, Westminster School was another planet.' That girl turned out to be the daughter of a Bangladeshi cab-driver who could barely make ends meet; she had never been to Westminster Abbey or the Houses of Parliament and couldn't afford the tube fare. Today that girl, and others like her, mixes freely with the Westminster pupils as if she had grown up with them, oblivious to the difference in their backgrounds. The new Westminster headmaster, Patrick Derham, told me that, when he first joined, 'I couldn't tell who was from which school.'

In its first Ofsted inspection, Harris Westminster was awarded the top rating for every aspect of its work. The inspectors said it had created 'a community of scholars with a passion for learning', which is precisely what Dan and I set out to do, with the support of the dean. 'Students make excellent progress in their learning,' said the Ofsted inspectors. 'On the majority of subjects their work is of a higher standard than is expected of them given their prior attainment.'

In 2016, our first graduate year, a third of our students applied to Oxford and eight were offered places. In the second year it was twenty-three, about 10 per cent of the students. James Handscombe says his '1,000-year target' is to get that to 50 per cent – but to do it in ten years.

There was plenty of criticism of our new establishment of course – I expected nothing less. Tristram Hunt, Labour's shadow Education Secretary, called it Michael Gove's 'vanity project', and Margaret Hodge, the MP for Barking and Dagenham, a borough which usually sent nobody at all to Oxbridge, called it a waste of money. Dan Moynihan could not resist making the point that both Hunt and Hodge had gone to expensive private schools, and then to Cambridge and the London School of Economics respectively.

One of the newspapers called us 'the most ruthlessly elitist state sixth form in the country', but I took pride in that. We couldn't lift every kid in London to the standards achieved by the public school down the street, but we could make a difference for the deprived kids who were good enough to get this far. We now have our own Harris teacher training college on the top floors of the Tothill building, offering initial teacher education to graduates and career changers joining the teaching profession. After just two years it has been awarded 'Outstanding' rating.

* * *

All the Harris schools are personal to me and I visit them at every opportunity, getting to know as many of the teachers and boys and girls as I can remember. Where there was once apathy and hopelessness in many of these schools, there is real pride now. I ask questions all the time, just as I would in one of my stores: why is attendance down? Why are we not doing better at sports? It is the same as in business: motivation is everything and people respond to seeing the person at the top taking an interest.

Andrew Adonis always says that when he meets me in the House of Lords, I reel off a battery of statistics which sends his head reeling. But I make no apology for that – nothing gives me a bigger uplift than to get a phone call from Dan telling me about yet another upgrade to 'Outstanding', and fortunately there have been plenty of them in the past few years. I can't resist updating Adonis – and anyone else who will listen.

In total, as of September 2017, we have a total budget of £150 million a year and 30,000 school children, or students as we call them, in for-ty-five schools; twenty-five of them are secondaries, three 'all the way through' (primary and secondary), and nineteen are primaries. Twen-ty-seven were 'failing' or 'requiring improvement' when we took them on but twenty are now rated 'Outstanding', twelve are 'Good' and, as of September 2017, twenty-one are waiting to be inspected by Ofsted.

At secondary level, of those already rated by Ofsted, 83 per cent of our schools are 'Outstanding' and the rest are 'Good' – that's about four times the national average and we are going up every year. No other academy federation comes anywhere near that.

Our secondary school results are top in five of the nine boroughs where we operate and second in two. Two of our schools, Greenwich and Chafford Hundred, have been recognised by the World Class Schools Quality Mark, which means they have moved beyond Ofst-ed's highest rating of 'Outstanding' into a different category altogether (and, as I have described, got a chance to row the Queen's Royal barge).

We also have a 'referral unit' for children who have been expelled from their schools and find no one else will take them. Previously, these were the kids who had little hope of getting back into the system and would almost certainly have led blighted lives. The government works closely with us on this programme and has financed a new centre in Norwood which we will run.

Each school has two parent governors and the others come from a wide range of professions, including banking, the City, lawyers – anyone who wants to help. Our board of governors are one of the secrets of our success, not properly recognised. In the summer of 2017, I gave a certificate to each of the governors who had been with us for more than three years – and there were a lot of them.

These are not just numbers – they are people's lives, and our schools are making a difference to them. Suffice to say, I don't think there's a single measure where we don't rank well above the average and in many cases our schools are among the best in the country. We have never had a school that didn't show significant progress in the first year and all of them have gone on getting better.

In 2014, *The Economist* remarked that 'the academy system has transformed Britain's educational landscape' but there's a lot more to be done and not enough time to do it. I hope to go on adding new schools, maybe three of four a year, as long as we can go on showing the improvement we have been able to achieve so far. Most of these schools will still be there a century from now and teachers and students will wonder who this man Harris was and why he founded them in the first place. I hope this book will give them some concept of what has driven me – and will go on driving me as long as I've got breath in my body.

Modestly, I shall leave the last word to Michael Gove, who told a meeting in Haringey: 'They called Phil Harris a threat – but he's transformed the lives of hundreds of thousands.'

POSTSCRIPT

This book has emerged as a series of apparently disconnected chapters in my life story: business, hospitals, schools, showjumping, Westminster Abbey, Oxford and politics, all of them presented here as if they were distinct and self-contained episodes. It was never like that of course. Although I have always had the ability to live my life in self-contained compartments, I never had the luxury of being able to concentrate on just one issue for more than a few hours at a time, a day at most. My restless nature wouldn't let me anyway. In the early 1990s, when I was executive chairman of Carpetright, I was also chairman of Guy's and Lewisham hospitals, I was treasurer of the Conservative Party, I had my school in Crystal Palace and I was chairman of the Westminster Abbey restoration fund. On any given day, I probably had to deal with all of them as well as a myriad of other issues that came my way. I was also on the board of a number of public companies, including the clothes retailer Matalan, GUS, Fisons and, for a time, Virgin Group, all of which needed attention and energy.

Yet I never felt overstretched or stressed and didn't believe I was taking on too much. I liked being busy and I thrived on challenges. I devoted as much time as I could to the family but after that my business took priority. Fortunately, I learned to delegate and it says a lot for the Carpetright team that the period when I was at my busiest included some of the company's most prosperous years.

But I don't think any of my other activities suffered from pressures of time or commitment. I put a great deal of energy into the Harris

City Technology College in Crystal Palace, and it responded, paving the way for the Harris Federation of today, which is the number one academy group in the country. At Guy's and Lewisham, which was at the forefront of Mrs Thatcher's plans to transform the NHS, we got the costs down across the board but still treated more patients and reduced waiting times; a government audit report showed that, in my time as chairman, we were one of the best performing hospitals in the country. As treasurer of the Conservative Party, working alongside my friend Charles Hambro, I helped raise £118 million, and we left the party finances in a lot better shape than we found them. Busy as I was, when Prince Philip asked me to, I took on the job of raising £10 million for Westminster Abbey and, with a powerful team to help me, ended up bringing in £24 million – enough to keep the 1,000-year-old institution standing for another few centuries at least.

All my life I have passionately believed that management – and life – is all about people, and my good fortune was to have exceptional people around me in each of my endeavours. In business, it was my first mentor, Mr Smith (I shall still call him that), who advised me to organise my rapidly growing carpet business into a proper company, and it was David Stockwell who did it for me. As the company grew, my team of raw youngsters matured along with it: Ted Wright, Kingsley Elton and my cousin Ron Poole were with me from the very early days, and when I got the opportunity to acquire Keith Royle, probably the single most important acquisition I ever made, the team was ready for it.

That's when I recruited Tony Behar, and a few years later Stephen Fearnley came along with Poundstretcher to complete the team, which grew Harris Carpets and then Harris Queensway through the 1970s and 1980s. Above it all sat the wise and observant figure of Hugh Sykes, my deputy chairman, who stayed with me loyally through thick and thin. He was my counsellor and sage, the perfect antidote on the board to what I can only describe as a boisterous lot.

But I couldn't have done it without the 'honorary' members who, whether they liked it or not, I seconded onto the team. David Biderman walked in off the street one day and for no particular reason that I could ever fathom befriended me and taught me the skills of buying carpets and dealing with the big manufacturers – and even how to dress properly. It was through David that I met Neville Cormack, who introduced me to the tufted carpet, a revolutionary development which opened up the mass market of lower income households. Thanks to Neville, I was one of the first retailers to offer tufted carpets, and they transformed my business. Both David and Neville became life-long friends as well as mentors.

Then there was Harvey Spack, the property arm of my team as well as my great friend until he passed away in 2012. Harvey never actually worked for me but he devoted so much time and energy to us that we both thought he did. He had a genius for identifying properties and sniffing out deals, and was also heavily involved in the Hardy's and Queensway acquisitions, important milestones in the history of Harris Queensway.

I mustn't forget the City bankers, who I also adopted as team players: first there was Charles Villiers, affable, courteous and always constructive, who gave me my first break by lending me £750,000. Then came Andrew Deacon, whose ingenuity got us Queensway and also took us public in 1988. Poor Andrew, like Harvey Spack, became the butt of many of my practical jokes, and I can well remember him getting soaked to the skin at a Horse of the Year Show in Wembley as the rest of the team, led by me, threw buckets of water over him. Being a member of the team required many sacrifices. David Reed, who took over from Andrew, suffered a similar baptism.

That basically was the group of people who built Harris Queensway into a £450 million company. We had thirty-one good years followed by just one bad one and we could have steered the company through the roughest of economic storms if circumstances had given us the chance. Many of the old Harris Queensway team proved their worth when they came with me to Carpetright and made a great success of it. Some of them are still with me.

I was, if anything, even luckier with the people I worked with outside business. At Guy's, Peter Griffiths and Cyril Chantler were brilliant professionals who, with the right support when it was most needed, could have helped transform the way the NHS manages its hospitals. In the schools, I don't think I've ever come across a better manager than Dan Moynihan, and the results prove it. At Westminster Abbey, John Hall has been a joy to work alongside, easily the best dean in the thirty-odd years I have been involved. And at Harris Manchester in Oxford, I can't speak highly enough of Ralph Waller, who has transformed the college.

Last but not least, there was David Broome, surely the most influential figure in British showjumping since the war, and also a great friend. The crowning achievement of my showjumping adventures, which Pauline started me on in my mid-teens, was watching the young Scott Brash bring home Olympic gold in 2012 on Hello Sanctos in Greenwich Park, home turf to generations of Harrises who lived and died in nearby Peckham. That's a day I shall never forget, and I owe it to David, who found both Scott and Sanctos for us.

*   *   *

I've now been in the retail trade for sixty years and I hope I have learned a thing or two that might inspire some young entrepreneurs as I was inspired by some of the great retailers of the past. There were three in particular in my area of the industry who I think were giants. I would bend the knee any time to Stanley Kalms, a man with a colossal intellect and brilliant commercial mind who built Dixons into a world-class electrical retailer at a difficult time in the high street. Noel Lister, co-founder of MFI, was probably his equal, a superb marketer who pioneered low-cost attractive furniture in the 1970s and once boasted that six out of ten British children were conceived on an MFI bedroom suite and one in three Sunday lunches were eaten in its fitted kitchens. The third great retailer and inspirational figure of my time has been my great friend Graham Kirkham, creator of the DFS furniture chain, whose marketing skills I stand in awe of.

I mustn't neglect my own children in all this, because they were there for me too. I tried to encourage an entrepreneurial spirit in them and from their mid-teens the boys worked in the shops in their holidays, learning the same trade their grandfather and father had before them. All three joined the business after they left school (or university in Peter's case) and I was delighted they did. All of us dream of dynasties, however unfair a burden that places on the next generation, and I was no different.

Charles started his retail career with Poundstretcher and then did a stint on the floor of Hamleys before moving on to Harveys. But, wisely perhaps, he decided to strike off on his own, which I could only admire him for. One day he called me to say he had bought a 50 per cent share in a gun shop in Tunbridge Wells, which initially didn't sound like a good business to me. He suggested, however, that before I blew my stack completely I should come and see it. I expected to find an empty shop, but when I arrived on a Saturday it was packed and Charles was too busy serving customers to talk to me. Despite my misgivings, he and his business partner Chris Potter have a very successful business and I'm very proud of him. He has two lovely children, William and Emma, and recently became a grandfather to a delightful little boy called Harry, my third great-grandchild, who has the reddest hair you've ever seen. William has set up his own gardening company called Harris Gardens, which is doing well, and has seven people now working for him.

Charles's twin brother Peter, who learned his trade at both Harris Carpets and Carpetright, is now responsible for store openings at our new carpet business. From the beginning, he has been committed to the schools' project and he served as a governor of Harris Crystal Palace (as did Pauline) for over twenty years, and he is now a governor of three other schools. He's married to Denise and has two children, Liam and Aran.

Martin, who went through the rougher times of Carpetright with me, is married to Zoe and he has three children, the youngest of whom, Suki, has inherited her grandmother's love of horse-riding. His daughter Lauren recently got married and her brother Charlie is at Newcastle University.

Our daughter, Susan, born the day before my mother died, also inherited her mother's love of horses and they are frequently away together with the showjumpers. She and her husband Mick Clifton have taken on the task of coordinating the travel itinerary to the shows around Europe for the horses owned by her mother and Pauline Kirkham, and she is the one who keeps us abreast of results and our standing in the world rankings. She has three children, Christopher, Philip and Dominic. She's now a governor of a Harris Federation school, as is young Christopher. She also has two grandchildren, Sophia and Lily.

*   *   *

I am now on my third carpet company, Tapi Carpets, which is run by my son Martin and backed by some of our oldest supporters, who have invested in it alongside the family. By the end of 2018 we hope to have 150 shops which incorporate all the innovations and improvements we have learned in a lifetime of dealing with customers. The pace of change is all the time accelerating but there are still age-old principles that remain constant: buying the right product at the right price and selling it competitively remain paramount. I still have some contribution to make there.

Right now, in the autumn of 2017, it's the future of this country I'm much more anxious about. I supported, and voted for, Brexit, and firmly believe it is the right thing for Britain. But I don't think we are going about negotiating our exit in the right way, and I am concerned that we are drifting towards decline under a government that lacks direction. In the build-up to the publication of this book, I gave an interview to Rachel Sylvester and Alice Thomson, two *Times* journalists who I admire, at my flat in London. The idea was that we would talk about the book and range over my life story, but inevitably I got drawn into controversy when they asked me what I thought of Theresa May.

'I'll tell you one thing,' I responded without thinking, 'Theresa May is no Thatcher. Thatcher used to make decisions. Not everyone liked her but you knew where you stood.'

I should have stopped there, but these clever journalists drew me on. 'I'd much rather have a strong Labour government than a weak Conservative one,' I added, although I wouldn't want it under Jeremy Corbyn. 'Tony Blair when he first got in now would be very good for this country.'

I had no desire to attack Mrs May – or anyone else in the party leadership – but unwisely I dug myself in deeper. 'I thought for the first three or four weeks she did well,' I told the interviewers. 'Then she did the election and she was hopeless. She's changed her mind too many times. I think she was shell-shocked, but she's got to start making decisions … she has a great opportunity if she lets [her ministers] work and leads them. I don't know if she can lead them or not.' I said I was dismayed with her attitude to business, and compared it to that of Thatcher 'who used to have twenty of us round every month, all from different levels – I was the youngest'.

I thought no more about the interview until over a week later, when, on 9 September 2017, I awoke to find myself on the front page of *The Times*, which led with the headline:

THERESA MAY IS 'HOPELESS AND WEAK', SAYS LORD HARRIS OF PECKHAM

The strapline was: 'Top Tory party donor accuses prime minister of mishandling Brexit and alienating business.' It wasn't quite what I had said, of course, and the full interview inside the paper put it all in proper context, but I had only myself to blame. I expected an irate call from Downing Street, which would certainly have occurred under Thatcher, Major or even Cameron, but Mrs May maintained an icy silence. Instead I received over 100 messages of support, many of them from fellow Conservative peers, agreeing with what I said. One of them, from (Lord) Irvine Laidlaw, read: 'It is time that people of your stature and experience did stand up and say that things are going badly,' and most of the others made the same point. 'It's what many of us are thinking,' said one fellow peer.

I was shaken at the time, but in retrospect I am glad I said it. I meant every word of it.

* * *

At the age of seventy-five, I am far from done. I still work (almost) as hard as I ever did, although writing this book has made me realise I may have slowed down a bit. How I was able to do five jobs at the same time, as I did at my peak in the 1990s, I can't now imagine. But I still get through a respectable workload: I spend two or three days a week on my schools, whose success gives me immense satisfaction and pleasure, and I probably talk to poor old Dan Moynihan half a dozen times a day. I also enjoy helping Martin with Tapi, seeing suppliers, looking at new sites, and going around the stores, just as I always did. Then there are charities, boards, Harris Manchester and other things to keep me busy.

I have no intention of stopping here, however. I still have plans, dreams, projects, new worlds to conquer, ambitions to fulfil and a future to experience. I believe, as I always did, that my best years lie ahead – and I will go to my grave proving it.

ACKNOWLEDGEMENTS

I could not have written this book without the help, support and assistance of a wide variety of people. I particularly want to thank Judy Willett, my personal assistant, who patiently delved into dusty archives and files to find long-forgotten documents and photos which I thought had been lost in our many changes of homes and offices.

She has been my life-saver these past twenty-five years and succeeded three other ladies who also played a major role in keeping me on track. Ruth Penny joined me when I didn't even have a proper office, working above our shop in Balham; Liz Chapman came all the way down from Norwich after we acquired Queensway to take up residence in our first real headquarters in Orpington; then Maritsa Blackman joined from the world of Fleet Street to take responsibility for organising my life.

I am also grateful to a long list of people who helped jog my memory as I worked on this book. These include Terri Askew, David Broome, Scott Brash, Andrew Deacon, Sir Harry Djanogly, Sir Cyril Chantler, Sue Fallon, Stephen Fearnley, Russell Field, Peter Griffiths, Dr John Hall, Peter Holmes, Sir Dan Moynihan, Vivienne Parry, Ron Poole, David Reed, David Stockwell, Sir Hugh Sykes, Charles Villiers and Dr Ralph Waller. But I am especially grateful to Pauline, keeper of the family albums and scrapbooks, who is really my memory and mentor as well as the most wonderful wife a man could have.

Re-tracing my father's military career proved a major task, and my researcher, Bill Bloom, spent many days and weeks deep in the military archives and museums. When we hit a blank wall, Robert Cranborne, Marquess of Salisbury, and Sir Michael Fallon at the Ministry of Defence helped open the way. I am grateful to them and to the many people who helped us find our way through the military archives. Dominic Butler, assistant curator, and his colleagues at Lancashire Infantry Museum, Fulwood Barracks, Preston, Lancashire, were very helpful and I also want to thank Jeanie Smith, assistant librarian at the Guildhall Library.

There are some excellent and detailed histories of both the East Surreys and the South Lancashire regiments which I relied on to set the background to my father's military experiences. Unfortunately, more than seventy years after the events, I could trace no veterans who had served with my father.

Sir Cyril Taylor and Lord Adonis both published books about their CTC/academy experiences and I have relied on them for some of the politics and background to the initiative. Michael Gove has already written and spoken at length about his involvement.

I am grateful to John Jay and Sir Harry Djanogly for reading the manuscript in draft form and feeding me back their comments which I have tried to include.

Finally, I want to thank Sir John Major for agreeing to write the foreword, and Ivan Fallon, who lived through many of the experiences described here both as a City Editor and member of various committees in Guy's and Westminster Abbey, who has put it all down in what we both hope is a readable and compelling form.

Lord Harris, Orpington, September 2017

INDEX